UFO SIGHTINGS

UFO SIGHTINGS

Alan Baker

New York

First published in 1997 by The Orion Publishing Group Ltd., London.

Publisher's Cataloging-in-Publication Data
Baker, Alan, 1964–
    UFO sightings / Alan Baker
       p. cm. — (True life encounters)
       Includes bibliographical references.
    ISBN: 1–57500–022-9
    1. Unidentified flying objects—Sightings and encounters. I. Titles.
    TL789.3B35 1999   001.9'42
                            QBI99-14

TV Books, L.L.C.
1619 Broadway, Ninth Floor
New York, NY 10019
www.tvbooks.com

Interior designed by Rachel Reiss
Manufactured in Canada

Contents

This book is dedicated to my parents

Introduction

Ever since that fateful day, 24 June 1947, when American pilot Kenneth Arnold made the first "modern" UFO sighting over Mount Rainier in Washington State, people from every walk of life across the world have been fascinated by the idea that we are the target of scrutiny by beings from elsewhere in the Universe. Although the numerous sightings that followed Arnold's gave rise to initial speculations that the strange objects were secret weapons developed by the United States, the Soviet Union, or both, this suggestion rapidly gave way to what has come to be known as the Extraterrestrial Hypothesis (ETH), which holds that the "flying saucers" were (and are) piloted spacecraft from other planets. While many distinguished and responsible people have supported this contention, it has resulted in an unfortunate misapprehension that has been reinforced by sensation-hungry journalists throughout the decades since the late 1940s. This grave misapprehension is that UFOs are, by definition, alien spacecraft. Nothing could be further from the truth.

It is essential to remember what the acronym "UFO" stands for: Unidentified Flying Object, with the emphasis on the *unidentified*. There is absolutely no doubt that UFOs exist. Any object seen in the sky that resists identification—even for a few moments—is a UFO. In approximately 90 per cent of cases, these objects become IFOs (Identified Flying Objects), either at the time of the sighting or through subsequent investigation. In the vast majority of UFO sightings, it sooner or later becomes apparent that what the witness actually saw was a man-made aircraft viewed at an unusual angle, or a flock of birds whose bodies were reflecting light from the ground, or astronomical phenomena such as meteorites, stars and planets. In the latter case, a planet can often be given the illusion of movement if viewed through passing clouds.

It is remarkably easy for untrained observers to be misled by what they see in the skies, as I can confirm from my own experience. In 1994 I was living in Reading, England, where I had attended the university. At about eight o'clock one Saturday evening, I left my house to visit some friends, and immediately noticed something very strange in the sky directly overhead. As is often the case in England, the sky was completely overcast, with a thick blanket of cloud dimly illuminated by the street lamps. In sudden confusion, I watched as a diffuse light flitted through the clouds, moving at what seemed like incredible speed, stopping and starting almost instantaneously, at one moment directly overhead, at the next above houses several streets away. As I stopped dead in my tracks and gazed into the sky, it seemed to me that the light was coming from something that was obscured by the heavy clouds.

As might be expected with anyone interested in UFOs, I immediately wondered if this might be the night I would finally see one. And I have to admit, I also felt a sudden twinge of fear: what if the abduction reports were true? I was all alone in the street . . . would I be next? These rather unsettling speculations were short-lived, however. It quickly occurred to me that there might be a more down-to-earth explanation for what I was seeing. The way the light was flitting about put me in mind of a searchlight beam playing upon the underside of the cloud cover . . .

Assuming that this was the answer, I made my way to my friends' house and told them what I had seen. They told me that a spotlight had recently been fitted to the roof of the Students' Union building on the university campus, and was switched on every Saturdy night.

I thought no more about the matter until several months later, when I read the March/April 1995 issue of Quest International's

UFO Magazine, which carried a report from the Reading *Evening Post* of 29 November 1994. The report stated that hundreds of people around Reading had witnessed strange, "disc-shaped" lights in the sky. One person who called the paper said she had run home in fear, thinking Martians were about to land, while another said: "I rushed in and told my husband. What he said back to me was unrepeatable. But at the time we just didn't know what it was." The *Post*, of course, provided the correct explanation for the lights, which had indeed been caused by the large spotlight on the Students' Union roof.

I mention this as a cautionary tale against making rash assumptions when spotting something unusual in the sky. The light I saw was a UFO . . . until I figured out what it actually was. And yet, like many other people in Reading who saw it, I had (albeit briefly) entertained the notion that it was an alien spacecraft. Such is the power of the cultural icon the UFO has become.

And from now on, things can only get more confusing, as our own aerospace technology improves, resulting in aircraft that display many of the attributes of alleged UFOs. This is especially true of military technology: it is generally conceded that developments in this field occur at least a decade before the public is allowed to know of them. A case in point is the F-117A Nighthawk covert strike aircraft. A full-scale mockup of this remarkable machine was constructed at the Lockheed Corporation's advanced projects factory, the Skunk Works, in Burbank, California, in 1979, nearly ten years before it was first revealed to the public. It follows that research and development work began earlier than that; photographs released a few years ago show a test prototype of the F-117A that was constructed in 1975. If we assume that developments in aerospace technology proceed approximately 15 years ahead of what is actually acknowledged to exist, we are led to the inescapable conclusion that what we might expect to see around the year 2015 is being developed right now!

We can therefore be forgiven for asking whether some UFO

sightings in the late 1970s and 80s were of Stealth-type aircraft. Likewise with the famous Belgian UFO wave of 1989–90, in which approximately 2,000 witnesses described overflights by a large, triangular object. This wave, which eventually extended throughout much of Europe, ranks as one of the most intriguing and impressive in the history of ufology, not least because the object (or objects) was reported by the Belgian police and Air Force, the latter subsequently releasing its radar tracking tapes for public scrutiny via the media. According to Colonel Wilfred De Brouwer, Chief of Operations for the Belgian Air Force, the objects tracked could not possibly have been conventional aircraft (nor could they have been misidentifications of the B-2 Stealth Bomber or F-117A Nighthawk), such was their speed and manoeuvrability.

When two Belgian Air Force F-16s were scrambled to intercept one such object, they were vastly out-performed by the UFO, which was capable of descending from 10,000 to 500 feet in less than five seconds. As with many UFOs, these bizarre "flying triangles" displayed inertial characteristics that would have proved instantly fatal to any human pilot. What should we conclude from this? That the "pilots" were not, in fact, human? Or would it be more prudent to suggest that there *were* no pilots?

It may come as a surprise to some that not all military aircraft are piloted. Those that aren't are known as RPVs (remotely piloted vehicles) and UAVs (unmanned aerial vehicles), and are much faster and more manoeuvrable than piloted aircraft. RPVs and UAVs have been used successfully in reconnaissance missions in many contexts, most recently in the Gulf War, and it is extremely likely that they account for a significant percentage of UFO sightings by people who are unaware of their existence and capabilities.

However, it is surely unlikely that such machines would fool highly trained fighter pilots of the Belgian or any other air force into thinking that they were dealing with something beyond conventional explanation. The fantastic flight characteristics of these UFOs included the ability to hover in absolute silence, as testified by ground witnesses. Surely, then, *this* must imply an extraterrestrial origin? Not necessarily . . .

Several years ago, it was reported in the media that scientists in Japan were investigating the apparently extremely peculiar properties of spinning discs which, when rotated at very high speeds (thousands of revolutions per minute), appeared to shed their mass! To be sure, this mass loss was tiny, requiring sensitive instruments to record it. (One researcher stated that in order to lose all of its mass, a disc would have to be spun at several hundred million revolutions per minute.) Yet, apparently, the mass loss was real, and repeatable in the laboratory. Bearing in mind that military technology is at least 10–15 years ahead of what the public is allowed to see (as mentioned above), would it not be reasonable to speculate that a major breakthrough in the struggle against gravity may already have been achieved, and been put into practice in the form of large, Stealth-like craft capable of hovering in absolute silence before hurtling away at colossal speeds? This would surely account for the undeniable presence of highly unusual craft at places like the now world-famous Area 51 in Nevada—a short hop from Lockheed's Skunk Works in California. Of course, this view does not take into account the assertions of those who maintain that such advances in aerospace technology are the results of reverse-engineering projects conducted on captured alien spacecraft, assertions that will be examined later in this book.

The presence of strange objects and lights in the sky is merely the tip of a very large iceberg. When venturing into the field of ufology, we quickly encounter some extremely bizarre events, which demand a much wider context of enquiry than that briefly discussed above. Indeed, the idea of a genuine extraterrestrial presence on Earth is only one of a host of theories that have been put forward over the years to account for human encounters with anomalous phenomena. While many researchers are of the opinion that the ETH is the theory that best fits the evidence thus far accumulated, the public remains largely unaware of the alternatives which might, in the long run, offer a greater insight into what is happening in these cases.

This, it seems to me, is the central problem of ufology. The assumption of an extraterrestrial origin for sightings of unusual objects, which has been consistently reinforced by the very same media that seeks to deride the people who report such sightings, has resulted in a set of preconceptions that can only obscure the underlying nature of the phenomenon. My own position is one of tentative acceptance that there is, indeed, something very strange happening . . . something that defies explanation in terms of our current scientific paradigms. In the pages that follow, I will present a number of cases which I hope will provide a representative sample of the wider field of ufology, and which will illustrate not only the dangers of accepting certain cases at face value, but also the inadvisability of ignoring those cases that strongly imply the presence of a genuine and profound mystery.

The first half of this book will include cases that fall into the famous categories invented by J. Allen Hynek: Close Encounters of the First to Fourth Kinds. Thereafter, I shall present seven further sections, which will include cases that illustrate additional important aspects of ufology that have arisen in the years since the Second World War.

I hope that, by the end of the book, the reader will agree with me that the field of ufology represents a puzzle of potentially colossal implications, one that demands serious study, rather than the closed-minded approach of the sceptics who maintain that there is absolutely nothing here worth dwelling on. Surely, in view of our rapidly expanding knowledge of the Universe and its myriad wonders, such a negativist viewpoint belongs to yesterday. As Abraham Lincoln said in somewhat different circumstances: "The dogmas of the quiet past are inadequate for the stormy present."

1

Close Encounters of the First Kind

Observers report a close-at-hand experience without tangible physical effects. *

Mystery Fliers and Ghost Rockets

Contrary to popular belief, the history of UFOs in the twentieth century does not begin with Kenneth Arnold's sighting in 1947; nor did the early UFOs correspond to the familiar disc-shaped objects that have been so frequently reported in the years since the Second World War. In fact, in terms of sheer strangeness, the phenomenon started very much as it meant to go on, with the arrival in the early 1930s of the so-called "mystery fliers."

Far from appearing as sophisticated "spacecraft," the mystery fliers were frequently described as large, multi-engined aircraft, which circled towns, railways and even ships out at sea. The main theatre of this activity was northern Scandinavia, although some sightings were made in Britain and the United States. According to the American researcher John Keel, these machines, while resembling conventional aircraft in terms of configuration and propulsion, were far larger than should have been expected for the time. A group of five witnesses reported seeing an enormous plane with no fewer than eight propellers!

---

* Close Encounter definitions 1–3 after Hynek, *The UFO Experience*. Definition number 4 is author's own.

In addition to this, the pilots of these machines often exhibited a cavalier attitude to the dangers of aviation in the inhospitable regions of Norway, Sweden and Finland. Not only were the mystery fliers reported during raging blizzards (which would have quickly forced any conventional aircraft to the ground), they also had a habit of cutting their engines and circling in silence through the driving snow.

The Swedish Government became alarmed at these outlandish claims, and in 1934 dispatched 24 Air Force biplanes to search the remote areas where the "ghost fliers" had been seen. The search failed utterly to resolve the puzzle; in fact, two of the Air Force planes succumbed to the harsh conditions and crashed. Fortunately, their pilots survived, which cannot be said for the hapless Georg Engelhard Wanberg...

A lieutenant in the artillery regiment based in Gotland, Norway, Wanberg set out on skis on a journey from Tannas to Storlien, on a path that would take him directly through the region where the ghost fliers had most often been reported. He was never seen alive again. Extensive searches by the Norwegian Air Force failed to find him. On 4 January 1934, a group of three men joined in the search, heading out into the vast and increasingly sinister northern wastes. When they failed to return on schedule, new search parties were dispatched to find them....

On 12 January, the three men arrived at the New Styl Station. The reason for their absence was never divulged. Five days later, Lieutenant Wanberg's frozen body was discovered a few miles from his tent. Apparently, he had left the tent without equipment or skis, despite a raging blizzard, and had walked into the mountains to meet his fate. No explanation was ever given for this suicidal act of an experienced outdoorsman.

As with more modern UFOs, the mystery planes seemed interested in areas of strategic or military importance, and often directed powerful searchlights at the ground. On 23 January 1934, a large, grey aircraft circled the Norwegian freighter *Tordenskiold* near Tromsø, Norway, and directed an immensely powerful searchlight beam on to the ship's deck. According to Captain Sigvard Olsen, the pilot of the plane was visible in the illuminated cockpit, and wore a hood and large goggles.

As more and more reports came in from the inhabitants of the rugged Scandinavian hinterlands, the military authorities became yet more alarmed. The ghost fliers were performing manoeuvres that would have proved fatal for any conventional aircraft (does this sound familiar?), such as circling at less than 100 feet, in violent storms, with their engines switched off. On 30 April 1934, Major-General Reutersward, based in upper Norrland, Sweden, issued this press release:

> Comparison of these reports shows that there can be no doubt about illegal air traffic over our secret military areas. There are many reports from reliable people which describe close observations of the enigmatic fliers. And in every case the same remark has been noted: No insignias or identifying marks were visible on the machine.... The question is: Who are they? And why have they been invading our air territory?

One of the factors that so perplexed the Scandinavian military was the apparent lack of logistical support for the fliers. The number of reports that were being received suggested that a very large number of aircraft were involved, perhaps hundreds. Large aircraft operating in the harsh conditions of the Arctic regions would have required considerable back-up in the form of bases, mechanics, fuel, spare parts and numerous other supplies—none of which had been revealed by the extensive search expeditions that had been mounted. As John Keel states, no other country could seriously be suspected of these bizarre infringements on Scandinavian air territory; certainly not Germany, which had yet to build the *Luftwaffe*; and certainly not the Soviet Union, which had neither the equipment nor the desire to mount such a dangerous and apparently useless reconnaissance.

In spite of the intensity of the military investigations of these sightings, the ultimate origin of the ghost fliers was never discovered. However, Scandinavia was eventually to play host to an equally perplexing mystery.

Following the Second World War, the ghost fliers were replaced in the cold skies over Scandinavia by the "ghost rockets," which exhibited even more extraordinary aerobatics. These cylindrical, wingless objects were reported to leave fiery trails in their wake as they shot across the sky at fantastic speeds, diving, climbing and occasionally even landing.

Once again, the Scandinavian military authorities were extremely concerned about these unauthorized overflights of their territories, and enlisted the aid of a US Army Air Force intelligence expert, Lieutenant-General James Doolittle, and an expert in aerial warfare, General David Sarnoff. British researcher Timothy Good states that a press blackout was quickly established, for which there were two reasons. The first was that, since the ghost rockets were assumed to be missiles, a standard procedure was followed, whereby nothing of the rocket sightings would be revealed, thus denying their builders any information regarding the accuracy of their targeting. The second reason was that the origin of the rockets was still unknown, and the authorities (perhaps understandably, given that the war had just ended) were anxious to avoid public panic.

In July 1946 a special committee was set up to investigate the sightings. Chaired by Colonel Bengt Jacobson, head of the Material Department of the Air Administration, the committee also included representatives from the Defence Staff, the Research Institute of National Defence, the Defence Radio Institute and the Naval Administration. Although about 80 per cent of the sightings were found to be explainable as mundane objects and "celestial phenomena," the remaining 20 per cent resisted such identification, prompting the speculation that the Soviets were secretly testing V2 missile technology, with the aid of captured German scientists. However, the Swedish Government announced, in the results of its official enquiry into the sightings, that the objects "were not the V-type bombs used by the Germans in the closing days of the war."

Although some witnesses stated that they had seen ghost rockets crashing, no wreckage was ever discovered. Some fragments, allegedly having fallen from some of the objects, were turned in for analysis, but were found to be nothing more unusual than lumps of coke. This did nothing to alleviate the sense of concern that continued to be felt by the US State Department which, according to Timothy Good, had upgraded its communications with the embassy in Stockholm to top secret.

The fact is that, as with the earlier mystery flier sightings, no ultimate explanation regarding the ghost rockets was ever forthcoming. The idea of a Soviet origin, while briefly mooted, was discarded, since the ghost rockets' performance far surpassed that of the V2 missiles. Although vast improvements in ballistic technology were not far away, they had certainly not been achieved within a year of the end of the Second World War.

As the ghost rocket sightings gradually decreased in frequency in the months that followed, all official investigations into their origin were halted, and a worldwide curtain of secrecy was lowered over the entire subject of unexplained aerial objects.

The "Saucers" Arrive

Although the unfortunate term "flying saucer" gained popular currency as a result of Kenneth Arnold's description of the nine objects he saw over Mount Rainier in Washington State, he was not referring to the shape of the objects themselves, but rather to their mode of flight. (They flew, he said, with an undulating motion, "like a saucer would if you skipped it across water.") The objects he reported were, in fact, crescent-shaped—more like flying wings than flying saucers.

The encounter occurred on the afternoon of 24 June 1947, when Arnold, a 32-year-old successful businessman from Boise, Idaho, was flying his private plane at 9,200 feet over the Cascade Mountains, aiding in the search for a missing Marine Corps transport aircraft. A sudden flash caught his attention, and he looked into the distance to see "a chain of nine peculiar looking aircraft flying from north to south at approximately 9,500 feet elevation and going, seemingly, in a definite direction of about 170 degrees"—in other words, towards the distant peak of Mount Rainier.

Arnold estimated the wing-span of each object to be about 100 feet. Having never seen aircraft of this type before, he attempted to gain some idea of their velocity by timing their passage from the peak of Mount Rainier to the peak of Mount Adams. As the first object passed the first mountain, he noted that the cockpit clock read exactly 2.59 P.M. By the time the last object passed Mount Adams, Arnold saw that 102 seconds had passed. He later established the distance between the two peaks as 47 miles, which gave a ground speed for the objects of 1,700 m.p.h. The most advanced aircraft of the time had yet to achieve half that speed. Using various landmarks as reference points, he estimated the nine objects to be 20–25 miles away, forming a chain approximately five miles long.

After the sighting, Arnold flew on to Yakima, where he told some friends what he had seen, before continuing the final leg of his journey to Pendleton, just over the state border with Oregon. When he arrived, he found several sceptical reporters waiting for him. However, when his respectable background became evident, their scepticism largely vanished, to be replaced by intense curiosity . . . a curiosity that has been shared by people all over the world for the last 50 years.

In view of that fact, it is rather ironic that the Arnold sighting was probably *not* of genuine UFOs. A number of possible explanations were put forward after the encounter over Mount Rainier. These included a mirage of distorted mountain peaks caused by temperature inversions, in which light rays are bent in their passage through layers of air of different temperatures, resulting in the apparent projection of mundane objects into locations where they shouldn't be. Alternatively, according to the US Air Materiel Command, Arnold might have seen a collection of large, flat hailstones which had formed under the icy conditions at high altitudes; or perhaps the sun reflected on low clouds; or perhaps the destruction of small meteors entering the atmosphere. Several scientists quoted in the newspapers at the time dismissed these suggestions as nonsense.

However, when Dr. J. Allen Hynek was consulted by the authorities several months later, the Ohio State University Professor of Astronomy pointed out some serious problems with Arnold's speed calculations for the objects he had seen. According to Hynek, the objects could not have been 20–25 miles away, *and* recognizable as crescent-shaped craft: they would have had to be virtually the size of mountains—thousands of feet wide, instead of 100. If they really were no more than 100 feet wide, then they must have been only a few miles away, and this would drastically reduce the estimate of their speed to well below that of sound.

As a result of these considerations, the final report on the Arnold sighting listed it as a "mirage." Not surprisingly, Arnold himself vehemently disagreed with any notion that he had misidentified an entirely natural phenomenon, reiterating that he had turned his plane and opened the side window to get a completely unobstructed view of the objects. Hynek's findings, however, would seem ultimately to tip the balance in favour of a mundane explanation for what has come to be known (however erroneously) as the first "modern" UFO sighting.

Near Miss with a Flying Torpedo

Exactly one year and one month after Kenneth Arnold's sighting, Eastern Airlines Flight 576 was *en route* from Houston, Texas, to Atlanta, Georgia, when Captain Clarence S. Chiles and First Officer John B. Whitted spotted an object approaching their DC-3. At 2.45 A.M. Chiles spotted a dull red glow above and ahead of the aircraft. According to his co-pilot, Whitted: "We sighted an object coming toward us.... This strange object had a stream of red fire coming from its tail and I could see it was much larger than anything I had seen or read about."

The night was clear, with good visibility, an almost full moon and only a few scattered clouds about 1,000 feet above the aircraft. Travelling at about 700 m.p.h., the cylindrical, wingless object passed the DC-3 on its right side. Owing to the clear conditions, both pilots were able to get a good look at the thing as it passed them. "It was about 100 feet long, shaped like a cigar [with] two rows of windows, an upper and lower, that were large and square." These windows were glowing very brightly, and there was an intense blue light underneath the object. Although Chiles estimated that the UFO missed their aircraft by about 700 feet, Whitted put the figure at half a mile.

The only other witness to the encounter was one of the passengers, Clarence McKelvie, who described how he saw something flashing, a "cigar with a cherry flame going out the back. There was a row of windows and [it was] going in that direction fast."

After reaching Atlanta, Chiles and Whitted reported their sighting to the Air Force. A subsequent Air Intelligence report stated that the object remained unidentified. According to Report 102–122–79, the Air Technical Intelligence Center (ATIC) made a thorough check of 225 flight schedules, both commercial and governmental, which revealed that the only aircraft Chiles and Whitted could conceivably have encountered was an Air Force C-47 *en route* from Robins Air Force Base to Olmstead Field, Pennsylvania. However, the report conceded that the "speed, direction of flight, maneuvers, configurations, lights and other factors rule[d] out this one possibility."

The report went on to note that other objects of similar configuration had been reported in Denmark, Norway and Sweden (see above). In a section entitled *Flying Fuselages (Torpedo or Cigar-Shaped Body)*, the report stated:

While the cigar or torpedo-shaped body represents an efficient form for the fuselage of an airplane or the body of a guided missile, in neither case has it been used as a primary lift producing surface. However, an extension of the Prandtl theory of lift indicates that a fuselage of the dimensions reported by the Eastern Airlines pilots Whitted and Chiles in the Montgomery, Alabama, incident could support a gross weight of approximately 12,000 pounds at an arbitrarily chosen stalling speed of 150 miles per hour, conservatively estimated. The Prandtl theory probably gives very conservative values of maximum lift for bodies of this shape. If a lift coefficient twice as great were used (such a value has been given by a German scientist from memory of his wind tunnel researches in Germany), a gross weight of 24,000 pounds could be supported at the assumed stalling speed....

While no stabilizing fins were apparent on the "flying fuselage" reported by Whitted and Chiles, it is possible that vanes within the jet, operated by a gyroservo system could have provided static stability, longitudinally, directionally and laterally. The same vanes could also have been used for accomplishing static balance or trim, as well as control for maneuvering. A square-tailed body of the type reported with the center of gravity sufficiently far forward can develop, approximately, a neutral stability and the possibility exists that definite static stability could be produced by a judicious use of flow-control slots located somewhere along the fuselage.

If nothing else, this proves that the Air Force was taking such reports very seriously. According to Project Sign, which investigated UFO reports at that time (more of which later), Chiles and Whitted had seen an alien spacecraft. The object, the report concluded, "remains unidentified as to origin, construction and power source."

Air Force consultant Dr. Hynek took a different view, and suggested that the object might have been a meteor, citing records from amateur astronomers that described a large number (part of the Delta Aquarid shower) on the evening previous to the Chiles-Whitted sighting. According to Hynek, the bright, flame-like trail and the sudden disappearance implied the presence of a meteor. Dealing with the reported "windows" on the object, Hynek commented: "It will have to be left to the psychologists to tell us whether the immediate trail of a bright meteor could produce the subjective impression of a ship with lighted windows."

Chiles and Whitted disagreed with this explanation, maintaining that the object had behaved as if under intelligent control. "The object," said Chiles, "flashed down and we veered to the left and it veered to its left." Then it pulled up "with a tremendous burst of flame" and disappeared into the clouds, "as if the pilot had seen us and wanted to avoid us."

The Gorman Dogfight

On the night of 1 October 1948, George F. Gorman was flying with the North Dakota Air National Guard. After the squadron had landed at Fargo, Gorman decided to get some night flying practice, and took his F-51 back up. Flying conditions were extremely good: visibility was unlimited, and there was no moon.

At 9.00 P.M., Gorman spotted a small Piper Cub aircraft flying below him. A moment later, he saw another apparent aircraft, or at least a light, which was blinking as it travelled from east to west. Gorman tried to distinguish some structure behind the light (which was easy to do with the Piper Cub), but could see none. He contacted the Hector Airport control tower, asking if there were any other aircraft in the vicinity, apart from the Piper. The tower replied in the negative, but the pilot of the Piper also saw the blinking light.

At that point, Gorman decided to try to intercept the light, but quickly realized that this would not be possible by flying a straight course: the light was moving too fast, even though Gorman's F-51 was flying at between 300 and 400 m.p.h. When the light altered its course, Gorman decided to try for a head-on pass. The two craft were heading straight for each other at an altitude of 5,000 feet.

At the very last moment, the light instantly climbed and passed 500 feet over the F-51. The object disappeared momentarily from Gorman's field of view, but quickly reappeared and started another head-on pass. It made the same vertical manoeuvre as before, but this time Gorman pulled his own aircraft into a steep climb in an attempt to keep up with the unknown object. The F-51 managed to maintain the climb until it reached 14,000 feet, whereupon it stalled out, leaving the object to continue its race into the night sky.

The dogfight continued as the object circled back and began yet another head-on pass, although this time it altered course much sooner and headed out over the airport. Gorman immediately gave chase. Since he was now at 14,000 feet, with the object below him at 11,000 feet, he decided to dive at it. However, the UFO eluded him, climbing vertically once again and finally disappearing for good in the night sky. The encounter ended at 9.27 P.M.

US Air Force Project Sign investigators were on the scene within hours, and interviewed Gorman, the pilot of the Piper Cub and the control tower operators. Gorman described the object as a ball of light, about eight inches in diameter. On 23 October, Gorman gave a sworn statement which ran, in part, as follows:

I am convinced that there was definite thought behind its maneuvers.

I am further convinced that the object was governed by the laws of inertia because its acceleration was rapid but not immediate and although it was able to turn fairly tight at considerable speed, it still followed a natural curve. When I attempted to turn with the object I blacked out temporarily due to excessive speed. I am in fairly good physical condition and I do not believe there are many if any pilots who could withstand the turn and speed effected by the object, and remain conscious.

The object was not only able to out turn and out speed my aircraft . . . but was able to attain a far steeper climb and was able to maintain a constant rate of climb far in excess of my aircraft.

Gorman's F-51 was checked for radiation by the investigators, who discovered significantly increased readings, as compared with an F-51 that had not been flown for several days. The Project Sign team returned to Wright-Patterson Air Force Base, and concluded that Gorman's UFO sighting was a genuine unknown. The UFO had apparently been nuclear-powered, capable of reaching 600 m.p.h., and out-performing a human pilot with ease. According to aviation historian Curtis Peebles, the radiation was the first recorded physical effect from a UFO sighting.

How Fast Do Ducks Fly?

On the night of 25 August 1951, an Atomic Energy Commission executive and his wife were relaxing in their garden in the Texas town of Lubbock, when they looked up to see a large, V-shaped formation of approximately 36 bluish lights, travelling silently across the sky. At the same time, in another part of town, a group of four professors from the Texas Technological College at Lubbock saw the same thing. The lights were apparently attached to a wing-shaped object, about one-and-a-half times the size of a B-26 aircraft.

Over the next few days, hundreds of people would report the same or similar objects gliding through the Texan skies. On 31 August an amateur photographer named Carl Hart Jr. took five photographs of the mysterious V-formation as it flew over his house. When the photographs were analysed by the Photo Reconnaissance Laboratory at Wright Field (later Wright-Patterson Air Force Base), it was concluded that the V-formation of lights had crossed approximately 120 degrees of sky, at 30 degrees per second angular velocity. (The professors from Texas Technological College had made similar measurements during their sighting, and had come up with exactly the same result.) The object was also tracked on radar, at a speed of 900 m.p.h., which corresponds to the visual and photographic measurements.

The Lubbock reports were also studied by a group of rocket scientists, physicists and intelligence experts, who came to the conclusion that a large object with a "highly swept-back wing configuration" had indeed been seen. They also speculated that the V-formation of bright lights (which were much more intense than the surrounding stars) were caused by the object's propulsion system, a series of jet-like orifices on the "wing's" trailing edge.

However, sceptics were (and are) unimpressed, maintaining that the Lubbock Lights were actually caused by ground light reflected from the bellies of ducks flying overhead. While this is possible, and has been convincingly cited to explain other, similar sightings, it does, in view of the radar evidence, beg the question: what kind of duck flies at 900 m.p.h.?

The Washington Invasion

If the objects tracked by radar around the US capital on the night of 19 July 1952 were truly anomalous, then it is hard to avoid the conclusion that whoever (or whatever) was controlling them had decided to make a serious point. Since some of the UFOs were tracked in the prohibited airspace over the White House and the Capitol, it is possible to draw the inference that the mysterious interlopers were perfectly well aware of the significance of these two buildings, and of the reaction that would be invoked by an overflight.

The so-called "Washington Invasion" began 20 minutes before midnight, when a controller at Air Route Traffic Control (ARTC) at Washington National Airport noticed eight targets moving at about 120 miles per hour—targets that were confirmed by the control tower's short-range radar. Since the targets were in the vicinity of Andrews Air Force Base, airport controller Ed Nugent decided to give the base a call, to confirm that they were military aircraft. An airman at the base said that he could see the objects in the sky, and told the Andrews tower to look south. A tower operator did so, and saw an orange fireball perform a circular manoeuvre before shooting away at a fantastic speed. A few moments later, another of the objects left the area.

Since three independent radar systems (the long- and short-range systems at the civilian airport, and the military radar at Andrews) had all tracked the same objects, a malfunction was clearly not to blame for the objects. One of the ARTC controllers then asked the pilots of several civilian aircraft in the vicinity if they could see anything unusual in the skies. The pilot of a Capital Airlines flight responded: "There's one—off to the right—and there it goes." Glancing at his screen, the controller immediately saw a target to the right of the Capital aircraft disappear.

At about 2.00 A.M. EST, another object was tracked by the civilian ARTC flying over Andrews AFB; however, the military radar failed to pick it up, prompting an Air Force captain to go outside to check visually. He spotted an orange-red light between 10 and 15 degrees above the horizon

Meanwhile, another civilian aircraft had reported a light pacing it as it made its final approach to National Airport. This visual sighting was confirmed on radar. Harry Barnes, the senior ARTC controller, waited until 3.00 A.M. and then called the Air Force Command Post to ask if anything was being done about this highly unusual situation. He eventually got through to the Combat Officer, who told him that all the information was being forwarded to "higher authority," and that he would not discuss it any further. According to the Combat Officer, the Air Force were "not really concerned about it anyway," and that "somebody else was supposed to handle it."

In spite of these rather impressive "radar-visual" sightings (in which the radar tracks had been corroborated by witnesses on the ground and in the air), Captain Edward J. Ruppelt, head of US Air Force Project Blue Book (which was then investigating UFO reports), did not learn about them until Monday 21 July, when he read about them in the newspapers! When he flew to Washington from Blue Book headquarters at Wright-Patterson AFB in Dayton, Ohio, he was treated in a most puzzling way.

When he asked for a staff car to go and interview witnesses, he was told that none were available, and that he should use the bus. Adding insult to injury, his superiors informed him that he was not authorized to be away from Wright-Patterson, and that if he did not return immediately he would be declared AWOL.

At 9.30 P.M. on the night of 26 July, the UFOs returned to Washington. When journalist Robert Ginna of *Life* magazine telephoned Ruppelt in Dayton to ask him what was being done (once again, the Air Force had neglected to inform its principal UFO investigator that the nation's capital was again the centre of UFO activity!), Ruppelt replied in exasperation: "I have no idea what the Air Force is doing; in all probability it is doing nothing."

Nevertheless, Ruppelt contacted Major Dewey Fournet, an engineering consultant to Blue Book who lived in Washington, and Lieutenant Holcombe, a Navy electronics expert, and asked them to get to National Airport as quickly as possible. When the two men arrived at 1.15 A.M. EST, they found Al Chop, the Air Force Press Officer, already there, and together they watched intently as two F-94 interceptors, which had been scrambled from New Castle County AFB, closed in on the objects on the radar scopes.

While this was happening, the reporters who had gathered at the control tower were ordered out, ostensibly because communication techniques with an interceptor were confidential. This seems to have been a rather weak excuse to clear the tower of the press, since it was perfectly possible for anyone with a radio set to listen in on such communications. According to British researcher Jenny Randles, the real reason was that the Blue Book personnel must have suspected that they were on the brink of securing absolute proof of the interplanetary nature of UFOs, and were anxious to evaluate what happened next *before* informing the press.

This final proof, however, never came. As the jet interceptors, which had been joined by two more from New Castle AFB, approached the unknown targets, the targets vanished from the screens, only to reappear when the F-94s had passed. Eventually, the jets ran low on fuel and were forced to return to base. The unidentified targets then began to leave the scopes. Although Major Fournet and Lieutenant Holcombe remained in the control tower until 5.15 A.M. EST, no more targets were detected.

At a press conference held two days later, Major-General John Samford, Director of Air Force Intelligence, presented the Air Force's conclusions on the Invasion of Washington. The anomalous radar targets were, he said, almost certainly caused by atmospheric phenomena; to be precise, temperature inversions. The visual sightings could most reasonably be accounted for by stars and meteors which, in the excitement, had been assumed to correspond to the false radar images.

This had not been the conclusion reached by those in the control tower at the time of the sightings, however. Dewey Fournet felt that the radar tracks were "very probably caused by solid metallic objects." In addition to this, it is reasonable to assume that experienced radar operators might be qualified to distinguish between false targets caused by temperature inversions, and those caused by large, solid objects. Indeed, according to Fournet, there *were* weather-related targets present on the scopes, and the operators had no difficulty in spotting them.

Although the press were fairly satisfied with the official Air Force explanation, Ruppelt, Fournet and Chop were certainly not. As Jenny Randles reminds us, Ruppelt left the Air Force less than three years later to write a book confirming his belief in the reality of alien spacecraft; Fournet resigned to join a leading civilian UFO group; and Chop resigned to work on a Hollywood documentary dealing with UFOs.

The McMinnville Photographs

As mentioned earlier, there is a large catalogue of photographs, taken by people from all over the world, allegedly depicting anomalous aerial objects. While many of them are no more than vague smudges that could have mundane explanations, including flaws on the film and lens flares, some are much more impressive. There are many photographs depicting definitely structured disc-shaped objects, apparently in flight near the witness. In cases such as these, there seem to be only two conclusions that can be drawn: either the photographer hoaxed the pictures, with a small model or through other means; or the pictures really do depict what they are alleged to depict. It should be borne in mind, however, that even if the latter is true, that does not automatically mean that the object photographed is an alien spacecraft (see Introduction).

It has been said that extraordinary claims demand extraordinary evidence. The sighting of an intelligently controlled disc-shaped flying object certainly qualifies as an extraordinary claim, but, unfortunately, capturing that object on film does not constitute extraordinary evidence: it is *another extraordinary claim*. Consequently, UFO photographs are often subjected to a battery of comprehensive tests designed to establish whether they can, with reasonable confidence, be said to be genuine.

One of the most impressive cases of this kind is the McMinnville, Oregon, case. On 11 May 1950, a strange object appeared over the small farm of Mr. and Mrs. Trent. Mrs. Trent was out feeding the farm's rabbits when she saw the object gliding soundlessly overhead, from the north-east to the north-west. She called her husband, they found their camera and took two photographs of the object from vantage points a few feet apart.

The Trents were, apparently, not greatly perturbed by what they had seen, since they waited for several days, until they had used up the remainder of the film, before taking it to be developed. The couple did not attempt to publicize the photographs, and it was only by chance that a local newspaper got to hear about them. The photographs eventually found their way into *Life* magazine and became world-famous.

They were included in the US Air Force's Condon Report, which was produced by a team at the University of Colorado, headed by the respected physicist Dr. Edward U. Condon. The findings of the two-year study, which were published in 1969, were highly sceptical. Indeed, Condon and his chief administrator, Robert J. Low, declared their disbelief in UFOs at the very outset, placing their negative conclusions at the beginning of the report rather than at the end! Even so, the Trent photographs occupied a unique place in the Condon Report, as the only ones that resisted all attempts at explanation. According to investigator William K. Hartmann, his examination of both the photographs and the scene of the sighting led him to conclude that "all factors investigated, geometric, psychological, and physical appear to be consistent with the assertion that an extraordinary flying object, silvery, metallic, disc-shaped, tens of metres in diameter, and evidently artificial, flew within sight of two witnesses." He continued: "It cannot be said that the evidence positively rules out a fabrication, although there are some physical factors such as the accuracy of certain photometric measures of the original negatives which argue against a fabrication."

Ground Saucer Watch, one of the most highly respected UFO investigation groups, subjected the photographs to sophisticated computer analysis techniques, such as colour contouring and edge enhancement. The former technique converted each shade of grey on the Trents' black-and-white photos into a certain colour, which made it easier to pick out details in the images; the latter technique exaggerated the edges of every feature in the image (including blemishes on the film). Thus, it would immediately become evident if the object were a model suspended from a wire. The results of GSW's analysis of the Trent pictures were that the object shown was a disc between 65 and 100 feet in diameter, and probably made of polished metal.

However impressive the Trent photos may be, they have not escaped the attentions of sceptics, most notably Robert Shaeffer and Philip J. Klass (the latter the most famous and outspoken of all UFO debunkers). While Hartmann maintained that the haze on the photos implied a large distance between the observers and the UFO (he put the figure at about 1,400 yards), Shaeffer suggested that it might be due to grease on the camera lens, implying that the object might have been quite close to the camera. For Shaeffer, there was an inconsistency in the shadows of the garage eaves appearing on the wall in the photos and he pointed out that this wall faced east, which suggested that the photos were taken early in the morning, rather than the evening, as the Trents claimed.

According to Klass, it was plausible that the Trents had claimed a time in the evening for their sighting because other farmers would have been out in their fields earlier in the day, and would surely have seen any large discs gliding through the sky (no such reports were made). Another investigator, Bruce Maccabee, disagreed, claiming that the garage shadows indicated a diffuse light source, perhaps the evening sun reflected off a large cloud. He added that lens grease does not necessarily mean that the object was definitely close to the camera, and claimed that, even allowing for lens grease, the McMinnville UFO was more than 1,000 yards away from the camera.

Klass pointed to the shift in attitude of the UFO between photographs as strongly implying that it was indeed a model suspended close to the camera, although, as we have noted, the edge-enhancement process would have revealed this. . . .

The controversy surrounding the Trent photographs continues, more than 45 years after they were taken, and shows no sign of letting up. As the great American anomalist Charles Fort once said, for every expert there is an equal and opposite expert; and it is this fact that will guarantee the continuation of the UFO controversy in general, in the absence of the "final proof" for which the world is still waiting.

The Salida, Colorado, Footage

On 27 August 1996, the town of Salida, Colorado, became the centre of the UFO map when restaurant owner Tim Edwards captured video footage of an astonishing object sailing through the skies. The footage was shown on American TV news broadcasts and syndicated shows such as *Sightings*.

According to Edwards, "The first experience was truly awesome. I felt deeply at the time that I was witnessing something of great scientific and historic importance for the world. I believe that the August 27th craft was sending a message to the world and wanted to be photographed, that its appearance was somehow just the beginning of more to come and that I was really fortunate to be part of it."

The object Edwards videotaped was cigar-shaped and apparently flying at high altitude. Its behaviour was described as "unprecedented," even for a UFO, and included intense white lights that hurtled around its base. Edwards also recorded several smaller UFOs, which appeared as bright "balls" that performed numerous darting manoeuvres around the "mother ship."

The UFOs were subsequently seen by hundreds of other witnesses in and around Salida. According to the National UFO Reporting Center Edwards' sightings resulted in a nationwide wave of reports, numbering thousands.

The Salida footage was sent for analysis to Village Labs, a video and film design facility in Glendale, Arizona. It was also analysed by Dr. Jack Kasher of the University of Nebraska, and other media technology facilities in San Antonio, Texas. According to Vance Davies, a Village Labs staff consultant formerly with the National Security Agency (NSA), the object witnessed by Edwards and others was flying at 10,000 m.p.h., at an altitude of approximately 60,000 feet. Davies has classified this object as an "Alien Visitation Craft" or AVC—apparently an NSA term to designate a vehicle that is "definitely not one of ours."

One of the most astounding aspects of this sighting is the sheer size of the UFO, estimated by Village Labs to be somewhere between 700 feet and almost a mile in length! It was also noted that the object must have had prodigious energy requirements—not only to keep it in the air, but also to power the gigantic lights around its base, each of which was estimated to be between 100 and 200 feet square. According to Jim Dilettoso, the founder of Village Labs, the power requirements of this object were equivalent to taking the twin towers of the World Trade Center in New York, laying them end to end and trying to make them fly up into the atmosphere.

The Salida footage was also described as unusually clear, with a large number of additional objects (such as a roof line, birds and airborne debris) providing excellent frames of reference in the calculation of the distance between the object and the camera. By this means, the object was also shown to be definitely three-dimensional, and not a reflected image.

According to the British *UFO Magazine* (September/October 1996), recent examination of the footage has revealed photographic evidence for a "self-contained energy field" or "envelope" surrounding the large object. Features of this kind have frequently been suggested by ufologists to be the only way that genuine "alien craft" could defy gravity and perform the astonishing manoeuvres reported.

Since he has taken more footage of strange objects over Salida, acquiring to date over 20 hours' worth, Tim Edwards has entered the category of so-called "repeat witness," and has come in for some close scrutiny from sceptics and debunkers. Undaunted by this adverse attention, Tim Edwards told newspaper reporters: "This time, with dozens of witnesses here in Salida and many others that were hundreds of miles away that I have talked directly to over the phone, there is no denying that something very unusual has been going on up there."

UFO over Hawaii

When Mike Page, a 36-year-old piano polisher from Hertfordshire, England, went to Hawaii for the holiday of a lifetime, he had no idea that he would also take the photograph of a lifetime. On the spectacular island of Maui, along with the many other tourists marvelling at the beautiful scenery, Page took a number of photographs and some Super 8 cine footage, before returning to his hotel and taking the film to be developed.

When he collected the prints and inspected them, he saw something that astonished him. In disbelief, he said to a friend: "Look at this, it's a flying saucer, I've taken a picture of a flying saucer!" In one photograph of a tall, monolithic hill, an elongated, cigar-shaped object seemed to be hanging eerily in the background. According to Page, he had not seen anything unusual when he took the picture; he was concentrating on getting a good, panoramic shot of the scenery at the time, so this seems understandable, since the object itself is partially cloaked in a humid haze.

Although these photographs were taken in 1989, and copies of them have been in the files of various researchers since then, it was not until 1996 that a serious effort to analyse them was undertaken by *UFO Magazine*. Prior to 1996, several possible explanations had been put forward, such as a flaw in the emulsion of the photographic film, and even a secret visit by the Northrop B-2 Stealth Bomber.

When Page contacted *UFO Magazine*, they began an investigation in which Kodak was enlisted to provide an analysis of the image. The negatives were sent to John Griffiths of Kodak's Customer Care department at Hemel Hempstead, Hertfordshire. Griffiths told Mark Birdsall of *UFO Magazine* that, over the years, Kodak has examined many photographs of "unusual" objects, including UFOs and the Loch Ness Monster. He thus considered his department to be "experienced in these matters."

On 25 November 1996, Griffiths telephoned Mark Birdsall, after having examined the photographic negatives. This preliminary examination had been intended to confirm that there were no emulsion flaws. According to Griffiths, there was no problem with the film itself. "It appears whatever is in the sky—is in the sky. The grain of the object is consistent with an object photographed in the distance. However, my gut feeling is that the object could be an airliner in ascent."

This opinion was later endorsed by Mike Manning, head of the department, who wrote to Mark Birdsall, saying that, although there was no evidence of any disturbance to the emulsion of the film, they nevertheless believed that the object photographed was an airliner flying from left to right, with light hitting the wing and tailplane, resulting in the two apparent lights on the image.

However, when *UFO Magazine*'s editor, Graham Birdsall, subsequently attended a conference in Hawaii, he asked local UFO researchers to comment on Kodak's conclusions. The consensus was that no airliner uses that flight path out of Maui's small airport. In addition, it seems likely that Mike Page would have heard the engine noise from a large aircraft at fairly close range; yet he maintains that he heard nothing of the sort when he took the photographs.

As to the idea that the object might be a Northrop B-2 Stealth Bomber, that too seems unlikely. For instance, if the photographs show the front of the aircraft (that is, approaching the camera), then the two bright lights are in the wrong position to be running lights which, on the B-2, are mounted on the undercarriage and thus would not be visible unless the undercarriage were down. If, on the other hand, the photograph shows the rear of the aircraft (travelling away from the camera), then the two lights are in the wrong position to be engine exhausts, since the engine nozzles on the B-2 are located on the upper surface of the aircraft, whereas the lights on the Hawaii UFO are clearly on its underside.

These considerations mean the object in Mike Page's photographs (which, the reader will note, is strikingly similar to the Salida, Colorado object) remains unexplained. The editors of *UFO Magazine* are continuing their analysis of the image, and will be subjecting it to computer enhancement in the near future. Perhaps then, hopefully, this enigmatic image will reveal its secrets.

Sightings by Astronauts: Is the Truth Out There?

If some UFOs are actually spacecraft operated by beings from other worlds, we might expect their presence to be observed on occasion by our own astronauts during space missions. Although many people lament our lack of manned planetary exploration in the wake of the triumphant Apollo programme in the late 1960s and early 70s, we are nevertheless establishing a greater presence in near-Earth space, with the now-routine flights of the American Space Shuttle, and the Russian *Mir* Space Station. In addition, when the international Space Station *Alpha* is finally constructed, it will most likely serve as a "shipyard" and jumping-off point for manned missions to the Moon and Mars. So, if extraterrestrial UFOs have been observed by people on the surface of our planet, then surely they must have been seen in outer space by our astronauts . . .

It would seem that this is indeed the case, with many UFOs having been seen and reported by NASA crews. An early sighting was made by James McDivitt during his Gemini IV flight with Ed White on 4 June 1965. During the capsule's drifting flight, McDivitt noticed a cylindrical object "with a high fineness ratio" ahead of their spacecraft. From one end of the object protruded a long, cylindrical pole "with the approximate fineness of pencil." Owing to the conditions in the vacuum of space, McDivitt was unable to determine the size of the object, or its distance from the Gemini capsule. According to him, it could have been very small and near, or very large and far away. Nevertheless, he turned on the capsule's control system, in case it became necessary to take evasive action.

McDivitt tried to photograph the object with the two cameras they had on board, but since it was only in his field of view for a few seconds, he had to use the cameras at whatever settings they had at the time. After the object had disappeared from view, he was unable to relocate it.

The camera films were flown back to Houston as soon as

Gemini IV landed. According to McDivitt, a film technician at NASA selected what he thought were the relevant photographs of the UFO, and subjected them to analysis. However, these photographs showed "sunspots," or flares, on the window, and *not* the object McDivitt had seen and photographed. When the astronaut returned from the aircraft carrier three days after landing, he went through the photographs himself, but could find nothing that looked like the UFO. Evidently, the camera settings had been wrong after all.

According to James Oberg of NASA, the object encountered by Gemini IV was actually the second stage of the Titan which had launched the capsule into orbit. However, as ufologist Timothy Good states, it is rather puzzling that McDivitt should fail to recognize his own rocket. For his own part, James McDivitt maintains that, although he does not think the object was genuinely anomalous, it was still unidentified, and was certainly not the upper stage of a rocket. When he checked the records, they revealed that there were no upper stages or rockets anywhere near the Gemini capsule at the time of the sighting.

The next NASA encounter with a UFO occurred aboard Gemini V, crewed by Gordon Cooper and Charles Conrad. On the third day of their mission, 24 August 1965, as they were passing over Cape Canaveral (then Cape Kennedy), the Gemini Flight Director, Christopher Kraft, asked them if they could see anything flying alongside them. Kraft radioed to them: "We have a radar image of a space object going right along with you from 2,000 to 10,000 yards away. Their radar return is approximately the same magnitude as Gemini V." The object was tracked until both it and Gemini V were lost beyond the curvature of the Earth. By the time the capsule came within range of the tracking station at Carnarvon, Australia, the UFO had departed.

Another UFO was encountered by the crew of Gemini VII, Jim Lovell and Frank Borman, as the following transcript attests:

SPACECRAFT: Bogey at 10 o'clock high.

CAPCOM: This is Houston. Say again 7.

SPACECRAFT: Said we have a bogey at 10 o'clock high.

CAPCOM: Gemini 7, is that the booster or is that an actual sighting?

SPACECRAFT: We have several, looks like debris up here. Actual sighting.

CAPCOM: Estimate distance or size?

SPACECRAFT: We also have the booster in sight. . . .

In his assessment of the case, Condon Committee investigator Franklin Roach suggested that the "bogey" might have been a large fragment from the launching of Gemini VII; however, he qualified this by adding that it would be impossible if the UFO was travelling in a polar orbit, as was apparently the case.

The crew of Apollo XI are also alleged to have encountered extraterrestrial vehicles, both during transit to the Moon and after making the historic landing there on 21 July 1969. The first sighting occurred when the Moonship was only one day out from the Earth. After spotting an unusual object between their craft and the Moon, they radioed Mission Control to ask if it was the Saturn V booster rocket. Houston replied that the booster was 6,000 miles away. Neil Armstrong described the object as being "like an open suitcase."

Viewed through a sextant (with the instrument just off focus), the UFO took on a different shape, now appearing as "two hollow cylinders." As it rotated, its interior could clearly be seen. When the sextant was focused correctly, the object returned to its "open book" shape.

According to persistent rumours, as soon as the Lunar Excursion Module *Eagle* arrived at the Sea of Tranquillity, Neil Armstrong and Edwin "Buzz" Aldrin watched a number of very large spacecraft land near them. Dr. Vladimir Azhazha, Professor of Mathematics at Moscow University, claims that Armstrong's message to Mission Control, confirming the presence of UFOs on the Moon, was censored by NASA, and that the UFOs departed soon after the astronauts began their Moonwalk. Another even wilder story has it that a number of alien beings disembarked from one of the UFOs, and stood on the lunar surface, watching the *Eagle*. Mission Control then ordered Armstrong to remain inside the LEM, and under no circumstances to venture out onto the surface while the aliens were nearby—an order he disobeyed. (Personally, I find it hard to imagine Armstrong making his cool and collected "one small step for a man" speech, with a number of possibly hostile alien beings a few hundred yards away!)

Some of these claims were supported by Maurice Chatelain, a former NASA communications specialist, who said in 1979 that NASA interrupted Apollo XI's radio transmissions on several occasions, to keep the truth from the people of the world. According to NASA's chief spokesman John McLeaish, however, the agency did no such thing; the only delay in the transmissions from the Moon occurred as a result of processing through electronic equipment, and this delay was very slight. The only actual break in transmissions occurred when the spacecraft was on the far side of the Moon, and the only conversations that were never made public were those of a private nature between the astronauts and doctors.

An Object Headed for the Moon in 1958?

In his 1959 book *Stranger Than Science*, the American journalist Frank Edwards tells an intriguing story from the early days of the Space Age. In October 1958, exactly one year after the Soviet Union launched Sputnik 1, the first artificial satellite to orbit the Earth, the Cape Canaveral Missile Center in Florida began to pick up powerful radio signals from an unknown object that was apparently moving between the Earth and the Moon. The signals were detected for approximately three hours each day, and the scientists at the Cape quickly alerted their colleagues at radio tracking stations around the world, each of which recorded the signals and immediately set to work attempting to plot the precise position of the device.

The most incredible discovery they made was that the object was headed for the Moon at approximately 9,000 m.p.h., although this speed was constantly changing! It had been assumed that the object was a Soviet rocket that had been launched in secret, but the variations in the object's speed ruled out this explanation: no known rocket could speed up and slow down, as this object appeared to be doing.

In addition, US intelligence sources confirmed that the Soviets had not made any launches during the period that the unknown device came to the scientists' attention. The calculations were rechecked. The object had first been detected approximately 3,000 miles out from the Earth, following a course that would take it to the Moon. However, as the scientists on Earth continued to track it with astonishment, it reduced speed, then twice accelerated rapidly, before finally altering its course and heading off into deep space.

Since the initial assumption had been that the object was a secret Soviet Moon probe, Cape Canaveral had no qualms in releasing the information to the public. However, when it became apparent that they were dealing with something else entirely, there was a frantic scramble to explain the object. As Frank Edwards puts it, "The customary pattern of multiple-explanation was pursued. This consists of having several allegedly explanatory statements released in rapid sequence, varying in nature but all dealing with the same incident. This achieves the desired goal of creating doubt and confusion while explaining nothing."

Thus, one of the "explanations" was that the signals detected were "similar" to those transmitted by Sputnik 1. This was not terribly helpful, since Sputnik 1 no longer existed, having re-entered the Earth's atmosphere and been destroyed. Another statement had it that Cape Canaveral and the other tracking stations had detected the ionized gases from rocket exhaust fumes. Of course, radio telescopes cannot track rocket exhaust fumes.

The object tracked on its way to the Moon has never been adequately explained. All we know is that it was there, and was doing things that no human-built crafts were capable of doing in 1958. . . .

The Bridge in the Sky

Frank Edwards also tells us of an astonishing mystery discovered on the Moon several decades before the recent controversies that have gained popular attention (more of which a little later). It began on the night of 29 July 1953, when John O'Neil, science editor with the *New York Herald Tribune*, decided to spend a while observing the Moon. Slipping a 90-power eyepiece into his telescope, he began his observation, and saw something he could never have imagined in his wildest fantasies. Stretching across one edge of the Mare Criseum (the Sea of Crises) was a long, straight shadow, apparently cast by a gigantic bridge. O'Neil estimated its length as approximately 12 miles!

Anxious for a closer look at the structure, he switched eyepieces, placing a 250-power lens in the telescope. He was rewarded with a crystal-clear image of the bridge, a truly colossal piece of engineering, and one that was all the more impressive for having, apparently, been erected in about five weeks, for it had not been there the last time O'Neil had observed the Mare Criseum.

In a courageous move, considering the nature of his discovery, O'Neil reported on the presence of the bridge to the Association of Lunar and Planetary Observers. Although he prudently referred to the bridge as a natural structure, he was predictably attacked by his peers. However, he was supported by the highly respected astronomer Dr. H.P. Wilkins, who announced that he had seen the bridge, too, a month after O'Neil first saw it.

A month later, the British astronomer Patrick Moore also spoke up in support of O'Neil, stating that he had spotted the bridge as well, observing it for more than an hour.

The Mare Criseum has something of a reputation for unexplained activity. In 1869 a series of bright lights was seen by astronomers prompting the Royal Astronomical Society to ask their members to observe and record the strange, geometric patterns. Over the next two years, they recorded more than a hundred such patterns, including vast rectangles and triangles. The phenomena lasted until 1871, whereupon they ceased.

However, other strange phenomena were noted in the early years of the twentieth century. In 1912, the American astronomer F. B. Harris watched an enormous object sailing across the face of the Moon. He estimated the black object, which cast a shadow on the lunar surface, to be 50 miles in diameter.

Thirty-eight years later, Dr. H. P. Wilkins was observing the crater Aristarchus, when he saw a glowing, oval-shaped object hovering just above the crater floor. This (or a similar) object was seen by another American astronomer, Dr. James Bartlett Jr.

Over the years, a large number of white domes (more than 200) have been seen on the Moon's surface. They appear to be mobile, since they frequently disappear from one location, only to pop up again somewhere else. As Edwards says, "if these markings on the Moon are not artificial, then they constitute a natural phenomenon without parallel."

Junkyard of the Gods?

In 1979, a group of respected Soviet scientists made a claim that astounded the world. According to the astrophysicist Professor Sergei Boshich, the shattered wreckage of an alien spacecraft—possibly containing the bodies of its crew—is in orbit 1,240 miles above the Earth. There are ten major pieces of debris, two of which are 100 feet across; these two large pieces apparently give a clue as to the shape and size of the original craft. Professor Aleksandr Kazantsev stated that the ship "was at least 200 feet long and 100 feet wide. It had small domes housing telescopes, saucer antennae for communications, and portholes. Its size would suggest several floors, possibly five. We believe alien bodies will still be on board."

Having plotted the orbits of the lumps of wreckage, which were first discovered in the 1960s, the Soviet researchers found that "they all originated in the same spot on the same day—December 18, 1955 [two years before the first artificial satellite, Sputnik 1, was launched]. Obviously there had been a powerful explosion."

Dr. Vladimir Azhazha dismissed suggestions that the debris were from a meteor: "Meteors do not have orbits. They plummet aimlessly, hurtling erratically through space. And they do not explode spontaneously. All the evidence we have gathered over the past decade points to one thing—a crippled alien craft. It must hold secrets we have not even dreamed of."

Soviet geologist Professor Aleksei Zolotov suggested that a "rescue mission" should be launched. "The vessel, or what is left of it, should be reassembled here on Earth. The benefits to mankind could be stupendous."

These findings were greeted with great interest by American scientists. Dr. Henry Monteith of the top secret Sandia Laboratories in Albuquerque, New Mexico, suggested that a space shuttle be launched to salvage the wreckage, while Dr. Myran Malkin, Director of the NASA Space Shuttle Office of Space Technology, said: "We would consider a joint salvage attempt if the Russians approached us."

Dr. Desmond King-Hele, a researcher at the Royal Aircraft Establishment in Farnborough, England, said: "There are more than 4,000 pieces of wreckage orbiting the Earth. Each has a catalogue number to identify it. We would like to know the catalogue number of this wreck. It is possible to date wreckage after a considerable number of observations. Like the Americans, we would be interested to look at this if the Russians make the information available."

In 1969, the US magazine *Icarus* carried an article by the astronomer John Bagby, which described how "ten moonlets" had been discovered in orbit around the Earth. They had apparently broken off from a larger body. The date of this disintegration was 18 December 1955.

Of course, little more has been heard of this potentially historic find. In view of the fact that the reasons for space shuttle missions are not always made public, it is possible that this mysterious wreckage has indeed been salvaged . . . in which case we can only wonder at the fabulous secrets it contains. . . .

A UFO in Orbit around the Sun?

It could be a comet or an asteroid . . . or perhaps something else. The discovery of an unidentified object orbiting the Sun has called into question the most fundamental assumptions of astronomers concerning the nature of the Solar System. The object, designated 1996PW, is being tracked by NASA scientists, who describe it as an "interplanetary oddball."

1996PW is about ten miles wide, and is following a highly elongated orbit which implies that it is a comet. However, there is no trace of the bright plume that invariably accompanies a comet during a close approach to the Sun; in this case the plume from 1996PW should have been easily visible from the Earth. Although analysis of the light reflected from it suggests it contains the ice and gases typically found in comets, the object is actually inert, behaving more like an asteroid. According to Eleanor Helin, a planetary astronomer at NASA's Jet Propulsion Laboratory in California: "This is a misfit in the grand scheme of things."

The great puzzle of 1996PW involves its orbital path, which does not correspond to the roughly circular orbit around the Sun followed by asteroids. The shape of these orbits (corresponding to those of the planets) has led most astronomers to conclude that the asteroids are the rubble left over from the formation of the Solar System about 4,500 million years ago, perhaps the remnants of a planet that didn't quite make it. Comets, on the other hand, are thought to have formed as a result of the gravitational effects of the Sun as the Solar System passed through interstellar dust clouds, thus creating their elongated orbits.

The orbit of 1996PW is 3.5 million miles long and takes 5,000 years to complete. Its discovery would seem to indicate either that there are deep flaws in current theories of comet and asteroid formation . . . or that 1996PW is neither a comet nor an asteroid.

Hale-Bopp's Curious Companion

In the wake of rumours reported by British astronomy writer Andrew Pike, that the Hubble Space Telescope photographed a "floating city in space" on 26 March 1996 (and that President Clinton and Pope John Paul II are being kept informed of developments), a leading astronomer—allegedly of Duke University in America—photographed a gigantic object orbiting comet Hale-Bopp in late November. The unnamed astronomer is said to be a pioneer in the field of planetary astronomy, and has known about the object for several months.

Astonishingly, the object appears to be self-luminous, lighting up the surrounding cometary debris, and has also been photographed moving about the comet, which seems to imply that it is under intelligent control. In addition, a complex radio signal has allegedly been transmitted by the object, and has been taped by radio astronomers, who are attempting to decipher it.

In an article in the January/February 1997 issue of *UFO Magazine*, Graham Birdsall draws attention to the fact that scientists all over the world have recently been holding meetings to discuss the potential threat to life on Earth posed by space objects. Senior Pentagon figures have also met with their Russian counterparts several times in recent years, first in a remote Sicilian town, then in northern Italy, France and finally London in 1996. Birdsall suggests a possibly sinister connection between these meetings and the discovery of 1996PW (which apparently defies the laws of physics), the alleged presence of a "city in space," and the colossal radio signal-transmitting object accompanying comet Hale-Bopp.

It has been claimed for many years that the military and intelligence communities in a number of countries know far more about UFOs than they are letting on. In view of the fact that there are more than 100,000 near-Earth asteroids, each of which would cause a global catastrophe if it impacted the Earth, it seems eminently sensible for scientists to discuss the best course of action to take, should such an object threaten our planet. In view of the bizarre discoveries mentioned above, it might also be sensible to combine this asteroid defence programme with a defence programme of a different kind. . . .

2

Close Encounters of the Second Kind

Measurable physical effects on the land and on animate and inanimate objects are reported.

The Maury Island Mystery

The world of the close encounter with the unknown can be a very murky place, inhabited by unscrupulous sensation seekers as well as those who are genuinely mystified by what they have seen. In view of this unfortunate fact, it is worth including at least one generally-accepted hoax to illustrate the importance of vigilance in dealing with extreme claims. Although total scepticism is just as unhelpful—and unhealthy—as total credulity (indeed, they are actually opposite aspects of the same belief system), it is nevertheless essential to maintain an initial scepticism, erring on the side of the mundane until impressive evidence to the contrary can be gathered and evaluated. In this respect, the so-called "Fortean" approach, in which what is accepted remains constantly open to reinterpretation in the light of new evidence, is by far the best. As Charles Fort (from whose name the adjective "Fortean" is derived) said: "I conceive of nothing, in religion, science or philosophy, that is more than the proper thing to wear, for a while."

With this in mind, let us take a look at one of the most famous close encounters of the second kind, the Maury Island incident. At about 2.00 P.M. on 21 June 1947, Harold A. Dahl, a harbour patrolman in Tacoma, Washington, was in a boat off Maury Island. With him were his 15-year-old son, his dog and two crewmen. According to their story, they saw six large, doughnut-shaped objects overhead. The objects seemed to be flattened spheres, with a hole in the centre and portholes around the rims. Five of the objects were circling around the sixth, which seemed to be experiencing some kind of difficulty in keeping aloft. The witnesses watched as one of the other objects descended toward and then touched the one in trouble, which immediately began to discharge a metallic substance and a black material resembling rock.

Harold Dahl had beached the boat on Maury Island, and was taking photographs of the spectacle. Some of the material from the centre object fell on them, killing the dog and injuring Dahl's son. The six objects then left the area, heading out over the sea. Dahl and the others then loaded the damaged boat with some of the material that had fallen from the object.

Dahl told his boss, Fred Lee Crisman, what had happened. Crisman, angry over the damage to the boat and suspicious of the fantastic story he had been told, took another boat out to the island. There he found a large amount of material scattered on the beach. At that moment, another UFO emerged from a cloud.

The Maury Island sighting had been brought to the attention of Raymond Palmer, the editor of *Amazing Stories* magazine, who sent Kenneth Arnold to investigate. Since his own sighting on 24 June 1947, Arnold had become deeply interested in the subject of "flying saucers," and interviewed both Dahl and Crisman on several occasions in late July.

Dahl had another strange tale for Arnold. He claimed to have had breakfast with a mysterious man on the morning following the sighting. The black-suited man told Dahl he had seen something he shouldn't have, and threatened both him and his family with dire consequences if he spoke to anyone else about it. When Arnold asked him for the photographs he had taken of the objects, Dahl replied that they were covered with spots, perhaps caused by radiation.

Together with United Airlines Captain E. J. Smith (who had seen a formation of UFOs during a flight on 4 July 1947), Arnold examined the debris from the Maury Island UFO, which looked to them like lava rock and scrap aluminium. They then enlisted the help of two Army Air Force intelligence officers, Lieutenant Frank M. Brown and Captain William Davidson, with whom they had been in contact regarding previous UFO sightings. The two intelligence officers agreed to interview Dahl and Crisman, and to examine the alleged UFO debris. They arrived in Tacoma on the afternoon of 31 July.

After the interviews and the debris examination, Brown and Davidson concluded that the whole story was a hoax. Subsequent Army Air Force investigations revealed that Dahl and Crisman were not harbour patrolmen, as they had claimed, but rather were salvagers of floating lumber. The official AAF report summed up the case by saying that both Dahl and Crisman admitted that the rock fragments had nothing to do with flying saucers. They admitted sending the rock fragments to Raymond Palmer as a joke, while telling him that they might have been part of a flying saucer.

According to the 4 August issue of the San Francisco *News*, Dahl told the *United Press* Bureau at Tacoma that he had never had any pieces of a flying saucer. He had several "metallic stones," which he had picked up on the beach at Maury Island just before the "flying saucer craze swept the country." Likewise, the mysterious man who had threatened Dahl was no more than a figment of his imagination.

With this, the Maury Island incident should have been consigned to the wastebasket of ufology, one of the many lamentable hoaxes that have plagued the subject since its birth. This surely would have been the case, were it not for a tragic accident that claimed the lives of the two AAF intelligence officers, Davidson and Brown. On 1 August, the B-25 aircraft in which they were flying back to Hamilton Field crashed as a result of a burning exhaust stack that set one of the wings on fire. The wing broke off and smashed into the tail, crippling the aircraft and sending it plummeting into the ground.

As aviation historian Curtis Peebles states in his sceptical analysis of ufology, *Watch the Skies!*, these facts were woefully absent from the *Tacoma Times* report of the following day. Under the headline SABOTAGE HINTED IN CRASH OF ARMY BOMBER AT KELSO, the report said that the B-25 "had been sabotaged 'or shot down' to prevent shipment of flying disk fragments." An intelligence officer had evidently confirmed that the aircraft had been carrying "classified material." The classified material, however, was merely a collection of reports that had nothing to do with UFOs. There had been nothing sinister about the crash: it had been caused by an aircraft malfunction, and nothing more.

The Maury Island incident, together with its tragic conclusion, serves as a prime example of the ease with which certain UFO reports can take on a life of their own, and remain the subjects of furtive rumours long after they have been proved to be spurious. Cases of this kind are extremely irritating to serious UFO researchers, since they not only provide grist for the mills of ardent debunkers (who maintain that there are no genuinely anomalous UFOs, and never have been), but also muddy the waters around the subject in general, making it even harder to approach a possible solution to its central mysteries.

The Death of Captain Mantell

Although there have been a number of deaths over the years that have been linked to UFO or alien activity, the first widely publicized incident of this kind was the fatal encounter between Captain Thomas Mantell and a strange object sighted in the skies over Godman Air Force Base, Kentucky. This "classic" case began on 7 January 1948, at about 1.20 P.M. CST, when the Kentucky State Police contacted the Military Police at Fort Knox, alerting them to the presence of an unidentified aircraft, "approximately 250–300 feet in diameter," over Mansville, Kentucky. Fort Knox then passed on this information to nearby Godman Air Force Base. The object was sighted in the south-west at 1.45 P.M. by personnel in the Godman control tower, who described it as resembling "an ice cream cone topped with red."

According to the Operations Officer, Captain Gary W. Carter, "the object . . . was easily discernible with the naked eye. The object appeared round and white (whiter than the clouds that passed in front of it) and could be seen through cirrus clouds."

At about that time, four F-51 Mustang aircraft took off from Marietta AFB, Georgia, on a low-altitude navigation training flight. The flight leader was Captain Thomas F. Mantell of the Air National Guard 165th Fighter Squadron, an experienced pilot with a total of 2,867 hours' flight time. At about 2.40 P.M. the four F-51s were in the vicinity of Godman AFB, and Mantell was asked if he could check out the mysterious object that was still hanging in the skies over the base. One of the Mustangs, short on fuel, had to continue on to Standiford AFB (the flight's intended destination), while Mantell and the remaining aircraft climbed on an intercept course toward the object.

When the Mustangs reached 15,000 feet, Mantell, ahead of the others, radioed to Godman: "The object is directly ahead of and above me now, moving at about half my speed. . . . It appears to be a metallic object or possibly reflection of Sun from a metallic object, and it is of tremendous size. . . . I'm still climbing, the object is above and ahead of me moving at about my speed or faster. I'm trying to close in for a better look."

The two remaining Mustangs abandoned the chase at 22,000 feet, due to lack of oxygen. (Since they had been on a low-altitude flight, they had not taken oxygen supplies.) Mantell informed Godman that he would go to 25,000 feet for ten minutes. When he reached that altitude, he evidently passed out from lack of oxygen, while his aircraft continued to climb to 30,000 feet before finally levelling off. With no one to guide it, the plane succumbed to the torque of its own engine and began a left turn,

which gradually steepened into a spiralling dive. At around
15,000 feet, the Mustang disintegrated.

The shattered wreckage was located, on the farm of a William
J. Phillips near Franklin, Kentucky. Mantell's body was still in
the cockpit. His watch had stopped at 3.18 P.M.

The two other pilots flew on to Standiford AFB, unaware that
Mantell had crashed. One of the pilots, Lieutenant A. W.
Clements, refuelled and secured an oxygen supply before taking
off again in search of the UFO. Although he climbed to 32,000
feet, he could find no trace of the object.

Shortly after the Godman tower lost the object at 3.50 P.M., it
was sighted to the south in Tennessee. At about 4.40 P.M., an astronomy professor at Vanderbilt University watched an object
through binoculars, and later described it as a pear-shaped balloon with cables and a basket.

The Mantell incident was investigated by personnel from Project Sign, who concluded (at least publicly) that the pilot had
died chasing the planet Venus. Although this explanation
sounded plausible (Venus was in the area of sky in which the
UFO had been sighted, was at the same 33-degree elevation and
moving at 15 degrees per hour, a pace consistent with the
planet's apparent movement), it suffered from the fact that the
planet was at only half its maximum brightness, and was therefore hard to see against the brightness of the sky.

News of Mantell's death spread quickly, and the press had a
field day with the possibility that a military officer had died in
pursuit of a flying saucer. Strange rumours quickly followed:
Mantell's body had been discovered riddled with bullet holes;
his head was missing; his entire body was missing; the F-51 had
been soaked in radiation. None of this was ever verified, and it
seems that all of the rumours were spurious.

According to the accident report, the emergency canopy lock
was still in place, implying that Mantell had indeed passed out
from lack of oxygen, without making any attempt to bail out. The
throttle and propeller pitch controls were in positions that

would have slowed the aircraft down, which seemed to indicate that Mantell had regained consciousness long enough to attempt to pull out of the dive. This manoeuvre was evidently too much for the aircraft, which disintegrated under the strain.

As to the object itself, Captain Ruppelt re-examined the case in 1952, and discovered that a Skyhook balloon had been launched from Camp Ripley, Minnesota, early on the morning of the sightings. These experimental, high-altitude balloons were being secretly tested by the US Navy at the time, and were unknown to Air Force officers. In addition, weather charts for 7 January 1948 indicated that such a balloon would indeed have floated over Kentucky and Tennessee.

However, there remains one unanswered question in the Mantell case, which, ironically enough, arises from similar considerations to those that more or less proved the illusory nature of Kenneth Arnold's UFOs the previous year. According to Project Sign's analysis of the incident:

> It has been officially reported that the object was a Navy cosmic-ray research balloon. If this can be established, it is to be preferred as an explanation. However, If one accepts the assumptions that reports from various other localities refer to the same object, any such device must have been a good many miles high in order to have been seen clearly, almost simultaneously, from places 175 miles apart... no man-made object could have been large enough and far enough away from the approximate simultaneous sightings.

The implication is that, just as Arnold's UFOs could not have been 25 miles away *and* recognizable as structured craft, the Skyhook balloon explanation in the Mantell case could not account for the size of an object observable from such widely separated vantage-points; it was simply too large and too far away from the various observers. It is also worth bearing in mind Mantell's description of the object as "tremendous" in size. If it were tremendous in size while still thousands of feet above him, it seems unlikely that it was a 100-foot long balloon; and yet, if it were tremendous in size because he was actually quite close to it, surely he would have recognized it as a balloon—even one belonging to a secret project.

Although the Mantell case is generally regarded as having been solved, this puzzling question does remain, casting a faint shadow of doubt over it. We will never know with absolute certainty what Captain Mantell was chasing when he died; perhaps it was a balloon... or perhaps it was something that left behind the most extreme of physical traces: a shattered plane and its dead pilot.

A 30-Ton UFO

Although apparent alien beings were encountered in the following case, it is more significant as a close encounter of the second kind, in that definite, measurable physical traces were left behind. The 15 September 1954 issue of *France-Soir* carried the following report of Marius Dewilde's experience.

Three investigators for the air police arrived at Quarouble Nord, yesterday to interview M. Marius Dewilde, the man who saw two "Martians" near his back-yard gate. They left the village convinced that, during the night of Friday to Saturday, a mysterious craft had indeed landed, as claimed by M. Dewilde, on the tracks of the Saint-Amand-Blanc-Misseron railway line, near crossing No. 79.

Their inquiries seem, in effect, to confirm the statement made by the metal-worker. The witness declared that on Friday, about 10.30 P.M., he had seen a machine of an elongated shape, three metres high, six metres long, sitting on the tracks a few metres away from his house. Two beings of human appearance, of very small height and apparently wearing diving suits, could be seen nearby. M. Dewilde walked toward them, but at that moment a beam of greenish light was focused on him from the craft and he found himself paralysed. When he was able to move again the machine had started to rise and the two beings had disappeared.

The investigators have found no trace of the existence of these beings. The ground, examined metre by metre, shows a trace of footsteps. However, there are traces on the sleepers that could have been made by a machine landing on it. In five places the wood of the sleepers is compressed over an area of about four square centimetres. These markings all have the same appearance and they lie symmetrically, on one line. Three of them—those in the middle—are 43 centimetres apart. The last two are 67 centimetres away from the preceding ones.

A craft landing on legs instead of wheels like our own aircraft would leave just such traces, one of the inspectors of the air police has declared.

M. Dewilde's story is also confirmed by several inhabitants of the region. In Onnaing, at about 10.30 P.M. (the time indicated by M. Dewilde), a young man called M. Edmond Auverlot and a retired man, M. Hublard, saw a reddish light travelling in the sky. The same light was seen from Vicq by three young men.

The air police investigators consulted various railroad specialists about the markings on the wooden sleepers. After examining the sleepers, the specialists concluded that the marks had been made by something exerting a pressure of 30 tons. In addition, the marks had sharply defined edges, which supported the conclusion that an extremely heavy weight had been involved. The police also examined the gravel of the railroad bed, and made another, perhaps even more intriguing discovery. According to the great French ufologist Aimé Michel, writing in his 1958 book *Flying Saucers and the Straight-Line Mystery*, they found that the stones at the site of the landing were brittle, as if they had been calcined. In other words, they had apparently been subjected to intense heat, which had raised their temperature to just below their melting or fusing point, causing a chemical reduction or oxidation. Blackish traces were also found at the landing site. According to the report, the ground around the landing site was hard.

Therefore, the fact that there were no footprints did not cast doubt on Marius Dewilde's story. In fact, when compared with the positive physical evidence that was discovered, the lack of footprints in hard soil fades into insignificance.

The Rendlesham Forest Incident

Toward the end of December 1980, an event occurred that has come to be regarded as the most significant in the history of British ufology. Although, depending on whose testimony one takes as the most reliable, it could be considered as a close encounter of the third kind (the sighting of alien entities), the Rendlesham incident is most significant for the measurable physical traces left behind by the UFO.

In 1980, the twin Royal Air Force bases of Woodbridge and Bentwaters in Suffolk, owned by the Ministry of Defence but staffed by the US Air Force, formed a vital component of the NATO defences in Europe. On the night of 27 December, two USAF security personnel were patrolling the area around the East Gate sector of RAF Woodbridge. They observed a light moving through the trees in adjoining Rendlesham Forest and, thinking that it might be an aircraft in trouble, they radioed back to their superiors.

Although no aircraft were flying that night, both the Woodbridge control tower and the radar defence unit at RAF Watton had locked on to a target approaching from the north. Three more security personnel were dispatched to investigate. Searching the dense forest in the enveloping darkness, they eventually came to a large clearing, in which they saw a glowing, triangular object resting on three struts in a tripod arrangement. The surface of the object had a peculiar, "quilted" appearance, although it seemed metallic. There was a large red light at its apex, and a bank of intense blue lights around the base. As the airmen approached, the object glided away across the clearing. The airmen were not the only ones to be stunned by what they were seeing. Nearby farm animals became panic-stricken and virtually stampeded into a lane behind the field.

In an official memorandum to the Ministry of Defence, Lieutenant-Colonel Charles Halt, the deputy base commander, described the investigation of the area that was conducted the following day.

> ... three depressions 1½" deep and 7" in diameter were found where the object had been sighted on the ground. The following night (29 Dec 80) the area was checked for radiation. Beta/gamma readings of 0.1 milliroentgens were recorded with peak readings in the three depressions near the center of the triangle formed by the depressions. A nearby tree had moderate (.05–.07) readings on the side of the tree toward the depressions.

The mysterious object returned to Rendlesham Forest that night, and was witnessed by Colonel Halt and others, as the final paragraph of his memorandum states.

> ... a red sun-like light was seen through the trees. It moved about and pulsed. At one point it appeared to throw off glowing particles and then broke into five separate white objects and then disappeared. Immediately thereafter, three star-like objects were noticed in the sky, two objects to the north and one to the south, all of which were about 10° off the horizon. The objects moved rapidly in sharp angular movements and displayed red, green and blue lights. The objects to the north appeared to be elliptical through an 8–12 power lens. They then turned to full circles. The objects to the north remained in the sky for an hour or more. The object to the south was visible for two or three hours and beamed down a stream of light from time to time. Numerous individuals, including the undersigned, witnessed [these] activities....

According to sceptics, these bizarre light formations were actually caused by the lighthouse at Orford Ness, about five miles away. However, this explanation seems rather facile, in view of the fact that the USAF personnel had dimly spied the lighthouse beam while they were searching for the object in the forest, and had recognized it for what it was. Apart from this, it seems extremely unlikely that highly trained servicemen would mistake such a thing for a metallic, triangular object, resting a few feet away from them on three landing struts. In addition, lighthouse beams are not generally known for their ability to leave traces of beta and gamma radiation.

According to Airman Lawrence Warren, who was also present at the time of the landing, alien entities were visible inside the object. As he approached the UFO, Warren became aware that time seemed to be flowing at "half speed." A small object detached itself from the larger "craft" before splitting into three. Warren claims to have been able to see beings with large eyes inside these smaller objects.

At that point, says Warren, Colonel Gordon Williams, the overall base commander, entered the field and actually attempted to communicate with the beings by holding up his arms in a questioning manner. There was a sudden, sharp noise and the entities raised their own arms, either in reply, or perhaps for protection. A "protective membrane" then slid over their eyes, "and they got real bright."

There were apparently a great many military personnel in the field, equipped with video cameras and other recording equipment. In an interview with British ufologist Timothy Good, Warren estimated that there were about 80 people present, before the security police were dismissed. Apparently, Warren and some of the others were deeply disturbed by what they had seen. His retinas had been damaged by the intense lights, and he even ended up with a shock of grey hair. He also told Good that, during his debriefing following the encounter, he and the other security police were shown a 15-minute film of UFOs, taken during the Second World War and the Korean and Vietnam Wars. The reason for this was, allegedly, to justify the extreme secrecy surrounding the UFO phenomenon.

The Rendlesham Incident is important not only for the measurable physical traces left behind by the UFOs, but also as an example of how the authorities *do* cover up such encounters. The Halt memorandum, describing the UFO activity and the radiation traces left behind, was sent to the Ministry of Defence via Squadron Leader Donald Moreland, commander of the neighbouring base at Bentwaters. While researching their book about the incident, *Sky Crash* (co-authored with Jenny Randles), Brenda Butler and Dot Street met with Moreland in February 1981, and were told by him that he knew nothing about any incident at Woodbridge. It was not until 1983 that the Halt memorandum was released under the American Freedom of Information Act. It is rather ironic that British researchers had to wait for a document describing events occurring on British soil to be released in America, before the Ministry of Defence even admitted that anything unusual had happened, and that the memorandum was in their files, after all.

Incredible as it may seem, this document, released to Robert Todd of the US group Citizens Against UFO Secrecy (CAUS), is claimed by the MoD to be the *only* documentation they have on the Rendlesham Incident. Although questions were asked in the House of Commons, the British Government insisted that they took no action following the events in December 1980. As Jenny Randles states, if this were true, it would constitute an appalling neglect of duty in the defence of British territory. If, on the other hand, the MoD *did* take steps in response to this apparent intrusion by an unidentified craft, then why is official secrecy being maintained?

Burned by a UFO

Although radiation traces left on vegetation after a UFO sighting are impressive enough, when physical evidence is discovered on the bodies of the witnesses themselves, the events become truly disturbing, and virtually impossible to dismiss as misidentification or hoax. One such event happened in Texas on the night of 29 December 1980 (around the time that the US airmen were puzzling over the mysterious intruder in Rendlesham Forest!).

At 9.00 P.M., a solitary car was driving along the lonely Cleveland-Huffman Road, north of Lake Houston, headed for Dayton, Texas. In the car were Betty Cash, a 51-year-old restaurant and grocery store owner, Vickie Landrum, 57, who worked in Betty's restaurant, and Colby Landrum, Vickie's seven-year-old grandson. The night was cold, the temperature 40° F (4.5° C), and they had the car's heater on.

Colby was the first to see the UFO, gliding just above the treetops. At first they assumed it was an ordinary aircraft, but, as it gradually drew closer, they realized that the object was anything but ordinary. As it approached the road on which they were travelling, they could see that it was large, diamond-shaped and emitted a very bright light that was punctuated occasionally by a burst of fire, like a rocket exhaust, from its underside.

The UFO was now dead ahead of them, and Vickie screamed at Betty to stop the car, believing that if they passed underneath the object, they would be burned alive. As the three stunned witnesses watched, the UFO continued to hover erratically about 60 yards away, losing height, letting forth another rocket blast and then rising again. Vickie described it as "a diamond of fire." It appeared to be made of a material like dull aluminium; the glow from it was so bright that it lit up the surrounding countryside. The points of the diamond were rounded rather than sharp, and its centreline was ringed with blue lights. In addition, the UFO emitted a beeping sound.

The three witnesses left the car to observe the object. Despite assurances that it would not hurt him, Colby was extremely frightened, so his grandmother got back into the car with him. Betty continued to watch the UFO from outside, in spite of the intense heat it was generating, until Vickie screamed at her to return to the car. When she tugged on the driver's door handle, it was so hot that she recoiled, and had to use her coat as protection to get the door open. Inside the car the temperature was so great that they had to switch on the air conditioner.

Presently, the UFO rose into the night sky and left the area. Incredibly, the witnesses saw that it was being pursued by about 20 large helicopters! According to Betty, "they seemed to rush in from all directions . . . it seemed like they were trying to encircle the thing." As Betty started the car and they continued their journey home, they could still see the receding object, a gradually fading light ascending into the sky. The helicopters were still clearly in pursuit; some of them were illuminated by the object. The witnesses described some of them as having four wheels and two rotor blades, which implies that they were Boeing CH-47 Chinooks. Others were much smaller, single-rotor craft, which might have been Bell Hueys.

Badly shaken by their experience, the witnesses continued on to Vickie and Colby's house, where Betty dropped them off before returning to her own home. The time was approximately 9.50 P.M.

The fear engendered in the witnesses was far from over, however. They all began to feel ill upon their return home, suffering from headaches and nausea. Perhaps because she had been outside the car for longest, Betty fared worst, with swelling of the neck and red blotches on her face and head. In the days that followed, these symptoms worsened, with the blotches turning into blisters. Betty also began to suffer from diarrhoea, and her eyes swelled shut.

All three witnesses had to be admitted to hospital for treatment. Betty was treated as a burn victim. During her 12 days there, patches of her skin fell off, and some of her hair fell out. Vickie and Colby also suffered considerably, from swollen eyes, diarrhoea, hair loss (which was eventually replaced by hair of a different, frizzy texture), anorexia and diminished vision.

According to Lawrence Fawcett and Barry Greenwood in their book *Clear Intent*, the Cash-Landrum encounter was investigated by John Schuessler, a Project Manager for Space Shuttle Flight Operations for the McDonnell Douglas Corporation and

Deputy Director for Administration for the Mutual UFO Network (MUFON) in Seguin, Texas. Schuessler came to the conclusion that the symptoms were consistent with radiation sickness, although he was unable to say exactly what type of radiation was involved. It is possible, however, that they were exposed to ultraviolet radiation. This ionizing radiation is the most dangerous to living tissues, and causes exactly the symptoms suffered by the witnesses. Non-ionizing radiation, as from microwaves, also causes irritated skin (particularly if they are pulsed), which plagued Betty, Vickie and Colby.

Attempts were also made to discover where the helicopters had come from. An official at the Houston Intercontinental Airport Federation Aviation Administration said that all of the roughly 400 helicopters operating commercially in the Houston area were single-rotor types. There were no double-rotor CH-47 Chinooks. A reporter from the *Corpus Christi Caller* asked the press officer at the US Army's Fort Hood, near Killeen, Texas, whether they had any aircraft in the vicinity of the encounter on the night of 29 December 1980. He replied that there were none, but qualified this by adding: "I don't know any other place around here that would have that number of helicopters. I don't know what it could be...unless there's a super-secret thing going on and I wouldn't necessarily know about it." All the other military bases in Texas and Louisiana, when contacted, denied having any helicopters in the area at the time of the encounter.

Betty, Vickie and Colby were not alone in witnessing these helicopters, however. L. L. Walker, a police officer from Dayton, Texas, told Schuessler that he had seen a large number of helicopters, flying in groups of three with their searchlights on, several hours after the encounter on the Cleveland-Huffman Road. According to Walker, the helicopters, which he identified as Chinooks, seemed to be searching for something. In *Clear Intent*, Fawcett and Greenwood ask the questions that demand to be asked: why were the helicopters chasing the UFO? Were they actually attempting to capture it? If it really was an alien vehicle that was experiencing some kind of trouble, did they succeed? Or was the object actually an experimental human-built craft that had gone out of control?

Whatever the ultimate answer, the presence of CH-47 Chinooks strongly implies military involvement with the UFO. Believing that the object was definitely American in origin, Betty Cash and Vickie Landrum decided to sue the government for $20 million in damages. In August 1986, the case was finally dismissed on the grounds that no such object was owned or operated by the Army, Air Force, Navy or NASA.

John Schuessler was far from satisfied with this outcome, since the evidence regarding the presence of the Chinooks was ignored, the judge settling for the testimony of government experts as providing sufficient grounds to dismiss the case.

The Landing at Trans-en-Provence

Ironically enough, the Trans-en-Provence, southern France, encounter was brief, perhaps even run-of-the-mill, as far as UFO encounters go, and yet it qualifies as perhaps the most impressive case of its kind on record. The reason for this was that a large number of professional scientists actually bothered to examine the evidence—something that very rarely happens in UFO sighting cases.

At about 5.00 P.M., on 8 January 1981, Renato Nicolai, 55 and retired due to ill health, was working in his garden. The garden was rather unusual, in that it was on four levels, or terraces. Nicolai's attention was drawn to a whistling noise behind him, and he turned to see a small, saucer-shaped object descending toward the ground. Since he was on one of his garden's lower terraces, Nicolai quickly climbed toward the uppermost section for a better view of the strange machine.

The UFO then took off, kicking up some dust from the ground, and ascended to treetop level, revealing four openings in its underside from which "neither smoke nor flames were emitted." It then headed in the direction of the forest of Trans-en-Provence. As he walked toward the landing site, he noticed a circle about two metres in diameter. Nicolai described the object as being "just about one and a half metres high. It was the colour of lead."

According to the police, who examined the landing site the following day:

> We observed the presence of two concentric circles, one 2.20 metres in diameter and the other 2.40 metres in diameter. The two circles form a sort of corona ten centimetres thick.... There are two parts clearly visible, and they also show black striations. Nicolai thought he saw two kinds of round pieces which could have been landing gear or feet as the UFO took off. He felt no heat, no vibration, no illness, neither during the observation nor after. He was simply very impressed by the inexplicable spectacle.

The sighting was investigated by the French group GEPAN (Groupement d'Etudes des Phénomènes Aerospatiaux Non-identifiés), which had been established by the government in 1977. GEPAN was unique among UFO investigation programmes, as it was actually a part of the Centre National d'Etudes Spatiales, the French national space agency and equivalent of NASA in the United States, and had access to laboratories all over the country. Even the military were officially obligated to cooperate with the programme.

The police had taken samples of the vegetation around the landing site, which GEPAN took for biochemical analysis. Having checked with both civil and military aviation authorities that the UFO had not been a man-made aircraft, GEPAN took further samples of vegetation at various distances from the landing site, as well as closely examining the site itself. This revealed that the soil had been tightly compacted; pieces of flint in the soil had been fractured, either through intense pressure or extreme temperatures.

In its report on the case, based on research conducted at the Universities of Metz and Rangueill, GEPAN stated:

> The methods of analysis and microscopic observation brought

out elements that indicate that the terrain or soil where Nicolai claims to have observed the phenomenon underwent certain specific modifications.

There was a strong mechanical pressure forced on the surface, probably the result of a heavy weight.

The appearance of a superficial structural modification of the soil, with both striations and erosion.

A thermatic heating of the soil, perhaps consecutive to or immediately following the shock, the value of which did not exceed 600 degrees Centigrade.

An eventual residue of material in the form of detectable traces on the samples analysed, such as a weak quantity of oxidous iron on grains of calcium and minute quantities of phosphate and zinc.

The plant specimens were analysed at the National Institute of Agronomy Research in Avignon. According to biochemist Professor Michel Bounias, the specimens at the landing site (as opposed to others of the same strain, used as a control) exhibited alterations that "might be consistent... with an electromagnetic source of stress.... The amount of mutilation or transformation... is a function of distance from the centre." However, Professor Bounias conceded that the amount of information yielded from the plant deformations was "too scattered to form a whole picture, so that as of this moment, we cannot give a precise and unique interpretation to this remarkable combination of results." He remained confident, nevertheless, that *something* did indeed land at Trans-en-Provence on 8 January 1981.

Perhaps the most striking conclusions of the analysis were that the leaves of the plants had the "anatomic and physiologic characteristics of their age [but] had the biochemical characteristics of advanced senescence, of old age! And this does not resemble anything known to exist."

As Professor Bounias stated, "something certainly happened," something which resulted in measurable but inexplicable physical traces and biochemical effects. If we combine this hard scientific evidence with Renato Nicolai's description of the cause as a saucer-shaped object landing in his garden, it is difficult to escape the conclusion that Nicolai witnessed a concrete, objective phenomenon. Where that phenomenon came from, and where it went, are still unanswered questions.

Ruined Cities on the Moon and Mars: The Ultimate Artefacts?

In recent years, the subject of ufology has, to a certain extent, become fused with the subject of "extraterrestrial archaeology." Magazines that had previously dealt exclusively with UFO encounters are now devoting more and more of their pages to what might be called, potentially at least, the ultimate in close encounters of the second kind: unequivocal evidence of alien activity on other planets in our Solar System, in the form of massive, intelligently designed structures. These are perhaps the most exciting developments in the entire subject of extraterrestrial intelligence, since it is entirely possible for us to visit these places with unmanned space probes, and to verify beyond any doubt that alien artifacts do indeed exist there.

The most famous of these "artefacts" is undoubtedly the so-called "Face on Mars," which was first photographed by the *Viking* probes as they passed over the region of Cydonia in 1976. There are, however, numerous other unusual surface features in the vicinity of the mile-long Face, including pyramid-shaped structures and a most intriguing object known as the "Tholus," a low, conical mound apparently containing a spiral ramp.

When NASA first released the *Viking* photographs, they assured the press that the strange image of the Face was nothing more than a "trick of light and shadow"; but this claim was later disproved when another frame containing the Face was discovered. The second photograph had been taken with the Sun at a different angle of elevation in the Martian sky, and showed that, far from being a trick of light and shadow, the Face was a genuine three-dimensional object. Computer enhancement later re-vealed eyeballs inside the eye sockets, a mouth with discernible teeth, and regularly-spaced stripes that seemed to represent a kind of head-dress.

According to Richard C. Hoagland, former space consultant to NBC and CBS News in the United States, the upper sections of the surrounding pyramidal structures have collapsed in places, revealing them to be hollow. This has led him to speculate that the structures might be comparable to the "arcologies" (architec-tural ecologies) proposed by the architect Paolo Soleri in the 1960s. These colossal buildings would be completely self-contained, and capable of supporting millions of inhabitants. Some critics have asked why ancient space travellers (the as-sumption being that the Cydonia architects originally came from beyond the Solar System) would want to colonize an inhospitable planet like Mars when the comparable paradise of Earth lay right next door. Hoagland counters convincingly, saying that the archi-tects' home planet might well have been smaller than Earth, with a lower gravity. In this case, it would have been suicide to colo-nize a planet with a stronger gravitational field. Centrifuge exper-iments on animals on Earth have shown that higher gravity puts a lethal strain on the heart muscle, and also has adverse effects on blood chemistry and ion balances inside cells. Perhaps the Cydo-nia architects had no choice but to confine their activities to Mars.

Hoagland has also discovered a geometric pattern linking many of the Cydonia features. The geometry expresses two con-stants of nature: *pi* (the ratio of the circumference of a circle to its radius) and *e* (the base of natural logarithms). *Pi* divided into *e* give the ratio 0.865; this ratio is revealed throughout the struc-tures of the Cydonia complex.

The apparent dilapidation of many of the Cydonia structures implies that (if they are indeed artificial) they were constructed a long time ago. Attempting to date their origin, Hoagland looked for connections between the ground plan and the positions of the Sun over the Cydonia plain, and discovered that a line projected east from the centre of the complex across the eyes of the Face would have intersected the rising Sun on the summer solstice, 500,000 years ago.

Mars is not the only planet holding potentially shattering mysteries of this kind. At the centre of the disc of Earth's Moon, in the region known as Sinus Medii, or Central Bay, lies a 16-mile-wide crater called Ukert, containing a perfect equilateral triangle.

In 1967, the NASA probe *Lunar Orbiter III* photographed two colossal objects rising out of the moonscape to the south-west of Sinus Medii. One structure, known as the "Shard," is a one-and-a-half-mile-high column, with a central bulge containing a strange, hexagonal feature. The other, known as the "Cube," appears to be a glass-like structure (difficult to see without the aid of computer enhancement) towering seven miles above the moonscape, and apparently containing numerous smaller "sub-cubes" suspended in a darker matrix.

In 1994 the unmanned military probe *Clementine* photographed the entire lunar surface, sending back images that allegedly confirmed the presence of enormous artificial structures on the Moon. One of the most impressive photographs is of an object known as the "Castle," a "geometric, glittering glass object hanging more than nine miles above the surface of the Moon." Richard Hoagland speculates that objects such as this form the remnants of vast domes, designed to protect the now-ruined complexes on the lunar surface.

If this is true, the reader may ask, then why didn't the Apollo astronauts report their discovery? According to Hoagland, not only did the astronauts walk among the derelict lunar cities, but that was the very reason they were sent to the Moon in the first place! In the climate of Cold War mistrust, it was considered essential that the Americans should explore the ancient ruins before the Soviets.

When astronaut Alan Bean of Apollo XII was interviewed by reporters from CNN and the Associated Press regarding Hoagland's claims, his reply was rather disappointing, although perhaps not entirely unexpected. "I wish we *had* seen something like what he

[Hoagland] is describing. It would have been the most wonderful discovery in the history of humankind—and I can't imagine anyone, in my wildest dreams, not wanting to share that."

However, Hoagland believes that Bean and the other astronauts are simply maintaining their loyalty to NASA, which doesn't want the truth to be released to the public. Hoagland cites, as a possible reason for this, a report commissioned by NASA from the Brookings Institute in Washington, D.C. Entitled *Proposed Studies on the Implications of Peaceful Space Activities for Human Affairs*, the report dealt with "the need to investigate the possible social consequences of an extraterrestrial discovery and to consider whether such a discovery should be kept from the public in order to avoid political change and a possible 'devastating' effect on scientists themselves—due to the discovery that many of their own most cherished theories could be at risk."

Citing the dangers of contact between societies of differing technological achievements (amply demonstrated here on Earth), the report concluded that NASA would run a serious risk of undermining and perhaps ultimately destroying terrestrial culture were it ever to inform the public of the discovery of alien artefacts on the Moon, Mars or Venus . . .

Richard Hoagland is presently seeking funding for a private, unmanned mission to the Moon. Perhaps then (and perhaps only then) we will find out once and for all if the "tiers of grasslike ruins" have an existence outside our hopeful imaginations.

The Brief Mystery of the Roswell UFO Fragment

On 24 March 1996, a piece of metal marked with intricate lines was taken to the International UFO Museum and Research Center in Roswell, New Mexico, by a man who claimed that it was a piece of wreckage from the now legendary Roswell Incident, in which an extraterrestrial spacecraft allegedly crashed to Earth in early July 1947. The man informed the staff at the museum that the piece of metal, which had been mounted in a frame with a glass front, had been picked up and smuggled away from the crash site by one of the GIs who had been involved in the clean-up operations. The GI had then given it to another man, who framed it before eventually handing it on to the present owner.

The metallic fragment was a few inches long, twisted and roughly triangular in shape, with a large hole in the centre. Intrigued but cautious, the museum gave the fragment to the Roswell Chief of Police who, accompanied by one of the staff, took it to be analysed at the New Mexico Institute of Mining and Technology in Socorro. The initial analysis was carried out by Chris McKee, who concluded that it was composed of copper and silver, with traces of sodium, aluminium, silicon, iron, chromium, sulphur and chlorine. McKee was quick to point out, however, that the fragment was not cleaned prior to testing, and so these elements could have come from handling or soil. McKee also offered the opinion that the metal came from a larger piece, via a "catastrophic event," perhaps an explosion or a crash.

The US Air Force has recently claimed that the Roswell "crash" was actually a Project Mogul balloon, which was part of a top se-cret programme to detect Soviet nuclear weapons tests (this would, supposedly, have accounted for the inability of Roswell Army Air Field personnel to identify it). However, the analysis of the fragment in Socorro was attended by Charles Moor, a member of the Project Mogul team, who is quoted as saying that the frag-ment was not part of any Mogul balloon or instrument platform.

Nuclear physicist and UFO researcher Stanton T. Friedman, who originally investigated the Roswell Incident in the late 1970s, was also cautious about the veracity of this latest claim. Drawing attention to the fact that the GI who allegedly collected the fragment has not been interviewed, and may not even be alive, Friedman maintained that there is no direct link between the metal fragment and the Roswell Incident itself. "A very pre-liminary test done at a New Mexico university established that it contained mostly silver and copper and some impurities. There seem to be raised lines on the thin material as well. These tests certainly provide no reason for claiming that the specimen is of ET origin. However, they do rule out conventional iron, aluminium, nickel, alloys, etc.... [There is] no sign to date that the material is very flexible, hard or very strong."

As it turned out, Friedman was wise not to commit himself too hastily to a genuinely anomalous origin for the fragment. Responding to a claim from a Utah-based artist called Randy Fullbright, that the fragment was a piece of jewellery scrap from his studio, Miller Johnson, a board member of the Roswell UFO Museum, compared samples from his studio with the fragment, and concluded that he was right. The raised markings on its surface were actually ancient Japanese metal-working patterns. Fullbright said that he had given the piece of jewellery scrap to a friend, but had never claimed it was a piece of a UFO, and had nothing to do with its eventual arrival at the museum. Blake Larsen, the man who gave the fragment to the museum, said he believed it had been picked up from the site of the crash in 1947.

Although this affair had a mundane (and rather embarrassing) denouement, it does nevertheless prove that not all of those involved in UFO research are undiscerning, starry-eyed believers; the staff of the International UFO Museum proved themselves more than capable of getting to the bottom of the "UFO" fragment mystery. According to the museum's cofounder, Max Littell, the fragment will still be exhibited there, together with the full story of the research that went into establishing its true origin.

Vivisectors from Space?

In late 1967, the subject of ufology changed direction in a dramatic and sinister way, with the discovery in a Colorado field of a dead horse. The wire service dispatch, which alerted readers throughout the world to this new threat, was as follows:

ALAMOSA, Colo. (AP)—Snippy, a 3-year-old Appaloosa horse

didn't return to the Harry King ranch from her usual evening drink Sept. 7 and her owner is blaming a flying saucer or at least a radioactive surgeon.

The horse (which was actually called "Lady") was discovered in a strange and grisly state. She had been completely skinned, and her body had been unaccountably drained of blood. There were no tracks in the area although it had rained the previous night. However, there were signs that something extremely unusual had been present. A three-foot-tall bush close to the carcass had been crushed to a height of just ten inches, and there was a circle of six indentations, each two inches across and four inches deep. There were also several "exhaust marks," which were checked by a forestry official with a civil defence Geiger counter, and were allegedly found to be radioactive.

As with the Mantell case, the rumour machine shifted into high gear, and soon people all over the area were whispering that a Denver pathologist had found the brain and spinal column of the horse missing, together with the rest of the internal organs. This was never confirmed, however. Neither were the "exhaust marks" radioactive: a forestry official had checked them, but had found no evidence of radiation, and had concluded that the marks had been caused by black alkali fungus. The animal itself was examined by Dr. O.R. Adams of Colorado State University, who discovered a severe infection in one of the horse's hindlimbs, which could have proved fatal.

Although probably not the result of "alien" activity, the "Snippy" case was only the beginning of an epidemic of mysterious cattle deaths that has continued into the 1990s, and has been reported all over the world. In America, reports of unexplainably mutilated cattle and other farm animals have come in from many states, including Texas, Colorado, Nebraska, Wyoming, Idaho and Minnesota. The defining attributes of the deaths were that various body parts were excised with surgical precision, with no clue left behind as to the possible identity of the perpetrators. Tongues, eyes, ears and sex organs were almost always missing.

As far as the ranchers and farmers were concerned, the mutilations were a genuine mystery. Although sceptics pointed out that the missing organs were the soft parts that scavengers always ate first when coming upon a carcass, the cattle owners reacted with understandable indignation, countering that they knew perfectly well what scavenger action looked like, and it didn't look anything like this. The incisions on the carcasses were almost always perfectly straight, their edges blackened as if by a cutting instrument working at very high temperatures.

The San Luis Valley: Centre of Operations?

There seems to be a profound connection between cattle mutilations and UFOs, which are frequently sighted in the area where an unexplained animal death occurs. In recent years, nowhere has seen more anomalous activity than the San Luis Valley, which extends from southern Colorado into northern New Mexico.

On 4 July 1996 the *Rio Grande Sun* of Espanola, New Mexico, carried a long article listing recent UFO sightings and apparently associated cattle mutilations. Between September 1993 and April 1994, rancher Eli Hronich lost ten head of cattle, mutilated in a way he claimed never to have seen before. He described the deaths as "unnatural," adding that he had seen hundreds of cows die from various causes, "but I have never seen cows that have been cut up like the ones I lost."

On 30 November 1993, at 6.07 P.M., an ex-naval aviation navigator named Jack Cookerly saw a bright, white object hurtling through the sky above his home in the Baca Grants area of the San Luis Valley. As the object approached the horizon, "it flared up about 20 times its original size, turned into an oval shape and stopped dead. It was huge!" The object then changed colour to blue, descended toward the horizon and disappeared. According to Cookerly, "it couldn't have been a meteor.... It made a 90-degree turn, changed its colour, shape, size and velocity."

Another bright object, described as a "white strobe-light," was reported by six residents of Monte Vista in the Valley. Rio Grande County Undersheriff Brian Norton was called out to investigate, and saw the object flying just above treetop level. He estimated its speed to be between 200 and 250 m.p.h.

On 10 May 1994, two days after the above sighting, two cows were found mutilated in the area. The cows, which had "classic" incisions, were subjected to forensic testing, which revealed "cooked haemoglobin and cauterization" of the incisions.

At 11.00 P.M. on 27 June 1994, six residents of Moffat, San Luis Valley, were out sky-watching, when they saw a "triangular ship with no lights" slowly gliding at about 1,000 feet overhead toward the east. According to the witnesses, the craft was "so big it blotted out the stars," and was followed by a smaller craft, also triangular in shape.

About a month later, on 24 July, Eli Hronich found another mutilated steer on his ranch near Eagle's Nest, New Mexico. As he went to examine the animal, a grey, unmarked helicopter arrived and hovered over him. (The appearance of unidentified helicopters has become increasingly important in ufology, and is a subject to which we shall return later.)

Another triangular craft was reported by Maida and Toby Martinez of Taos, New Mexico, in September 1994. Together with a co-worker named Eric Tafoya, they saw a bright, white object surrounded by about 12 smaller objects gliding over their backyard. Moving at a height of no more than 20 feet above treetop level, the objects made a distinctive humming sound as they passed. According to Mrs. Martinez, "it was as big as my living room ... there was a round light and a series of red lights, about 12 or 15. It was the most spectacular thing I have ever seen. We could not hear the blades of a helicopter [or] hear the engine of a jet. As the object got closer to our home, we heard a hum." According to Toby Martinez, the object was shaped like a Stealth Bomber, but he was at a loss to explain the slowness of its flight.

On 17 August 1994, poor Eli Hronich found yet another mutilated cow on his ranch. The next day, three more carcasses were discovered 20 miles south on the Max Cordova ranch near Truchas. According to Cordova, the cows had been pregnant, but the foetuses were gone. Two members of his family who touched the cows suffered from "chemical-like burns," and the entire family reported "flu-like symptoms" the next day.

Strange, burn-like rashes have been reported by others who have touched mutilated cattle in the area, including Eli Hronich and New Mexico state livestock inspector Jerry Valerio. The latter examined a dead calf on a Questa ranch in May, and said that the meat looked like it had been microwaved or pressure-cooked.

Things were still looking bleak for the unfortunate Eli Hronich, who found *another* dead steer on 30 August 1994. "I wish I knew why they are picking on me," he said, adding that he has suffered a substantial financial loss as a result of the mysterious and gruesome activity in the area.

At about 10.00 P.M. on 8 October 1994, a large, disc-shaped object was sighted by two witnesses in La Veta Pass. The object was shining a spotlight on the ground. Not long after, a number of helicopters were seen overflying the area. Further UFO sightings occurred on 9 October and 6 November. In the former, a "glowing ball of bluish-white light" was seen over the Sangre de Cristo Mountains, making a "slow 70 degree arc over the mountains" before moving to the south-east. Five hours later, rancher Tom Reed of Questa saw a "bright blue floodlight lighting up the forest" near the Colorado border. The 6 November sighting was made by the well-known researcher Christopher O'Brien, who has written a book, *The Mysterious Valley*, dealing with anomalous activity in the area. O'Brien and a friend saw a "tight wedge-shaped configuration of three unblinking orange lights" moving overhead. They watched the formation through O'Brien's night-vision binoculars, which he has with him all the

time, and were able to discern a triangular shape behind the
lights. It was moving in absolute silence, which the witnesses
found puzzling: "It did not appear to be more than a couple of
thousand feet up and we should have heard something."

The Biotech Factor

One of the most puzzling aspects of these cases (and one which
researchers point to as confirmation that something "unnatural" is indeed going on) is the rate of decay of the carcasses.
Sometimes, they decompose much more slowly than normal;
sometimes much faster. In addition, contrary to the skeptics'
claims of natural predator action as the cause of the mutilations,
many carcasses are eschewed totally by normally eager scavengers. According to Eli Hronich, "the first thing you notice if
you think something's dead are birds." He describes the deaths
of his cattle as "a real clean deal [with] no blood, no flies, nothing." In one case, "the buzzards sat on the barn and just looked
at it. They never would touch it."

Cattle mutilations are potentially the most impressive of close
encounters of the second kind: the physical results of alien activity (if such be the case) are there for all to see and examine.
Yet, as is frequently the case in ufology, the cattle mutilations
have resulted in sharp divisions among researchers, with one
group maintaining that mutilations constitute a "fringe" subject
that may not be connected with UFOs at all, while another group
claim that aliens are slaughtering cattle and stealing parts of
their bodies for nutritional purposes, while yet another group in-
sist that the US Government itself is to blame.

This last claim is an example of how conspiracy theories have
a habit of merging into one another, confusing the issue with a
cloud of hazy and unsubstantiated rumours. According to these
rumours, the US Government is engaged in a nefarious conspiracy to test biological weapons, a programme that began in 1961,
when American involvement in Vietnam was increasing. When

biological weapons were banned in 1970, the programme became one of the notorious "black projects," which were ultra-secret and relied on untraceable funding. The goal of this program was to perfect the so-called "VX toxin," a biological weapon designed exclusively to kill Asians.

Testing was conducted on private land by government scientists, who monitored the spread of the toxin through the bodies of exposed cattle by excising the blood, eyes, lymph glands and other parts. Incredible as it may seem, the rumours claimed that the eyes of cattle are chemically similar to those of Asians!

Of course, such a race-specific weapon is (thankfully) biologically impossible, and so once again the rumour machine churned out plausible variations on the general theme. According to one, the cattle were mutilated in order to monitor a spillage of biological weapons or radiation. Another claimed that employees of sinister corporations were conducting geo-botanical prospecting, analysing the tissues from cattle, to detect mineral trace elements from the plants they had eaten and thus to locate valuable mineral deposits.

However, such speculations are of little help to people like Eli Hronich who, in common with many others who rely on ranching for their income, would just like the killings to stop. "This is my living," he says, "and it's cost me thousands of dollars already. . . . Why isn't somebody doing something about it?"

Whatever the ultimate answer to the mystery of the cattle mutilations may be, the fact remains that farmers and ranchers all over the United States and the rest of the world are continuing to lose valuable livestock in a way that seems to be incompatible with the normal activities of predators and scavengers. For this reason, their status as one of the most puzzling of UFO-related events seems assured for the foreseeable future.

3

Close Encounters of the Third Kind

*Animated entities (often called "humanoids, "occupants,"
or sometimes "ufonauts") have been reported.*

The Problem Of Evidence

UFO sightings are of course open to a number of different
interpretations; even a genuine "unknown" is not necessarily an alien spacecraft. As discussed in the Introduction,
highly unusual aerial objects might be explainable in terms of
very advanced—but nevertheless human—technology, such as
Stealth or remotely piloted vehicles. They might also represent
atmospheric phenomena that are ill-understood, such as ball
lightning. Likewise, physical traces left by UFOs present their
own problems for ufologists attempting to secure absolute
proof of an extraterrestrial origin.

The central problem lies in the fact that the Universe is made
of essentially the same stuff that is found on Earth, with the result that any fragments purporting to come from an "alien craft"
will more than likely be constructed from elements that are
found on our own planet, perhaps in abundance. If those elements are shown to be combined in unusual ways, then things
get a little more interesting, and yet even this might not constitute proof of an alien origin. For example, in the unlikely event
that a piece of a Stealth Bomber fell off during a flight and landed

on a ranch in New Mexico, prompting the bemused owner to hand it over to the local UFO group for analysis, the news would doubtless hurtle around the world and cause a media frenzy.

While many people would point to this strange fragment, with its unknown metallurgical and chemical composition, as the long-awaited "final proof" of an ET presence, the truth would, of course, be quite different. The Stealth coating on the skin of the B-2 and F-117A aircraft that enables them to slip through the skies virtually unnoticed by radar, is very highly classified. Were a civilian laboratory to attempt an analysis of the substance, they would doubtless be extremely perplexed, perhaps even astounded. It would contain elements that are commonly found on Earth, but put together in a totally novel way, and thus would constitute "proof" (at least to the more en-thusiastic extraterrestrialists) that we are indeed not alone.

With a phenomenon as elusive and perplexing as UFOs, this problem looks set to be with us for some time to come, and in-creases dramatically when we begin to consider its most bizarre aspects, namely the alleged sighting and interaction with the "occupants" of UFOs. Of course, one would assume that interaction with a vastly superior alien culture *would* be bizarre in the extreme, something which perhaps should be considered a criterion for authenticity. However, we must bear in mind that with so-called "high strangeness" comes a blur-ring of the distinction between what happens outside the mind and what happens within. Far from being a glibly sceptical dis-missal of alien encounter reports, this notion actually has the potential to open up a rich vein of surprising, and perhaps shocking, speculation on their ultimate nature.

Joe Simonton's Pancakes

Joe Simonton was a 60-year-old chicken farmer who lived alone near Eagle River, Wisconsin. At about 11.00 A.M. on 18 April 1961, Simonton heard a strange noise coming from outside his small house; he described the sound as similar to "knobby tires on a wet pavement." He went outside to investigate, and was confronted with an astonishing sight. Hovering a few feet above the ground was a saucer-shaped object of a bright, silvery colour, 30 feet in diameter and about 12 feet high.

Suddenly a hatch opened up in the side of the object, revealing three men inside, whom Simonton described as looking a little like Italians, with dark hair and olive complexions. They wore black, two-piece outfits with turtlenecks and balaclava-type helmets. One of the men produced a metal jug and motioned to Simonton, who assumed that they needed water. (This seems to echo the behaviour of the Great Airship pilots in the late 1890s, some of whom occasionally requested water and other consumables from witnesses.) Simonton happily obliged, filling the jug with water from his house and handing it over. When he did so, he noticed that one of the UFO occupants was cooking something on a "flameless grill" inside the craft! One of the men noticed Simonton's interest and handed him three pancakes. Another crewman then closed the hatch, and the object rose about 20 feet before heading off to the south.

Simonton then called Sheriff Schroeder, whom he had known for 14 years. The sheriff sent two deputies to Simonton's house. Although they could find no evidence to support the veracity of his claims, it was generally accepted that the old farmer had not concocted the story, and that he truly believed what he had reported.

The case was investigated by Dr. J. Allen Hynek on behalf of the US Air Force, who concluded that Joe Simonton was trustworthy, and that "Mr. Simonton felt that his contact had been a real experience." The pancakes were analysed by the Air Force. Simonton had eaten one of them and found it rather unappetizing, tasting like cardboard. The analysis yielded results that were perhaps unsurprising:

The cake was composed of hydrogenated fat, starch, buckwheat hulls, soya bean hulls, wheat bran. Bacteria and radiation readings were normal for this material. Chemical, infrared and other destructive type tests were run on this material. The Food and Drug Laboratory of the US Department of Health, Education and Welfare concluded that the material was an ordinary pancake of terrestrial origin.

This UFO sounds rather like some cosmic version of Aeroflot, whose cabin crews routinely cook in-flight meals on gas stoves in the aisles. This hardly bodes well for a literal interpretation of the encounter: genuine extraterrestrials may well be expected to behave in very unusual ways, but surely we must draw the line at frying buckwheat pancakes in their spaceships. And yet, if we accept that Joe Simonton genuinely believed what he reported, where does this take us?

Jacques Vallée, perhaps the most original mind in ufology, is most reluctant to regard the Eagle River case as solved, in spite of the US Air Force conclusion that Simonton had a waking dream, which his mind inserted into "the continuum of events around him of which he was conscious." Vallée believes that Simonton's encounter may indicate the activities of a non-human intelligence that has perhaps always existed alongside us here on Earth, and whose presence has, through the ages, been represented by us in a variety of different ways, each of which conforms to the world view prevalent at the time.

According to Vallée, the most striking parallel with modern "alien" encounters exists in the folk tales and legends associated with a race of beings known as the Gentry (in Ireland), or the Good People (in Scotland). In the Celtic traditions of western and central Europe, these supernatural beings had many contacts with humans (most commonly in remote places), frequently playing tricks on them, but also helping them in times of hardship. It was not unusual for a member of this fairy race to ask something of a human, perhaps as a test of good will (the "ufonauts" asked Simonton for some water); if the human gave what was asked, a gift was made, sometimes in the form of food (Simonton received some pancakes for his trouble).

Although this idea may sound completely outlandish to those encountering it for the first time (perhaps even more so than the idea that aliens would fry their dinners in their spacecraft), it actually offers one of the most intriguing and potentially useful ways of approaching the whole problem of encounters with non-humans. As such, it demands a section to itself, and will be dealt with in greater detail later in this book.

However, as far as Joe Simonton and his pancakes are concerned, it does seem more feasible (to this writer, at least) that he suffered a temporary although ultimately harmless aberration, in which he hallucinated his encounter. Perhaps he had just made himself some pancakes when the hallucination took hold (they *were* "ordinary pancake[s] of terrestrial origin"); perhaps, when he returned to normal consciousness, he looked down and saw the "evidence" in his own hands. . . .

The Socorro Landing

One of the most famous and impressive close encounters of the third kind occurred on 24 April 1964, south of the town of Socorro, New Mexico. Yet even this case contains certain elements that imply that the encounter was not quite what it seemed.

At about 5.45 P.M., Patrolman Lonnie Zamora was in pursuit of a speeding motorist when his attention was seized by the roar of an object descending in the distance. The object, which he described as resembling an upended automobile, was emitting a bright flame from its underside. As the object landed Zamora, fearing that the flame might ignite a nearby dynamite shack, abandoned his chase and drove his patrol car up and over a ridge, in search of a better vantage-point.

About 150 yards away, he saw not only the craft at rest, but also two small figures, dressed in what looked like white coveralls. The figures (which he estimated to be about four feet tall) were moving around the object, which appeared to be made of an aluminium-like metal, and rested on four diagonal landing struts. On the side of the object was an unusual red insignia which consisted of an upward-pointing arrow, bounded by a semicircle above and a horizontal line below.

At that point, one of the figures noticed his presence and appeared to jump, as if startled. Thinking that they might be in need of help, Zamora drove on a little way and radioed his headquarters, informing them that he was at the scene of a possible accident. As he climbed from his car, he heard several loud bumps, as if someone were shutting a door.

Zamora proceeded on foot, and got to within about 50 paces of the object, when it produced a loud roar and lifted off. The roar was so intense that the patrolman suddenly feared for his safety and ran to take cover, while the object rose to a height of about 15 feet and accelerated away over an adjacent mountain range.

A few moments later, Sergeant Sam Chavez arrived, and was struck by his colleague's agitated state. Together they inspected the landing site, and discovered four depressions, about two inches deep, and four burn marks in the brush, together with some shallower prints that Zamora assumed had been made by the occupants.

Both Chavez and Zamora were interviewed by representatives of Project Blue Book, including Dr. Hynek, who concluded that "Zamora, although not overly bright or articulate, is basically sincere, honest and reliable. He would not be capable of contriving a complex hoax, nor would his temperament indicate that he would have the slightest interest in such."

Zamora also exhibited a trait that Hynek had noticed in other UFO witnesses: the desire to have the sighting explained in conventional terms (in contrast to the common misconception that witnesses see what they *wish* to see), so that they may be relieved of the burden of having encountered something beyond their ability to comprehend. According to Hynek, "Both Zamora and

Chavez appeared to me to be hoping that I could tell them that this had been a secret Air Force device, so that they could dismiss the whole thing from their minds."

In fact, this case was a turning-point for Dr. Hynek, who had hitherto maintained a highly sceptical attitude to UFOs, and had aided the Air Force in explaining many previous sightings. In August 1964 and March 1965, he made two more trips to Socorro, satisfying himself completely that Zamora had not perpetrated a hoax. He had also been unable to uncover any Air Force projects that might account for what Zamora had seen. Thus Hynek began tentatively to entertain the notion that some UFOs might indeed be extraterrestrial spacecraft. . . . Since Project Blue Book could find no conventional explanation, the case was listed as "unidentified"—the only landing/occupant case so designated in their files.

However, there remain several inconsistencies in the Socorro case. For instance, a man named Felix Phillips and his wife lived approximately 1,000 feet away from the UFO landing site. They were both home at the time of the encounter, and yet neither heard the loud roar of the craft as it arrived and departed. Hynek explained this by pointing out that their house was downwind of the site, and a strong south-westly wind was blowing at the time, although this could not be confirmed, since Socorro did not have a weather station.

UFO sceptic Philip J. Klass investigated the Socorro case, and interviewed Felix Phillips. Phillips told him that several windows had been open, but nothing had been heard from 1,000 feet away. Zamora, on the other hand, had been in a speeding car, 4,000 feet away, and yet had heard the roar of the object's arrival.

Other inconsistencies came from Zamora himself, who changed his story in the years after the encounter, later saying that he had heard a roar but no flame as the object descended. He also claimed to have seen a rock that had been melted by the intense heat of the engine exhaust. However, the Air Force site investigation revealed no such thing, and also concluded that the sporadic burning of the brush was inconsistent with the powerful, rocket-like blast Zamora reported.

The landing prints left behind by the object also presented a problem, since their kite-shaped pattern meant that the struts would have been nonsymmetrical, of unequal lengths and angles. Any object that attempted to land on them would have promptly fallen over.

There was also the question of the location of the landing site—on land owned by the Mayor of Socorro, Holm Bursum. Plans were soon being made to turn the site into a tourist attraction: Socorro was not a particularly wealthy town, and would have benefited greatly from the interest generated by Zamora's sighting. This led sceptics such as Philip Klass to conclude that the encounter had been a hoax, designed to put Socorro on the tourist map.

So, what happened at Socorro? Did Lonnie Zamora encounter beings from another world, or was it all a cynical ploy to bring in tourist dollars? As the cliché goes, we may never know. . . . Before we move on, however, it must be mentioned that Ray Stanford, an investigator with the National Investigations Committee on Aerial Phenomena (NICAP) was at the landing site with Dr. Hynek, and discovered some tiny fragments of metal on a rock. Together with some other NICAP members, Stanford took the samples to NASA's Goddard Space Flight Center at Greenbelt, Maryland, in order to have it analysed by qualified space scientists.

According to Stanford, when the rock was returned to NICAP after analysis, every trace of the metal had been removed: "The whole thing had been scraped clean." Dr. Henry Frankel, head of the Spacecraft Systems Branch and director of the analysis, explained that they had to get enough of the material to make an accurate analysis. Frankel assured Stanford that the results of the analysis would be available in a few days.

In the meantime, Stanford spoke to a US Navy captain in Washington, who told him that, if something anomalous was discovered in the samples, NICAP would never get them back from NASA; national security considerations would see to that. It is unclear whether the samples were ever returned.

On 5 August 1964, Stanford phoned Dr. Frankel at the Goddard Space Flight Centre. Frankel had interesting news: the samples contained a material that "could not occur naturally," a zinc-iron alloy of a particular ratio that was not present on any charts of "alloys known to be manufactured on Earth, the USSR included. . . . This finding definitely strengthens the case that might be made for an extraterrestrial origin of the Socorro object." According to Frankel, the material would make "an excellent, highly malleable, and corrosive-resistant coating for a spacecraft landing gear."

Stanford made many attempts throughout the rest of August to get in touch with Frankel again, but was rebuffed on every occasion. Frankel, it seemed, was either "unavailable," or "in a top-level security conference," or "unprepared, at this time, to discuss the information [Stanford was] calling about."

Eventually, Stanford was contacted by Thomas P. Sciacca Jr. of NASA's Spacecraft Systems Branch, who notified him of the "official" conclusion of the analysis. According to Sciacca, everything Stanford had been told by Frankel was a mistake. Frankel was "no longer involved with the matter." The sample was "determined to be silica, SiO_2."

The Watcher in the Field

Photographs of UFOs are controversial enough, constituting additional "extraordinary claims" rather than "extraordinary evidence." In the five decades of "modern" ufology, they have provided food for intense discussion, given the relative ease with which they can be (and indeed have been) faked. When a photograph is allegedly taken of an alien, however, the controversy increases dramatically. While some researchers point to such photographs as unequivocal proof that we are not alone, more cautious ufologists (not to mention the sceptics!) point out that photographs of aliens are just as easy to fake as, if not easier than, photographs of the UFOs they are alleged to pilot.

However, once in a blue moon, a photograph comes along that sends a shiver ot terror and exhilaration down the spine. One such picture was taken by a fireman named Jim Templeton, during a family outing with his wife and two daughters in Cumbria, England. The weather on 24 May 1964 was warm and sunny, and Templeton was taking pictures of his family in a quiet area of marshland. Everything seemed normal; the family saw nothing unusual whatsoever during their day out.

When the family returned home and Templeton had the pictures developed, however, he saw something *most* unusual on one of the prints. A figure was clearly visible, standing behind one of Templeton's daughters; a figure that had not been visible when the photograph was taken. As if this were not bizarre enough, the figure appeared to be wearing a white spacesuit with a dark, featureless visor. Based on the apparent position of the "man" in the photograph, he is either floating a good several inches above the ground, or is *very* tall.

Looking for an explanation, the Templetons sent the photograph to Kodak, which had developed it. The initial cause which Kodak put forward, that the image was caused by an accidental double exposure, was abandoned because the girl's head completely obscures the lower part of the "man," which would not happen in a double exposure. According to Jenny Randles, who spent more time investigating the case than any other ufologist Kodak offered free film for life to anyone who could come up with an answer to the puzzle. The prize is still unclaimed.

Twenty-six years later, in 1990, the picture was blown up to life size as part of an advertising campaign for a local photocopying firm, revealing additional structures in the image. The visor was not entirely featureless, after all; it was semi-transparent, and revealed apparent ears within the helmet, and breathing tubes. Sceptics have claimed that this image is nothing more than a flaw in the photographic emulsion, an assertion that is somewhat unlikely in view of the fact that the image is clearly and unequivocally that of a white-suited figure in a helmet and visor. As Jenny Randles states, an emulsion flaw producing such an image would constitute "a coincidence as amazing as the proverbial monkey typing out the works of Shakespeare by chance."

In a curious postscript to a curious tale, Randles reports a conversation she had with Jim Templeton in 1990, in which he said that after the pictures had been developed he was visited by two mysterious men, claiming to be government investigators, who arrived in a dark Jaguar car. They took him out to the marsh where the "man" had been photographed, and asked him questions about the behaviour of the animals on the marsh at the time. When Templeton dismissed their suggestion that the strange figure was just an ordinary man, they became annoyed and promptly drove off, leaving him there, five miles from home. Randles points to the similarity between this puzzling encounter, and the activities of the so-called Men in Black, who have often been reported to harass witnesses to UFO-related events, and who will be discussed later.

It seems clear enough that this is one of those intriguing cases that are amenable to one of only two explanations: either the Templetons were lying and the entire episode was a hoax, or they were telling the truth, in which case they shared their day out with a person who was not only wearing a spacesuit, but who was invisible as well. Where that person came from, what he was doing there, and where he went are questions that will surely haunt anyone who sees the Templeton photograph.

Encounter at Valensole

Timothy Good has described the Valensole case as one of the most thoroughly investigated close encounters on record. It also seems to be one of the first widely publicized encounters with the entities that have come to be known as the Greys (or at least a variation thereof).

Maurice Masse, a farmer living near Valensole, Basses-Alpes, rose early as usual on the morning of 1 July 1965, and was in his lavender field by 5.45 A.M. (Some of the plants had recently been going missing.) He was working behind a pile of stones when he heard a whistling sound. Looking for the source of the sound, Masse saw an elliptical object on the ground, standing on six legs joined together at the centre of the under-side. There was an open hatch in the side of the object, through which Masse could see two seats, arranged back to back.

The farmer then spotted what he assumed to be two eight-year-old boys making off with some lavender plants. Although he had clearly discovered the culprits responsible for his missing plants, Masse was unable to do anything about it, since one of the "boys" pointed a tube-like device at him, which rendered him incapable of movement.

Masse told Jacques Vallée that he was not afraid of the "boys"; in fact he sensed a friendly curiosity on their part. They were about four feet tall and dressed in dark, grey-green one-piece suits. Their heads were large and entirely devoid of hair; they had fleshy cheeks, large eyes and lipless mouths. According to Masse, their facial appearance gave an impression of joviality, and he had the feeling that they were making good-natured fun of him. They communicated with each other by means of deep, gurgling sounds.

Presently, the entities returned to their craft through a sliding door that closed "like the front part of a wooden file cabinet." Still visible inside the transparent cockpit, they retracted the landing gear and guided the craft swiftly away.

Masse did not regain his ability to move for about 20 minutes, and became very frightened. Presently, though, he was able to return home. He noticed that the ground where the craft had stood was soaked with moisture, although it had not been raining. In addition, nothing would grow at the landing site for the next ten years.

A few days after the encounter, Masse's sleep cycle became

totally disrupted (as often happens in such cases); whereas he had hitherto required only five or six hours' sleep each night, after the encounter he needed 11 or 12 hours' sleep, and found it difficult to stay awake for longer than four hours at a time. This disruption lasted for several months.

The case was investigated by Lieutenant-Colonel Valnet of the Gendarmerie, Maître Chautard and the mayor and parish priest of Valensole, as well as UFO researchers such as Dr. Jacques Vallée. All concluded that Maurice Masse was telling the truth, as well they might: Masse was a former Resistance fighter, and was regarded as conscientious and absolutely trustworthy by all who knew him.

Visitors from UMMO

In the years since the late 1940s, millions of words have been written about the possible nature of UFOs and, by implication, the possible agendas of their pilots—if such exist. It is entirely understandable that such speculations should arise, given the genuinely mysterious nature of the phenomenon. Much has also been written of a "cover-up" by major governments, who allegedly possess a considerable amount of information about the interstellar visitors, including their biology, technology, history and social structure. And yet relatively little attention has been given to the ways in which governments might use the *idea* of an alien presence for their own ends. This is not to imply that there *is* no alien presence; however, it must be remembered that psychological weapons are among the most powerful in a government's arsenal. The "extraterrestrial alien" has become one of the most powerful cultural icons of the twentieth century—a fact that is surely not lost on those who have a vested interest in controlling our belief patterns.

Tales of alleged alien contact can be immensely convoluted affairs, and the controversy surrounding the arrival of explorers from the planet UMMO is no exception. In his remarkable book *Revelations: Alien Contact and Human Deception*, which slaughters a number of ufological cows, Jacques Vallée closely examines the UMMO affair, and arrives at some sinister conclusions none of which have anything to do with the genuine arrival of extraterrestrial voyagers.

The controversy began in Aluche, a suburb of Madrid, Spain, on 6 February 1966, when a number of witnesses reported the landing of a large, circular object. Beneath the disc was a curious symbol:)+(. The following year, another object bearing this insignia was seen by several dozen witnesses in another Madrid suburb, San José de Valderas. Five photographs of the UFO were taken by unidentified people, who submitted them to the newspaper *Informaciones*. A few hours after this sighting, an object was seen to land in yet another suburb of Madrid, Santa Monica.

In the days following these encounters, a number of metallic cylinders, each bisected by a thin disc, were discovered by local residents. When opened, the cylinders were found to contain pieces of tough, flexible material embossed with the UMMO symbol:)+(. When examined, the material was revealed to be Tedlar, a weather-resistant plastic used by NASA as a protective covering for rockets on the launch pads. The cylinders themselves were analysed by the Spanish Institute for Space Research. They were 99 per cent nickel, with "traces of magnesium, iron, titanium, cobalt, silicium and aluminum."

The UFO photographs were sent for analysis to a space research facility in Toulouse, France; at that time, the facility was preparing a sophisticated reconnaissance satellite for launch from French Guiana. Although it had been claimed that two photographers had taken the photographs independently, analysis revealed that they had in fact come from the same source: a tripod-mounted camera. Digital analysis of the photographs proved that the San José de Valderas UFO was 8.5 inches in diameter and ten feet away from the camera. It appeared to be constructed from plastic plates and a cup, and was suspended from a piece of string.

The respected Spanish researcher Antonio Ribera disputed these findings, drawing attention to the testimony of the many witnesses (including soldiers) who saw the objects in flight and on the ground. Jacques Vallée has an ingenious solution, suggesting that the witnesses really did see UFOs, but that they were man-made, remotely piloted vehicles. The implication here is that a complex and well-planned scheme was afoot, an implication borne out by examination of the "UMMO documents."

The documents were sent out to UFO investigators from a still-unknown source who mailed them from locations all over the world. The information contained in them, which covered diverse subjects from science and sociology to politics, allegedly came from UMMO, a planet of the IUMMA star system, 14.6 light years away. This system is said to be located 12 degrees 31 minutes of right ascension and 9 degrees 18 minutes of declination, placing it near the Galactic North Pole in a hydrogen-free, highly transparent region of the sky. Vallée points out that, given this location, IUMMA ought to be visible from Earth as a fifth-magnitude star . . . but isn't. According to the documents, the star is hidden by "absorbing matter," although no such matter has been detected in that area.

The information itself was impressive in that it was internally consistent, and was based on hard science rather than the woolly-headed mysticism so common to other "contactee" cases. According to a French physicist named Dr. Teyssandier, who examined several of the documents, the mathematical system used by the "Ummites" was base 12 (a "base" being the number that is raised to various powers to generate the principal counting units of a number system), rather than base 10 which is used on Earth. This and other information suggested that whoever had produced the documents had a scientific education, at least to degree level.

However, Ummite technology was not quite as astonishing as might have been hoped. As Jacques Vallée says: "[I]t matches the kind of clever extrapolations one finds in any good science-fiction novel of the last forty years. . . . There is an ingenious twist to the construction of the spacecraft used by UMMO which are self-repairing in case of collision with asteroids, but the very concept of space travel implied in such a technology barely reaches the level of the average *Star Trek* episode."

The UMMO affair contains many sinister elements perhaps more suited to an espionage novel than the field of alien contact. In 1955, Spanish investigators were sent a copy of a letter allegedly sent by the "UMMO source" to the CIA office in Madrid. The letter stated that two Ummites, claiming to be Danish doctors, had stayed at the Albacete house of a society lady, Doña Margarita Ruiz de Lihory y Resino, Marquise of Villasante, Baroness of Alcatrali, between 1952 and 1954, during which time they had conducted "psychophysiological experiments" on a number of domestic animals.

In 1971 the CIA received another document from UMMO, containing "tests for unmasking extraterrestrial beings who live on earth clandestinely." The same year, "W. Rumsey" (allegedly a CIA agent) sent out a circular letter to the citizens of Albacete, offering $1,000 for information leading to the apprehension of the two Danish doctors. Although the involvement of the CIA might lend an air of authenticity to these strange goings-on, Vallée reminds us that anyone can write a letter to a government agency; and the UMMO source's attempt to legitimize itself through these means becomes even more ridiculous when one considers how unlikely it would be for an organization like the CIA to canvass ordinary townspeople for information as to the whereabouts of two Danes.

In 1953 Margot Shelly, daughter of the Marquise of Villasante, who lived on the estate, became seriously ill and was examined by the two mysterious "doctors"; one said her illness was "benign," the other said it was probably fatal. After being treated by a number of respected physicians in Madrid, Margot Shelly died. While her body was awaiting burial, it was mutilated by an unknown person, who removed one hand, both eyes and the tongue. This was done using "surgical techniques." These body parts were subsequently found in the marquise's mansion by the police, as a result of a complaint filed against her by her son.

There were yet more macabre discoveries to be made on the estate, including the remains of a large number of dogs and cats, which had been experimented upon by the Danish "doctors." Some of the animals were mummified, while others had been eviscerated. Various animal heads were discovered in silver containers in one of the rooms in the house.

A criminal suit was instigated against the marquise and her husband, during which they were examined for a month in a Madrid psychiatric hospital. The examination concluded that they were both "of perfect mental state," and were normal in every way.

Their butler, Andres Gomes, was also interrogated by the police, and later told journalists that the marquise's ancient mansion contained a large network of underground chambers, which he described as "a horrible place." He told how the marquise would enter this cellar-network through a metal trapdoor in her bathroom, and would spend "many hours" there. "I don't know what she did there exactly, but she came up as pale as a corpse."

An UMMO document distributed in 1969 claimed a connection between the macabre events in Albacete in 1954, and the Ummites' mission on Earth. As Vallée states, it is likely that the UMMO source simply wove this 15-year-old scandal into its own elaborate hoax, to give it an additional air of authenticity (like the CIA "involvement"). Of course, the only person who could have shed any light on the true nature of the events at Albacete was Doña Margarita herself . . . but she died just before the 1969 document was distributed.

The UMMO affair is one of the most outlandish and intriguing cases in the history of ufology; indeed, its elements extend well beyond ufology, entering much darker terrain, with its tales of sadistic animal mutilation and a sinister castle holding unspeakable secrets in its cellars. Some researchers have come to the conclusion that UMMO was initially a psychosociological experiment, based on the idea of a "verifiable" alien presence on Earth, that eventually got out of hand, with a number of unknown individuals using it as a departure point for their own bizarre agendas. There is even a possible link, apparently being investigated in France, that the origin of UMMO is an intelligence agency in the former Eastern bloc, which was (and perhaps still is) conducting a programme in scientific espionage. According to one of Vallée's French colleagues, such a group would thus be in a position to gain access to "a lot of grass-root UFO information," and, since a number of physicists in Europe and America have become deeply involved with UMMO, would gain a "confidential insight into current scientific research ideas in Western laboratories."

Bulletproof Goblins

Although in recent years reported descriptions of alleged alien entities have been dominated by the so-called Greys (short, spindly, large-headed, obsidian-eyed ne'er-do-wells who abduct hapless humans and harvest their sperm and ova for diverse reasons), previous years saw wildly differing descriptions, of everything from entirely human-looking "people," to smelly hirsute dwarfs, to eyeless single-legged pseudo-robots with tentacles for arms.

One such sighting occurred at the home of the Sutton family in the tiny community of Kelly, several miles from the town of Hopkinsville, Kentucky, on the evening of 21 August 1955. Bill Taylor, a relative of the Suttons who was visiting, went out to get a drink from their well, when he noticed a saucer-shaped object descending into a nearby field. A few minutes after he had excitedly returned indoors to tell the Suttons what he had seen, they all saw a small figure approaching the house.

The sight must have been truly shocking: the creature was just over three feet tall, with a round head and enormous, bat-like ears. Its mouth was a wide slit extending from ear to ear. Its arms were long, almost ape-like, and ended in clawed hands. Perhaps most terrifying of all, the creature appeared to be self-luminous, casting an eerie, silver glow across the darkened yard.

This bizarre visitor was soon joined by several others, which began to wander around outside the house. Some of them climbed a nearby tree and from there dropped on to the roof. The terrified Suttons quickly armed themselves with shotguns, which they fired several times at the creatures. Incredibly, they claimed that whenever they hit one of the creatures, the bullets sounded as if they were "hitting a bucket"; the creature would then roll over and scurry for cover, completely unharmed. Although they walked upright, the creatures ran on all fours.

At one point, Bill Taylor attempted to leave the house, and was immediately confronted by one of the creatures, which was sitting on the roof just above the door, and which reached down and grabbed his hair. Needless to say, Taylor decided to go back inside.

Interestingly, whenever the creatures approached the house, they would raise their arms in a "stick 'em up fashion," and would move very slowly. Bud Ledwith, who worked at radio station WHOP in Hopkinsville and conducted an in-depth investigation of the case, suggests that this may well have been a friendly gesture on the part of the creatures, an attempt to let the humans know that they were unarmed and meant them no harm. Of course, when faced with such a creature, approaching with its taloned hands raised, the average person would be forgiven for placing precisely the opposite interpretation on the gesture.

This activity went on for much of the night, with the humans desperately trying to disperse their unwanted guests with flashlight beams and bullets. The creatures were, however, disinclined to leave, and continued to wander around the yard and climb nearby trees. Whenever they were caught by a beam or bullet, they would float gently to the ground—rather than jumping or falling—and then scamper for cover. At no time did they attempt to enter the house.

Eventually the situation grew unbearable for the Suttons and Bill Taylor, and they made a frantic dash for the family car and drove into Hopkinsville to report the encounter to the police. Deputy Sheriff George Batts went out to the house, accompanied by two Kentucky State policemen, but was unable to find any evidence of the little creatures or their craft. However, Chief of Police Greenwell was impressed with the Suttons' testimony, and concluded that "something scared those people—something beyond reason—nothing ordinary."

Bud Ledwith could find no motive for a hoax: not only were the Suttons not seeking publicity, they were subsequently harassed by reporters and numerous other curious people, to the point where (in common with many other UFO witnesses) they wished the story of their encounter had never emerged.

Although he did not officially investigate the case, Dr. Hynek did attempt to find out if there had been a travelling circus in the area, from which monkeys might have escaped. But, as he admitted, if the Suttons were to be believed, the creatures they encountered could not have been monkeys. Assuming that they had hit the creatures with bullets, at least one body should have been discovered. In addition, monkeys either jump or fall from trees; they do not float from them. In the event, Hynek was unable to find any trace of a travelling circus. . . .

An Alien Projection?

Encounters with apparent alien entities are strange enough, but the following case has an additional aspect that is yet more bizarre, but which might shed light on the origin of such creatures. The encounter happened in Argentina on the night of 13 June 1968, at about 12.50 A.M. The witnesses were Señor Pedro

Pretzel, the 39-year-old proprietor of the Motel La Cuesta, near the small town of Villa Carlos Paz, which lies about 500 miles to the west of Buenos Aires, in the province of Cordoba, and his 19-year-old daughter, Maria Eladia.

On the night in question, Senior Pretzel was walking home when he spotted a strange object about 55 yards beyond the motel, apparently resting on the highway that ran past the building. The object had two very intense red lights, which were projecting their beams at the motel. Although at first he thought it might have been a car, Pretzel realized that no car has taillights that can project laser-like beams. Almost immediately, the object vanished, and Pretzel hurried into the motel.

Entering the kitchen, he found his daughter lying unconscious on the floor, apparently having fainted. He managed to revive her, and asked her what had happened. Maria Eladia replied that, a few minutes before, she had said goodnight to her fiancé, seen some guests to the door, and then returned to the kitchen.

At that moment, she saw that the lobby was filled with light, which was impossible, since she had just switched all the lights off. She returned to the lobby to investigate, and was confronted by a six-foot-tall man, dressed in a single-piece suit that seemed to be made of blue scales. The man had fair hair, and was holding a gyrating blue sphere in the palm of his raised left hand. On the fourth finger of his right hand he wore a very large ring, which he moved up and down in front of her.

Maria's initial terror was rapidly replaced by uncontrollable lethargy, which increased as she was flooded with light emanating from the man's hands and feet. It seems that Maria's fear had been inappropriate (although understandable), since the man exuded "goodness and kindness," and smiled at her throughout the encounter. She also had the feeling that he was attempting to communicate with her: although his lips did not move, she could hear a faint voice that she compared to Chinese.

Maria was held like this for some moments, and then the man walked slowly and precisely to the side door, which was open.

When he had walked through it, the door closed behind him. As soon as the man had departed, Maria fainted.

Pretzel reported the incident to the local police. For some days afterward, Maria became prone to weeping fits, and was very nervous.

It seems possible that the "man" Maria Eladia encountered was not really "there" at all. He might well have been a projection, a moving hologram beamed into the house by the object that her father had seen outside. If this is the case, perhaps other UFOs and non-human entities are of a similar nature, projected into our reality from an unknown source. This idea will be considered in more detail later in the book.

A "Cerebral" Mystery

Alleged alien beings who contact humans are fond of uttering outlandish prophecies, which rarely come true. One case from the 1970s, which is as comical as it is bizarre, occurred in Palos Verdes, southern California. Two men in their late twenties were driving home from their friend's house one night, when they encountered two strange objects on the highway. As the car approached, its headlights illuminated the objects, which appeared to be human brains the size of basketballs. Stunned, the two friends slowed down and spent a few moments observing the "brains" through the car windows, before manoeuvring around them and continuing on their journey.

The driver took his friend home and then drove to his own house. In total, the journey should have taken about ten minutes, but the driver discovered that it had taken two and a half hours. He was at a total loss to explain the missing time.

The case was investigated by Ann Druffel, who gave the driver the pseudonym "John Hodges." During regressive hypnosis, he recalled being taken into a room (after he had taken his friend home), where he encountered one of the brains. The brain spoke to him telepathically, with a voice that seemed to come from within him. Also in the room were a number of tall, grey-skinned humanoids, apparently crewmen. They had "webbed features," as if their natural habitat was aquatic.

Hodges was shown a series of three-dimensional, holographic images of nuclear explosions. The brain then proceeded to lecture him on humanity's misuses of nuclear power (a favourite subject with aliens). It was during one of the hypnosis sessions that Hodges realized that the grey creatures were actually in control, and the brains were biomechanical translation devices. During the encounter, a tiny "translator cell" was inserted in Hodges' brain, through which the aliens would be able to communicate with him. He was then returned to his car.

In the years following his encounter, John Hodges received numerous messages from the aliens through his translator cell. Largely prophetic in nature (and totally inaccurate), the messages told of a war that would begin in the Middle East and then spread to Europe between 1982 and 1984, and in which nuclear weapons would be used. After the war ended, there would be a single world government, and the aliens themselves would land *en masse* in 1987.

While conceding that stories such as this sound like arrant nonsense, British researcher Jenny Randles comments on the apparent absurdity of many other close encounters, and wonders if there might be a common source for them. "They involve ghost-like beings, weird monsters, spirit entities, and a veritable menagerie of aliens from all over the Universe. Yet all of them share an underlying theme and many consistent internal characteristics. . . . Could these experiences stem from a source that is somewhat closer to home—namely ourselves?" This is an idea that we shall return to later.

The "Ghost" that Wore a Spacesuit

Another baffling and shocking case occurred on Cyprus in September 1968. At 3.00 A.M., a British Army NCO, stationed at

Dakelia barracks, was alerted to a possible intruder by his dog. The Turkish wolfhound, a formidable beast, rose to its feet and began to growl. Its fur was standing on end; clearly, it was perceiving a potential threat nearby. The soldier's first thought was of an imminent terrorist attack on the barracks. He moved silently to the door, intending to gauge the situation before deciding on a response. As he did so the wolfhound scurried under the bed and began to whimper in terror, a most unusual act for such a fierce animal.

At this point the soldier heard a high-pitched humming sound that gradually grew in intensity. Totally at a loss to explain either the strange sound or the stranger behaviour of his dog, the soldier decided to risk going out on to the landing to see what was happening. It was an act he doubtless wishes he had never even contemplated.

He opened the door and tentatively stepped on to the landing. A few feet away, a flight of wooden steps led down to ground level. When he looked down the steps the soldier saw something he would never forget, no matter how desperately he might try. Floating up towards him was a being—or rather, the head and shoulders of a being. . . .

As he watched in horror, the humanoid thing continued to approach; all that was visible was its upper portion. It was dressed in a light blue suit with a collarless neck. Its face, glowing bright orange, was inclined forward slightly, and had a strange, scowling expression. Its eyes were very large, round and unblinking beneath a shock of red hair. As it proceeded up the stairs towards the landing and the now petrified soldier, it looked around, swivelling its head a full 180 degrees.

By now the soldier had seen more than enough. In panic, he raced back to the safety of his room, slammed the door and sat on the edge of his bed, trembling in abject terror. The strange whining noise outside continued to rise in intensity, eventually reaching a nerve-shattering crescendo. It was now accompanied by a sliding sound, as if the being were moving towards the door. The soldier grabbed an underwater speargun, loaded it, aimed at the door and fired.

Whether because of this or for some other unknown reason, the sliding sound and the machine-like humming gradually faded away, and the soldier was left alone with his cowering wolfhound. There he stayed until he was found an hour later by a relief guard.

The soldier told his remarkable and frightening tale to Jenny Randles, who accepts his absolute sincerity. After his encounter, he suffered from muscular paralysis, but eventually made a full recovery. His poor dog was not so fortunate; its fierce spirit, which makes Turkish wolfhounds such excellent guard dogs, was completely shattered by its experience at the Dakelia base. It spent the rest of its days in a state of total fear, hiding and whimpering at every noise.

"The Story of the Century"

What the London *Times* described as—potentially, at least—"the story of the century" began sometime between 21 September and 2 October 1989 in the Russian city of Voronezh, 300 miles south of Moscow. Here, according to the Russian news agency TASS, in a report relayed to the rest of the world through the office of Associated Press in Moscow, a UFO landed in full view of many witnesses. In the words of the AP report, "Scientists have confirmed that an unidentified flying object landed recently landed in... Voronezh. They have also located the landing site and found traces of aliens who made a short promenade about the park."

At first, the only witnesses willing to come forward were children (who were doubtless unaware that reporting UFOs was not the done thing in the Soviet Union), but soon others began to endorse the children's claims. There were a number of sightings of disc- and sphere-shaped objects prior to the landing in the Western Park area of the city. Then, at 6.30 P.M. on 27 September, a large crowd of commuters saw a "pink haze" manoeuvring in the sky over the park. Suddenly, a silvery sphere emerged from the mist and descended to treetop level. As it settled into one of the trees, its shape apparently changed to that of a bulging cylinder, and a door opened in its side, revealing a humanoid entity that looked around for a few moments before retreating into the craft.

The object then descended further into the tree, until it was just a few feet above the ground. The hatch opened again, and several beings, between 12 and 14 feet tall, disembarked, accompanied by a small robot. As perhaps might be expected of people observing such a totally unusual event, there are a number of discrepancies in their accounts of what followed. For instance, according to some witnesses, the beings had three eyes, or perhaps a bright light in their foreheads. Some claimed that one of the beings fired some sort of pistol at one of the onlookers, who promptly vanished; after the UFO had left, the man reappeared, still in mid-stride. Other witnesses claimed that one of the beings climbed an electricity pylon, whereupon it had caught fire and been vaporized.

In her examination of the encounter, Jenny Randles states that the pylon episode actually belonged to the testimony of some children who allegedly had witnessed an earlier landing on 23 September, illustrating the ease with which descriptions of different events can become intermingled. Whatever the exact nature of the 27 September episode, it seems undeniable that the object left traces from its undercarriage, which touched the ground around the tree in which it had settled. The site was examined by several scientists, including Professor Genrikh Silanov, Director of the Geophysical Laboratory in Voronezh. The investigators concluded that the imprints had been caused by an object weighing 11 tons.

Seventeen samples were taken from the soil around the landing site, and were sent for analysis to the Department of Nuclear Physics at Voronezh University. They were found to contain two to three times the normal background gamma radiation. Although, on 28 October, a spokesman for the university said that this was merely due to residual fall-out from the accident at the Chernobyl nuclear power station in 1986, it does seem strange that the higher radiation levels were concentrated precisely in the indentations allegedly caused by the UFO's landing gear. In addition, as Randles reminds us, these levels were exactly the same as those found by the US Air Force investigators when they examined the indentations left by the Rendlesham Forest UFO.

The Voronezh landings were also investigated by Jacques Vallée, who took the trouble to go there and interview the Russian researchers who were intimately involved with the case. In his book *Revelations*, he remarks on both their professional kindness and their genuine interest in the global aspects of ufology. He also received some startling and immensely intriguing new information.

According to Dr. Vladimir Azhazha, Professor of Mathematics and Director of the (then) Soviet Commission for the Study of Paranormal Phenomena, it was true that several people vanished during the Voronezh landings, and reappeared when the UFOs had departed. He also stated that this had happened elsewhere; for instance, a woman in the village of Vologda vanished while in the vicinity of an "occupant," which also vanished at the same time. The woman immediately reappeared, in a great deal of distress, but with no memory of what had happened to her. This event was witnessed by several people. Azhazha claimed to have a number of such cases in his files.

According to the Russian investigators, the aliens' movements had been tracked by means of a curious technique called "biolocation," implying that Russian scientists were investigating UFOs using parapsychology. This should come as no surprise to anyone familiar with the old Soviet fascination with such subjects, which they attempted to utilize in an espionage capacity throughout the Cold War. Vallée reminds us that the concept of biolocation is found in the Russian literature on psychotronics, and refers to "radiesthesia" or dowsing, "the detection of hidden mineral, water, or living entities by paranormal means."

According to investigator Venceslaw Martinov, chief engineer at the Voronezh aviation factory, biolocation is "the detection of the bioenergetic field and its application to the analysis of terrain, including the geology." Professor Silanov measured the "magnetic field and the magnetic capacity of the soil at the landing site."

If the Russians were (and are) using techniques such as biolocation to track the movements of UFOs and their occupants, this carries intriguing implications for us here in the West. It is now widely accepted, for instance, that the CIA had their own parapsychological research programmes during the Cold War, with similar espionage-related intentions to those of the Soviets. It would surely not be stretching the bounds of possibility too far to wonder if biolocation techniques are being used by our own security organizations—whether to find an explanation for the phenomenon, or to monitor a phenomenon they already understand.

As one might expect, UFO sceptics were quick to dismiss the Voronezh landings; some commentators even voiced the notion that the traditionally active Russian imagination had finally rebelled against the repressive communist system, with the people of Voronezh confabulating the whole affair in a desperate attempt at escapism. In view of the global nature of the phenomenon (not to mention the physical traces left behind by the objects), this seems a little contrived.

Ironically enough, the Voronezh encounters were also dismissed by some members of the ufology community in the United States, who claimed that it had to have been a hoax, since the reported appearance of the tall, statuesque aliens did not correspond to that of the short and spindly Greys, which they consider to be the benchmark against which all alien encounter reports must be measured for authenticity. Vallée is rightly dismayed by this state of affairs, in which "many researchers actually select the cases that match their pre-existing expectations. This mockery of the scientific method can only lead to absurd results."

In spite of the sceptical attitudes mentioned above, the

Voronezh landings were merely a single part of a much wider UFO wave that extended across Russia at the time. As Vallée states, the UFO phenomenon "can drive our measurement tools and our analytical powers to their limit. But of its physical reality there cannot be any doubt."

Have Aliens been Captured in Brazil?

In mid-1996, news began to spread of incredible events in the southern Brazilian city of Varginha. According to the numerous rumours, not only had a UFO crashed in the region, but its crew had been captured and killed by the authorities. As a result, Varginha, which is situated 180 miles north-west of Rio de Janeiro in the state of Minas Gerais, has become the most important location on the UFO map; and the events there have been described as rivalling the Roswell incident in their significance.

In January 1996 there had been a large number of UFO sightings in the area, which is not unusual for Brazil, which in recent years has become the location of the most intense UFO activity in the world. On 13 January, Afranio da Costa Brasil and his nine-year-old daughter Emeline witnessed a submarine-shaped object near their home. One week later, the same (or a similar) object was seen by Eurico de Freitas and his common-law wife Oralina Augusta, who were woken at 1.00 A.M. by the barking of their dogs. The UFO was gliding across the fields, about five metres off the ground.

At 8.00 A.M. on the same morning, the Varginha City Fire Department received an anonymous phone call asking them to apprehend a strange animal that had been seen in a park in the Jardim Andere district. About two hours later, four firemen arrived at the park. Eventually they came upon an astonishing sight: crouching at the edge of some woodland was a small, humanoid creature, about three and a half feet tall, with large red eyes and brown skin. On its forehead were three curious, pronounced ridges.

The firemen immediately set about capturing the creature, while the officer in charge contacted the local military base at Coracoes, 25 kilometres away. Troops were then ordered by General Sergio Coelho Lima, the base commander, to seal off the park. By the time the military arrived, the creature had been placed in a wooden box, which was handed over to the soldiers and taken to the Sergeants' School at Tres Coracoes.

Although this in itself would have qualified as one of the most impressive close encounters of the third kind, the story was far from over. On the same day, at about 3.30 P.M., *another* humanoid was discovered by three young women as they were returning home from work in the Jardim Andere district.

Liliana Fatima Silva, her sister Valquiria, and Katia Andrade Xavier said that they saw the creature crouching on Benevenuto Bras Vicira Street. Its appearance, which was identical to the one captured in the park, terrified them and they ran away screaming, thinking it was the Devil himself.

One of the most impressive aspects of the case is the large number of witnesses to the creature's presence, which is extremely rare in close encounters of the third kind. As the girls fled the scene, a crowd gathered around the creature, which seemed disinclined to move. Some residents of the street telephoned the Fire Department, which promptly arrived accompanied by more military personnel, who bundled the poor creature up in nets and quickly took it away. It had apparently been injured by some children who had thrown stones at it. (The phrase "welcome to Earth" springs to mind!)

According to the Brazilian ufologists who investigated the case, more than 60 witnesses came forward, including several military personnel involved in the capture of the beings. The second being was allegedly taken to the Varginha Regional Hospital. It was then transferred to the nearby Humanitus Hospital, where it survived until 6.00 P.M. on Monday 22 January, apparently finally succumbing to its injuries.

The doctors who examined the creature noted a powerful

stench, similar to ammonia, that was exuded by its skin. Witnesses to its capture reported that the same stench remained after it had been taken away by the military. The being was naked, and had no sexual organs, no nipples and no navel. One of the doctors opened the being's lipless mouth and, using a pair of forceps, pulled out its black tongue. As soon as he let go, the tongue snapped back into the mouth. After the examination was over, the being was wrapped in black plastic sheeting, placed in a wooden box and taken away from the hospital by the military.

According to Brazilian investigator Rodrigues e Pacaccini, the capture of the first creature on the morning of 20 January resulted in a human casualty. A young policeman had been injured by the creature during the struggle to apprehend it. Two days later, he died in hospital, the official cause listed as pneumonia. His family were suspicious, but were treated unsympathetically by the authorities.

Pacaccini also revealed that he had interviewed a Brazilian Air Force radar operator, who claimed that the Brazilian Armed Forces had been alerted to the presence of a UFO by the United States. The UFO's coordinates were also supplied, although it was unclear whether the object was about to land or crash. Pacaccini is certain that this was the reason why the military were on the scene so unusually quickly.

In the months following the events at Varginha, Pacaccini has come to fear for his life; there have been numerous threatening phone calls, and he occasionally wears a bulletproof vest. The military have been screwing the lid down very tightly on the whole affair, forbidding all personnel from having any kind of contact with Brazilian UFO investigators. In addition, hospital administrators subsequently denied that any unusual creature had been examined, telling press reporters that the "body" was that of a university student, arrested for robbery who had committed suicide in his cell.

Nor has the apparent alien activity in Varginha ended there. Three months after the events described above, on 21 April

1996, Mrs. Terezinha Gallo Clepf was having dinner in a local restaurant when she decided to step on to the porch for a cigarette—and came face to face with another creature, identical to those captured in January.

Three weeks later, a motorist encountered yet another being as he was rounding a bend. The being raised its arms to its face, as if to protect its huge, red eyes from the glare of the motorist's headlights, before running away.

It would seem, from these later reports, that the UFO that came down in Varginha had a larger crew than originally supposed. Or maybe a "rescue mission" was mounted, with a number of creatures now searching the area for their lost colleagues. . . .

4

Close Encounters of the Fourth Kind

Human beings are taken from their normal surroundings against their will, and are forced to interact in various ways with non-human entities.

The Darkening Skies

The case of Barney and Betty Hill has been included in virtually every book dealing with alleged alien encounters, beginning with John G. Fuller's excellent investigation *The Interrupted Journey*, first published in 1966. Such is its importance, however, that it must be included here, not least because it is the first comprehensively examined example of a close encounter of the fourth kind: abduction by non-human beings. Prior to the Hills' experience in 1961, the only "communication" that had taken place between human beings and UFO pilots had been that reported by the "contactees," who claimed to have been visited by beautiful and benign "space brothers" who had come from various planets within our own Solar System with a message of peace and universal love.

The Hill case was to sound the death knell for such platitudes, serving as a prototype for subsequent encounters with the ruthless and almost militaristic Greys. In fact, as we shall see, the appearance of the aliens themselves seems to correspond to an intermediate stage between the entirely human-looking space brothers and the insectoid creatures that are so frequently reported today.

The Hills met their appointment with destiny on the night of 19–20 September 1961, as they were driving back from a holiday in Canada to their home in Portsmouth, New Hampshire. They expected to be home between 2.30 and 3.00 A.M. When they were just south of Lancaster, Betty Hill noticed a bright star, which seemed to be following the car. Betty looked at it through a pair of binoculars, and saw what seemed to be a row of windows.

Barney Hill assured his wife that the "star" was merely a plane. Nevertheless, he stopped the car, took the binoculars and walked a little way into an adjacent field to see for himself. He saw a group of strange men at the windows of the craft, staring back at him. Moments later, he was running back to the car, screaming hysterically that they were about to be captured.

As they drove away, the couple heard a strange beeping sound and became intolerably drowsy. Moments later they heard another, similar sound, and Betty turned to her husband, saying: "*Now* do you believe in flying saucers?"

"Don't be ridiculous. Of course not," Barney replied.

They continued their journey home without further incident, arriving just after 5.00 A.M., about two and a half hours later than they should have done. As they got out of the car, they noticed some strange, shiny spots on the paintwork. When a compass was later held to them (at the suggestion of Betty's sister, who had seen a UFO), the needle span wildly. This piece of physical evidence has never been satisfactorily explained.

About a week later, Betty began to have disturbing dreams of being captured by strange creatures. She wrote to Major Donald E. Keyhoe of NICAP, describing the UFO sighting. Two months later, the Hills were visited by several NICAP members who went through the encounter with them in minute detail. According to Barney:

They were mentally reconstructing the whole trip. One of them said, "What took you so long to get home?" they said, you were this distance and it took you these hours. Where were you? Well, when they said this, I thought I was really going to crack up.... I became suddenly flabbergasted to think that *I realized for the first time* that at the rate of speed I always travel, we should have arrived home at least two hours earlier than we did. [Original emphasis.]

Barney and Betty were referred to respected Boston psychiatrist and neurologist Dr. Benjamin Simon, who began a series of hypnotic regression sessions, in an attempt to probe the missing hours. It had been their collective intention to explore any possible links between the Hills' apparent UFO experience and certain physical problems (such as stomach ulcers) from which Barney suffered, in addition to psychological factors, including the couple's interracial marriage, their previous marriages and their social and civil rights work.

The Hills were hypnotized separately, and were not allowed to hear the tape-recorded results until Dr. Simon had completed the programme. The tale that emerged was unlike anything previously reported, and made headlines all over the world. According to their testimony, given under hypnosis, the Hills had been taken from their car by a group of bizarre humanoid creatures, who guided them into a landed UFO and subjected them to the by now familiar medical examination. This included a "pregnancy test" on Betty, by means of a long needle inserted into her abdomen.

When the aliens had finished, Betty asked the one she called the "leader" where they came from.

...I said that I knew he wasn't from the Earth...and he asked if I knew anything about the Universe. And I told him no. I knew practically nothing...And he went across the room...there was an opening. And he pulled out a map....It was an oblong map.... And there were all these dots on it.... Some were little, just pinpoints. And others were as big as a nickel...there were curved lines going from one dot to another. And there was one big circle, and it had a lot of lines coming out from it. A lot of lines going to another circle quite close but not as big.... And I asked him what they meant. And he said that the heavy lines were trade routes ... the solid lines were places they went occasionally. And he said the broken lines were expeditions.... So I asked him where was his home port, and he said, "Where are you on the map?" I looked and laughed and said, "I don't know." So he said "If you don't know where you are, then there isn't any point in my telling you where I am from." And he put the map ... back in the space in the wall.

One of the most intriguing aspects of the case (and one of the most significant in terms of UFO history) involves the attempt made by schoolteacher and amateur astronomer Marjorie Fish to create a three-dimensional model of Betty's drawing of the "star map." Fish created the model out of beads and string in 1968, trying to find a match between the map and the nearer stars to our Solar System. The result was inspected by astronomer Terence Dickinson, who concluded that the "star map" was a view from several light years beyond the binary star system Zeta Reticuli, looking back towards the Sun and the star 82 Eridani.

This seemed to offer astonishing confirmation of the presence of explorers from another star system, although sceptics argued, quite rightly, that there were so many stars out there that *some* sort of match was inevitable. And yet, largely thanks to the "Fish interpretation," Zeta Reticuli has come to be regarded by many ufologists as the origin of at least one of the alien species currently visiting the Earth.

The aliens themselves were, facially, not quite like humans. They were similar, but eerily different: their eyes were a little larger than ours, with a wider lateral field of vision, but with pupils and irises. Their noses were vestigial—little more than two holes; likewise with their ears. (Strangely, Barney described the aliens' noses as above, while Betty described them as being very large, like Jimmy Durante's!) Their heads, utterly devoid of hair, were only slightly larger than ours. In short, they were too strange to be taken for humans, yet not strange enough to be taken for Greys, whose basic characteristics (large eyes, large cranium, no nose or ears) they shared.

As far as Dr. Simon was concerned, the Hills' experience had been entirely subjective: in effect, a waking dream. While he accepted that they believed what they were relating, Simon noted several correlations between Betty's testimony and documented dream symbolism. For instance, Betty had asked the leader for some proof of their encounter, and he had complied by giving her a book containing strange symbols. However, this provoked an argument among the aliens; the leader told her he had to take the book off her, because they could not leave behind such concrete evidence of their presence. This ties in rather strikingly with a certain aspect of Betty's unhappy childhood. She had frequently sought escape from her depression in books, but her mother, an extremely stern character, had insisted on limiting her reading.

There were also some illogicalities in the encounter; for instance, the aliens were fascinated by the notion of "time" as experienced by humans, and asked Betty to define "old age," "life span" and "year." But when Betty and Barney were about to leave the craft, the leader asked them to "wait a minute." Dr. Simon pointed out that contradictions of this kind are frequently found in dreams, which are the mind's way of grappling with conflicts, fears, desires and other problems.

There is no doubt that the Hills' interracial marriage was a potential source of great stress: although they were very happy together, their situation was extremely unusual in 1960s America. In addition, they both had had previous marriages, and were separated from the children of those marriages. Dr. Simon suggested that these stresses and conflicts may have resulted in Betty's nightmares, which she related to Barney. The (perhaps genuine) UFO sighting on their journey home from Canada might have been a catalyst for the abduction scenario, which was based on those stresses and conflicts, and which was then relived by the couple during their hypnosis.

Notwithstanding these speculations, the fact remains that the ultimate nature of the Hills' encounter is still open to debate. In view of the other close encounters with non-humans discussed in this book and elsewhere, it remains well within the bounds of possibility that Barney and Betty Hill experienced something genuinely anomalous.

All in the Mind?

At 9.15 P.M. on 3 July 1972, Maureen Puddy, a 37-year-old housewife from Rye in Victoria, Australia, was returning home from a visit to her son, who was in hospital, when she had the first of a series of apparent close encounters. Her experiences were to give rise to intense debate in the ufology community, not least because it became clear that only her consciousness was being abducted!

On the first occasion, the road on which she was travelling suddenly became bathed in intense blue light (a frequently reported element in abductions). Mrs. Puddy looked up to see a disc-shaped object, which seemed to be generating a humming noise, similar to that of an elevator. The object paced the car and its alarmed driver for several miles, before streaking away.

Three weeks later, on 25 July, Mrs. Puddy was driving on the same road, when the UFO returned, this time causing her car's engine to stall. As the vehicle gradually came to a halt, she heard a disembodied voice saying, "All your tests will be negative. Tell the media, do not panic, we mean no harm." Then the voice said, "You now have control," and the car's engine started. The UFO streaked away into the sky again.

Mrs. Puddy reported both of her sightings to the Royal Australian Air Force (RAAF), who sent her forms to complete. She also contacted several television stations, and was interviewed by one of them.

In February the following year, 1973, Mrs. Puddy felt an "eerie presence" in her house. Once again, she heard a strange, disembodied voice, which said, "Go back to the same meeting place." Understandably unwilling to do so alone, she telephoned the Victorian UFO Research Society. Two members of VUFORS, Judith Magee and Paul Norman, agreed to meet her at the location.

One of the UFO "entities" arrived early, however, appearing in the front passenger seat beside her as she was on her way to the rendezvous. The entity had long, blond hair and was wearing a white, ski-type suit. It vanished immediately, and Mrs. Puddy continued without further incident.

At the location of her earlier sightings, Mrs. Puddy sat with the two VUFORS investigators in her car, and waited for the next development. It wasn't long in coming. Mrs. Puddy became aware of the same entity standing outside the car. It beckoned to her, but she refused to leave the car. Neither of the two investigators saw the "man."

It was at that point that the most unusual aspect of the case became apparent. Mrs. Puddy suddenly fainted and, although she seemed to be unconscious, began to describe what she was experiencing. She claimed to be in a circular, windowless room; rising from the floor was a mushroom-shaped object, covered with hieroglyphics. The "man" was there with her, and told her to describe what she was seeing. Since there was no apparent way of escaping, Mrs. Puddy became very frightened and started to cry. She then returned to normal consciousness in the car, with no memory of her experience.

About a week later, Mrs. Puddy was driving with her son sitting beside her in the front of the car. Without warning, the "man" appeared once again, on the bench seat between them. It was raining heavily, and visibility was very bad, but while he was there, the weather improved dramatically. Mrs. Puddy and her son were able to see for miles around. When the "man" disappeared a few moments later, the poor weather conditions resumed.

As we shall see a little later, many researchers are content to consider the abduction phenomenon in purely concrete terms, with solid, "flesh and brood" aliens kidnapping people and conducting various unpleasant experiments on them. But the experiences of people like Maureen Puddy would seem to indicate that this is not necessarily the case. Neither can many of these experiences be accounted for by any theories in mainstream psychology, although certain concepts such as lucid dreams, hypnagogic and hypnopompic imagery, and fantasy-prone personalities, may cast some light on these distressing events. We shall examine these possible explanations in the final sections of this book.

The Pascagoula Fishermen

On 11 October 1973, an abduction incident occurred that once again made headlines all over the world. Charlie Hickson, 45, and Calvin Parker, 18, of Pascagoula, Mississippi, had decided to go fishing in the Pascagoula River. Their experience was reported by United Press International the following day:

> PASCAGOULA, Miss.—Two shipyard workers who claimed they were hauled aboard a UFO and examined by silver-skinned creatures with big eyes and pointed ears were checked today at a military hospital and found to be free of radiation....
>
> Jackson County chief deputy Barney Mathis said the men told him they were fishing from an old pier on the west bank of the Pascagoula River about 7 P.M. Thursday when they noticed a strange craft about two miles away emitting a bluish haze.
>
> They said it moved closer and then appeared to hover about three or four feet above the water, then "three whatever-they-weres came out, either floating or walking, and carried us into the ship," officers quoted Hickson as saying.
>
> "The things had big eyes. They kept us about twenty minutes, photographed us, and then took us back to the pier. The only sound they made was a buzzing-humming sound. They left in a flash."

"These are reliable people," Sheriff Diamond said. "They had no reason to say this if it had not been true. I know something did happen to them."

The sheriff said the "spacecraft" was described as fish-shaped, about ten feet long with an eight-foot ceiling. The occupants were said to have pale silvery-grey skin, no hair, long pointed ears and noses, with an opening for a mouth and hands "like crab claws."

The sight of these creatures coming towards him had evidently been too much for the younger man, Parker, who fainted and remained unconscious throughout the rest of the encounter. Hickson described being placed in a horizontal, floating position and being scanned by an instrument resembling an enormous eye.

Dr. J. Allen Hynek, who was no longer working for the US Air Force, having established his own civilian research group, the Center for UFO Studies in Chicago, flew to Pascagoula to look into the case, along with investigative journalist Ralph Blum.

According to Sheriff Diamond, whom they interviewed, the two men had requested a lie-detector test, to prove that they were telling the truth. "And Calvin," he added, "I'm not easily convinced, but I heard that boy pray when he was alone and thought that nobody could hear. That was enough for me."

The police had tried to trick the two men into revealing a hoax; on one occasion, they left them in a room with a hidden tape recorder, but Hickson and Parker maintained their story even when they thought no one was listening:

> PARKER: I passed out. I expect I never passed out in my whole life.
> HICKSON: I've never seen nothin' like that before in my life. You can't make people believe it—
> . . .
> PARKER: You see how that damn door come right up?
> HICKSON: I don't know how it opened, son. I don't know.

PARKER: It just laid up and just like that those son' bitches—just like that they come out.

HICKSON: I know. You can't believe it. You can't make people believe it. . . .

Hickson and Parker were subsequently hypnotized by UFO researcher James Harder, who concluded that they had indeed been abducted by extraterrestrial creatures. Hynek, ever cautious, disagreed, saying that it was premature to make such a statement, although he did accept that the two men had undergone a "terrifying experience of some sort."

The case was also investigated by UFO debunker Philip J. Klass, an editor with *Aviation Week & Space Technology*, and Joe Eszterhas, a writer for *Rolling Stone* magazine. As might be expected, their sceptical standpoint resulted in a spirited slanging-match between the two sides of the UFO debate. Klass and Eszterhas located a bridge attendant and two 24-hour toll booth operators who should have had a clear view of the abduction, but who saw nothing at the time. The abduction occurred within a few hundred yards of the busy Highway 90; why, asked the sceptics, had no motorists witnessed the event? Hickson replied that their view would have been obscured by high bushes and the bridge railing. Sheriff Diamond came to Hickson's defence, and stated that three unnamed motorists had indeed seen a UFO "flying low in the direction" of the alleged abduction.

"Unnamed" witnesses did not impress Klass, who turned his attention to the lie-detector test that the men had passed. He discovered that the polygraph operator had only been in practice for one year, and had not even been certified by his training school, owing to his failure to complete his course. According to a licensed operator to whom Klass spoke, such a test would need to be conducted over a full day; but Hickson's test had only lasted about 20 minutes.

Joe Eszterhas did some digging of his own, and discovered that Hickson had been fired from his job at the Ingalls shipyards for "conduct unbecoming a supervisor." Apparently, he had been borrowing money from those working under him, and had paid them back by "trying to finagle them promotions."

The debate between the pro- and anti-UFO factions regarding the Pascagoula case continues to this day. It has become a "classic," which in effect means that it is used by the sceptics as a prime example of the ludicrous nature of the UFO phenomenon in general, and by some ufologists as an example of its puzzling variety and multi-faceted richness. As journalist Keith Thompson says: "For either side of the ongoing argument to truly win would violate one of ufology's unspoken rules: *the debate must continue.*"

Abduction at Cergy-Pontoise

Although extremely rare, UFO abductions lasting several days are not unheard of. In America, the most famous case of this kind is that of Travis Walton, who, in November 1975, disappeared for five days after encountering a disc-shaped object in the Apache-Sitgreaves National Forest in Arizona. A lesser-known but equally striking event happened in France in 1979, at Cergy-Pontoise, an overspill town situated 25 miles north-west of Paris.

The victim was 18-year-old Franck Fontaine, who was allegedly abducted in full view of his two friends, Salomon N'Diaye, 25, and Jean-Pierre Prévost, 26. The three men were market traders, rather shady characters who drove an unlicensed and uninsured car—without drivers' licences; Prévost was on file at the Intelligence Branch of the Gendarmerie as an anarchist. He and N'Diaye lived next door to each other in a cheap, drab apartment block called La Justice Mauve (Purple Justice); Fontaine lived two miles away.

In the early hours of Monday 26 November 1979, they began to load their battered old car with a stock of jeans and sweaters, which they planned to take to the market at Gisors, 35 miles away. An early start was required, since the car had a habit of breaking down, and they wanted to get a good spot in the market. Franck Fontaine helped to push-start the car, and then remained at the wheel to make sure it didn't stall, while his friends began to bring the merchandise down.

At this point, Fontaine noticed something unusual in the night sky: a bright, elongated light. Thinking that a photograph of the light might be worth some money to the newspapers, N'Diaye hurried up to his apartment to fetch his camera; Prévost also went inside to collect another load of jeans. Left on his own, Fontaine drove the car on to the main road adjacent to the apartment block, trying to get a better look at the object. Alerted to the sound of Fontaine driving away, N'Diaye and Prévost looked out of their windows to see the car coming to a halt, its engine no longer running.

Prévost was angry because they would probably have to jump-start the car all over again. Followed by N'Diaye, he rushed downstairs and out of the building, to be confronted by an incredible sight. The rear of the car was completely enshrouded by a sphere of glowing fog, around which several smaller spheres were moving. The small spheres entered the large one, which seemed to transform itself into the same elongated light they had all seen earlier; it then ascended into the sky and vanished. Fontaine, as his friends quickly discovered, was nowhere to be seen.

N'Diaye and Prévost immediately went to the police who, after listening to their story, told them to inform the Gendarmerie which, as a department of the Ministry of National Defence, handles all French UFO reports. The two witnesses were questioned for several days; various theories were put forward by the authorities, including that Fontaine had engineered his own disappearance to avoid his military service. They also briefly suspected that N'Diaye and Prévost might have killed him, and come up with the UFO story to cover their tracks. The questioning continued for a week, both by the authorities and the media, which by now had got their teeth firmly into the story. But the whereabouts of Fontaine were still a complete mystery.

At about 4.00 A.M. on Monday 3 December, one week after his

disappearance, Franck Fontaine awoke to find himself in a cabbage field near the Purple Justice building. Confused, he went up to Salomon N'Diaye's apartment and rang the bell. When N'Diaye saw his friend, he hugged him joyously. Fontaine was nonplussed by this behaviour, not realizing that a full week had passed—he was still expecting to begin the journey to Gisors. Although besieged by reporters and UFO investigators, Fontaine could offer no information about his experience, other than that he had been overcome with drowsiness while looking for the object, and had then woken up in the cabbage field.

One of the groups that had become involved with the case was the the Institut Mondial des Sciences Avancées (World Institute of Advanced Sciences), co-founded by Jimmy Guieu, a well-known science fiction writer. Guieu declared his absolute belief in the veracity of the three witnesses. As a result, Fontaine, N'Diaye and Prévost agreed to co-operate with him on a book, *Cergy-Pontoise UFO Contacts*, which became a huge bestseller. The book described how the investigation had taken a sudden left turn, when Prévost volunteered to be hypnotized (Fontaine himself had steadfastly refused). What emerged from these sessions was that Prévost—not Fontaine—had been the focus of the abduction. Fontaine had simply been used by the aliens to focus the world's attention on the events in Cergy-Poutoise.

The information Prévost provided turned out to be rather disappointing—similar, in fact, to the tired and trite pronouncements of the "contactees" of the 1950s and early 1960s. The aliens, calling themselves the "intelligences from beyond," were here to warn the Earth of the dangers of technology, etc. According to Prévost's account (expanded upon in his own subsequent book *The Truth about the Cergy-Pontoise Affair*), he was invited to a secret alien base, located in a railway tunnel containing an abandoned railway carriage from the Second World War.

The tunnel was near the small village of Bourg-de-Sirod, 225 miles away on the French-Swiss border, a place in which Prévost had spent time as a child. He was taken there by someone claiming to be a "travelling salesman," who had called at his apartment soon after Fontaine's return. Inside the tunnel, Prévost found many other people, some of whom were sitting around a fire. The people had been brought from all over the world, to be given the philosophy of the "intelligences from beyond," via a friendly and talkative alien called Haurrio.

The Cergy-Pontoise case was also investigated (without the cooperation of the three witnesses) by the French "Control" group, a highly respected, scientifically oriented organization, whose representatives discovered several inconsistencies in the story. Although Prévost professed no previous interest whatsoever in UFOs, Control investigators established that, at the time of the incident, he had been reading a magazine in which an abduction story very similar to Fontaine's was being serialized. It also became clear that two additional people had been present on the morning of the abduction: Prévost's girlfriend Corinne, and a young man called Fabrice Joly. Why had this been covered up by the witnesses? According to Control, a possible answer was that N'Diaye and Prévost had made much of their driving straight to the police after Fontaine's abduction—in spite of the fact that their car was uninsured and they had no driving licences. The intended implication was that they did not care if they got into trouble: it was more important to them that the police be informed of their friend's disappearance. The fact was that Joly had a valid licence, and had agreed to drive them to the market at Gisors.

Other contradictions became evident. The journalist Iris Billon-Duplan, who was covering the case, was conducting an interview with Prévost on the night Fontaine returned. Prévost had told her that he had no money or food, since the abduction business had been interfering with his ability to make his living, so Billon-Duplan invited him to her nearby apartment for a meal. This is consistent with Fontaine's assertion that Prévost was not at home when he tried his apartment, and that he then tried N'Diaye's. However, N'Diaye claimed that he had woken up at about 4.30 A.M. and looked out of his window. On the road below, he saw a ball of light, from which Fontaine emerged.

These and other discrepancies strongly imply that Fontaine, Prévost and N'Diaye concocted a hoax (probably for financial gain) that quickly got out of control owing to the intense world-wide media interest. While Prévost subsequently admitted as much, Fontaine has always maintained that he was abducted, which raises the possibility that the three men began to embellish what had been a genuine UFO event. Alternatively, Fontaine may have fallen (or been placed) into some altered state of consciousness, in which he hallucinated the abduction. For his part, he maintains that his only memory was of being in a strange room that appeared to be a laboratory of some kind.

In his book *Revelations*, Jacques Vallée presents some very intriguing information with regard to this last theory. Apparently, a French researcher was able to secure an interview with a representative of the French Ministry of Defence, who claimed that Franck Fontaine had been "abducted" in the course of an experiment designed to test the "reactions and the investigative abilities of local law enforcement agencies," in addition to the reactions of the scientific establishment. According to the man from the Ministry of Defence, Fontaine had indeed been placed in a drug-induced state of extreme suggestibility. (Vallée speculates that the inspiration for the scenario lay in the Travis Walton abduction in 1975.)

If this is true, then the fathomless waters of the UFO mystery become even muddier, with an unknown number of close encounters perhaps having been staged by secret government groups in an effort to gauge the reactions of the population to genuinely anomalous activity.

Abduction and Bilocation

Most UFO investigators tend to dismiss the claims of the "contactees" who came to prominence in the 1950s and 60s. In those days, the idea that UFOs might have pilots wishing to interact directly with humans was totally new, and not a little outrageous to contemporary researchers. The information they conveyed was also deeply suspect, consisting mainly of warnings to curtail our irresponsible development of nuclear weapons, which was having an adverse effect on the balance of the Universe, and jeopardizing the safety of a number of alien races. The aliens themselves—entirely human-looking in every respect—usually claimed to have come from various planets within our own Solar System. This claim was shown to be absolutely ludicrous in the light of subsequent unmanned exploration of those planets, all of which are totally unsuitable for the development of humanoid life.

In fact, as we learned more and more of the deeply unpleasant conditions on our nearest planetary neighbours, the ufonauts gradually claimed more distant origins: mysterious worlds with names like Baavi and Zomdic, orbiting unreachable stars. These beings were dismissed as figments of the imagination by investigators: their messages of universal peace, love and brotherhood were extremely distasteful to those anxious to discover a hard, scientific explanation for what was doubtless a genuine mystery.

And yet the field of ufology is an immensely complex one, whose individual elements resonate powerfully, subtly echoing down through the decades, altering their surface details while leaving their essence intact. Additional details are frequently added to the core scenario, integrating them into a modified whole. Take, for example, the case of Judy Doraty.

Judy's frightening encounter took place while she was driving in her car near Houston, Texas, in May 1973. Four members of her family were also present; all five people saw a bright light in the sky. The light seemed to be following them, so Judy pulled over to the side of the road, got out and walked to the back of the car to get a better view of it. She was unable to recall what happened next; however, when she underwent hypnotic regression with psychologist Dr. Leo Sprinkle in March 1980, disturbing memories surfaced.

Apparently, Judy had what is known as a "bilocation experience" which, as the name suggests, means that the percipient seems to be in two different locations at the same time. Judy reported standing beside her car, and simultaneously standing inside the UFO that had been pacing them. The occupants of the craft were in the process of mutilating a calf that they had captured, drawing it up through a beam of yellow light. The light seemed to be filled with strange, swirling particles, and Judy had the impression that it would feel solid, if touched.

The beings themselves were very similar in appearance to the Greys, in that they were short and spindly, with pale, sickly-looking skin, large heads and vestigial noses and mouths. Their eyes, however, were different from the jet-black, featureless orbs commonly associated with this "species"; they had yellow irises and vertical, cat-like pupils.

Judy's horror was increased immeasurably when she saw that her daughter was also aboard the craft, and was being examined by the beings. However, they assured her (communicating through telepathy) that neither of them would be harmed, adding that they had not intended to bring her into the craft; her bilocation had somehow been spontaneous.

As the ufonauts went to work on the live calf (which was surely pointlessly cruel), excising various parts of its body through tubes that deposited them in different receptacles, they explained to Judy that they were in the process of monitoring the spread of some form of toxin, whose presence in the environment would soon have an adverse effect on humans. During her hypnosis session, she told Leo Sprinkle: "It's like if we continue like we are now, it's going to involve not only us but possibly other . . . and they're trying to stop something that could cause a chain reaction. And maybe involving them. I don't know. . . . We're not the only ones to be concerned." When they had finished their procedures, the beings returned the dead calf to earth via the beam.

In his examination of the case, Richard L. Thompson makes a

cogent point, and one which is echoed by the sceptics who maintain that UFO abductions do not occur: the episode Judy described under hypnosis is illogical, given the apparent level of the beings' technology. "Beings capable of producing antigravity beams would presumably be able to detect pollutants in animals without harming them." Thompson believes that, if animal mutilations really are the work of non-human creatures, then they may be leaving their carcasses in farmer's fields (itself an apparently unnecessary act), in order to frighten humanity, or to demonstrate their displeasure with the way we are managing the Earth.

The reader will doubtless detect an echo of the concerns for the future of our planet expressed more politely by the "Space Brothers." Although the surface details have been radically altered (the appearance of the beings, their savage treatment of another living creature, their ongoing programme of taking people very much against their will), the core reason for their presence remains unchanged: they are here because humans are behaving irresponsibly, calling their very future into question. In the 1950s and 1960s, the "aliens" were concerned with atomic weapons testing, which would "upset the balance of the Universe"; in recent years, they seem to have shifted their attention to chemical, rather than nuclear, dangers.

And yet they still do not seem to have our best interests exclusively at heart: the implication remains that they themselves will somehow be adversely affected if we continue to treat our planetary environment in a cavalier fashion. They are looking after their own future as well.

There are a number of possible ways in which this may be interpreted. It is possible that when human percipients report that "aliens" are concerned about the environment, they are merely concretizing their own subconscious fears. On the other hand, it may be that, if these beings really do exist, they (or at least some of them) may be *indigenous to the Earth*, having always lived here alongside us, perhaps in an adjacent plane of existence. (This theory will be examined in greater detail towards the end of this book.) If they are truly extraterrestrial, having their home port on some distant planet, they may be caretakers of Earth (a position we had always assumed was already filled by ourselves!), given the duty of ensuring the survival of the biosphere. When they imply that ecological disasters will cause a "chain reaction" of adverse effects for "others," perhaps they are referring to certain consequences arising from the dereliction of a bestowed duty

Whatever the ultimate nature of Judy Doraty's experience, there remains a striking parallel with that of Maureen Puddy, discussed a little earlier. Like Mrs. Puddy, Judy in a sense "left her body," entering the UFO in an apparently non-physical state. In Mrs. Puddy's case, her apparently unconscious body was in full view of two investigators throughout the experience; in Judy's case, her family watched in bewilderment as she stood beside their car, apparently watching the UFO, while, from her perspective, she was simultaneously inside it.

Judy Doraty's encounter (like Mrs. Puddy's) is representative of the complex nature of UFO abductions, which carries implications far beyond the straightforward "nuts and bolts" interpretation favoured by many researchers. It is possible, even likely, that we are dealing with something rather more subtle than the arrival of explorers from another planet.

"Base City of Operation"

The following deeply disturbing case contains virtually all of the components currently to be found in the general subject of ufology: abduction, missing time, cattle mutilation, journeys to strange landscapes and underground bases apparently operated by both aliens *and* humans. The encounter bears certain similarities to that of Judy Doraty, and was likewise investigated by Dr. Leo Sprinkle, together with Dr. Paul Bennewitz, a physicist and member of the Aerial Phenomena Research Organization (APRO). As with Judy Doraty, Sprinkle needed to resort to hypnotic regression in order to liberate the memories of the alleged incidents experienced by the witness, 28-year-old Myrna Hansen. The sessions were conducted between 11 May and 3 June 1980. The story that emerged is as follows.

Myrna Hansen and her six-year-old son were driving near the town of Cimarron, New Mexico, when she saw five UFOs land in a nearby pasture and capture a cow. She and her son were then abducted by strange beings, who proceeded to mutilate the unfortunate cow in front of them. Once again, they seemed to be unconcerned that the animal was experiencing abject agony, as a long knife pierced its chest and its genitals were excised. Again, they informed their human captive (telepathically) that it had to be done, however unpleasant it may be.

Myrna and her son were then taken on a bizarre journey to a number of different locations. During the journey the beings forced her to disrobe, and gave her what has become the typical physical examination, including a vaginal probe. Apparently, she later suffered from a life-threatening infection, which she attributes to this intrusive procedure. As with the Hill case discussed earlier, the beings were fascinated by human physical attributes: in Myrna's case, the beings (who were totally devoid of body hair) found her hair, eyebrows and eyelashes extremely interesting.

After the physical examination, a tall, "jaundiced-looking" man appeared. He informed Myrna apologetically that her abduction had not been intended. (The reader will recall that Judy Doraty's encounter had likewise been a mistake.) The following event was even stranger and more unusual. After informing her that her son (who had been taken elsewhere) was unharmed, the tall man said that the other beings (apparently Greys) would be punished for their mistake.

She remembered seeing them naked from the waist up, described their terrible thinness and how they had "more ribs than we have." Her description of them ("one has a nose that's crooked, turned up and crooked. They shuffle and drag their feet") is more reminiscent of medieval goblins than the crew of a starship. Likewise, their mode of dress was a far cry from what one might expect. One being wore a "Franciscan monk's collar" with a belt and "military" boots, while another, square-headed female being wore a collar, "gathered at the neck like a pilgrim with ruffles."

Myrna was taken to a strange place full of control panels, TV monitor screens and other electronic equipment. At one point, she remembered seeing a window, with a starscape beyond. In the foreground was a planet, which apparently was not the Earth. Throughout her encounter Myrna was aware that the beings did not seem to know what they were doing, and this apparent incompetence frightened her more than anything else: "I'm scared, not of him, but his confusion. It worries me that they don't know what they're doing."

She was then taken outside by another group of beings, who were "attractively dressed" and three of whom looked entirely human. She immediately recognized the landscape as that of the Roswell region of New Mexico. The beings took her to a hidden elevator, which descended to a vast underground complex described by her as the "base city of operations." The strange, Grey-type entities were everywhere, but there were also many human beings, implying that the complex was jointly run by aliens and humans.

At this point, Myrna briefly saw her son, but he was immediately taken away again, causing her finally to lose control and run, screaming, off into the complex. Presently she found herself in a dimly lit room full of large tanks. When she looked into one of them, she saw that it was full of liquid . . . and contained something else: "Something is horrifying me. . . . Top of a bald head. . . . I think I see an arm with the hand—human! Other something red and bloody looking. Oh, God! I'm so scared at seeing this. . . . Tongues, huge; they look real big. They're under liquid, real dark. . . . They found me, but when they found me, I was in the corner on the floor crying."

The beings took her to another area where she and her son were subjected to intense flashes of light, apparently some process by which their memories of the encounter were erased. They were then flown back to the point of their abduction aboard a UFO, which was also carrying their car. The car was lowered to the ground, and Myrna and her son continued on their journey, now unaware of all that had happened.

It is alleged that later Myrna had several CAT scans, which revealed small devices in her brain. During her encounter, the beings had made "necessary alterations" to her, which included inserting these devices. Many abductees report similar procedures involving "implants," some of which have been retrieved through subsequent surgery. Although none of these objects has ever been proved to be of extraterrestrial origin, some of them do seem to have some remarkable characteristics.

For example, a doctor in Santa Barbara, California, named Roger Leir, has recently retrieved unusual objects from several patients. The objects are described as magnetic metallic fragments surrounded by a greyish "membrane," which apparently prevents them from being rejected by the body. According to Dr. Leir, "Always there's an inflammatory reaction to a foreign body. That's the golden, God-given rule. But the soft tissue analysis from around the objects produced no inflammatory changes whatsoever.... And not just from one site, but we're talking about three sites in two different individuals."

Analysis of the membrane revealed that it was composed of three common bodily substances: protein coagulum (a protein derived from blood), hemosiderin (an oxygen-carrying substance similar to haemoglobin) and keratin (the tough, protective substance that forms the main constituent of skin, hair and nails). Dr. Leir said that, if scientists could discover precisely how this membrane was put together, "we could probably stick anything inside the human body and not get a rejection reaction, which would certainly be a contribution to medical science."

Although the discovery of such artefacts implies an experience grounded in objective reality, encounters such as that of Myrna Hansen carry undertones suggesting something quite different. Her experience sounds more like a visit to Hell (complete with subterranean location) than an encounter with aliens. Their evil, goblin-like appearance and shuffling gait, together with the bodies of unfortunate humans being stirred in huge, liquid-filled vats, offer a scene whose horror seems grounded as much in religion or mysticism as in extraterrestrial science.

Of course, Myrna's testimony was given under hypnosis, as are those of many (but by no means all) abductees, and this is almost certainly part of the problem. In his introduction to John G. Fuller's account of the Hill abduction, *The Interrupted Journey*, Dr. Benjamin Simon wrote:

> The charisma of hypnosis has tended to foster the belief that hypnosis is the magical and royal road to TRUTH. In one sense, this is so, but it must be understood that hypnosis is a pathway to the truth as it is felt and understood by the patient. The truth is what he believes to be the truth, and this may or may not be consonant with the ultimate nonpersonal truth. *Most frequently it is*. [Emphasis added]

Although it must be said that Dr. Simon was here stating his position that the Hills *believed* that they had been abducted (and that this may or may not have corresponded to what *actually* happened), the possibility must surely be conceded that some memories retrieved through hypnotic regression refer to a core event experienced by the percipient, with certain details being obscured by material already present in the subconscious.

Anatomy of an Alien Race

The concept of the extraterrestrial alien, which is now one of the most powerful icons of the twentieth century, has come to be represented—in the eyes of many ufologists as well as the general public—by the mysterious beings known as the Greys. Although, in the earlier days of ufology, alleged alien beings came in all shapes and sizes, from hairy dwarfs to giant disembodied brains, the Grey is now the most commonly described visitor to our planetary shores.

They are usually described as being short (three and a half to four feet), with spindly limbs and torso. People who have encountered them often maintain that they have no visible elbow or knee joints, and some have the impression that the beings' physical make-up is totally undifferentiated: in other words, they appear to have been produced from the same material with a "cookie-cutter." The term "Grey" is apt in many cases, but not all, since their colour is also sometimes described as white, tan or pale blue.

By far the most striking feature of these beings is the head, which is disproportionately large, almost balloon-like, and tapers to a pointed chin. The mouth appears to be vestigial, no more than a narrow slit, while the nose is most often described as very small, if present at all. The ears are tiny holes, with no external structure to speak of.

Without exception, those who encounter the Greys speak with awe and terror of their eyes, which are enormous and usually jet black. It is through the eyes that much communication seems to take place, with the percipients feeling that they have no defence against the beings' penetrating stares. Looking into a Grey's eyes has been compared to looking into eternity itself, accompanied by a sense of being forced to surrender every aspect of the percipient's personality, as if the Greys were entering into and becoming one with their victims.

There has been much speculation on the reasons for the disproportionate size of the beings' heads. If we accept, for the sake of the argument, that the Greys are genuine, real beings, the products of their own evolutionary processes, then we can begin to discern possible similarities between them and humans. In his Pulitzer Prize-winning book *The Dragons of Eden*, which deals with the evolution of human intelligence, the late Carl Sagan drew attention to the fact that, in the past few million years, the size of the human brain has increased spectacularly. This increase was accompanied by a reshaping of the female pelvic girdle, doubtless to accommodate the larger cranium. Sagan also suggests that this is the reason for the pain of human childbirth, which is apparently unique in the natural world: "Childbirth is painful because the evolution of the human skull has been spectacularly fast and recent." He goes on to quote the American anatomist C. Judson Herrick's description of the development of the neocortex (the outermost, most recently developed part of the brain): "Its explosive growth late in phylogeny [evolutionary development] is one of the most dramatic cases of evolutionary transformation known to comparative anatomy." According to Sagan, the fontanelle (the open space at the top of the skull in newborn humans) "is very likely an imperfect accommodation to this recent brain evolution."

If we accept that our continued evolution over the next few million years will bring yet greater increases in cranial capacity, combined with a decreasing need to trouble ourselves with physical labour, might we not expect our distant descendants to resemble closely the Greys? Sceptics frequently argue that we cannot be visited by humanoid extraterrestrial beings because such things are biologically impossible. The colossal number of genetic mutations leading from the single-celled organisms of three billion years ago to the human beings of today could not possibly have been duplicated on any other planet. However, the theory of convergent evolution offers a possible counter-argument.

The British science writer Edward Ashpole, in his book *The UFO Phenomena*, reminds us that "similar-looking animals have evolved from different points within the same phylum [basic body plan].... The most striking examples are seen in the dolphin (mammal), shark (fish) and ichthyosaurus (reptile)." Although Ashpole goes on to qualify this by saying that these animals are all vertebrates of the same phylum, and that evolutionary convergence from isolated biospheres would be extremely unlikely, some evolutionary biologists do not dismiss the idea completely. If it is within the bounds of possibility that a successful oceanic predator would look something like a shark, no matter which planet we happen to be on, then there is a chance that, on a planet similar to Earth, a successful, rational creature with the capacity to develop a technological society would look something like us. In other words, it would possess a large cranium with two eyes located nearby for binocular vision at the highest possible elevation above ground level. It would have four limbs only, since any more would use up valuable processing capacity in the brain, and would have been selected out during evolution. It would also have developed something similar to hands in its earlier stages, in order to manipulate tools.

In considering the increase in cranial capacity that (in our case) harbingered the development of reason and, ultimately, technology, we are obliged to note that, while the shape of the pelvic girdle also underwent changes, it is not large enough to prevent the extreme discomfort of childbirth. As Sagan notes, in human females, the pelvis has probably reached its maximum size: to grow any larger would interfere with the ability to walk efficiently. If our cranial capacity continues to grow, this will present some rather obvious problems for our descendants; problems that, perhaps, the Greys have already experienced.

Many researchers have put forward the concept of neoteny (in which adult animals retain certain larval characteristics) to account for the similarity in appearance between the hairless, large-eyed Greys and human foetuses. There is clearly no conceivable way that the fragile, spindly form of a female Grey could withstand a natural full-term pregnancy. Therefore, according to the theory, they must reproduce through entirely in *vitro* methods. This would certainly account for the often-reported transparent vessels seen by abductees aboard UFOs, in which foetal Greys are suspended.

The beings frequently tell abductees that their sperm and ova are being harvested in order to strengthen the alien stock, which has become genetically weakened over the millennia; the infants seen in the tanks are "hybrids" of alien and human. It has thus been suggested that this is the ultimate reason for the Greys' presence on Earth. However, even if the Greys were the result of convergent evolution, this would still make no sense as an explanation, since human and alien genetic material would be utterly incompatible. Abduction researchers counter this by suggesting that perhaps the Greys have developed sophisticated methods of altering our genetic material to make it compatible with theirs. However, this does beg the question: if they are such consummate genetic engineers, why can't they repair their own stock without recourse to alien species?

In the absence of more comprehensive information, questions such as these must remain open; but in the final section of this book, I shall examine some additional theories on the possible true nature of these troublesome and elusive beings.

Death by Unnatural Causes?

Zygmunt Adamski, a 57-year-old Pole who had been a prisoner of war throughout the Nazi occupation of his country in the Second World War, settled in England after his release. Here, Adamski (no relation to the American contactee George Adamski) met his future wife, Lottie, worked as a miner for many years, was well liked by his neighbours, and had no apparent enemies. On 6 June 1980, he left his home in the Tingley suburb of Leeds, West Yorkshire, to buy a bag of potatoes. He was not seen alive again. Five days later, his body was discovered by Trevor Parker, who was loading his truck at his father's coalyard in the neighbouring village of Todmorden.

The body was lying on top of a coal tip. Although it had recently been raining, there were no tracks on the sides of the tip to suggest how he might have got there. At the inquest into Adamski's death, which was not held until 15 months later to give the police more time for their ultimately fruitless inquiries, it was revealed that he suffered from angina and, while his death could have been caused by heart failure resulting from exhaustion, a pathologist also said that he might have died of fright.

The post mortem also revealed the presence of strange burn marks on Adamski's head and neck, apparently caused by some corrosive substance, which forensic scientists were unable to identify. According to pathologist Dr. Alan Edwards, there were scratches on the palms of both hands and the knees. The coroner, James Turnbull, recorded a verdict of death by natural causes, although he added that foul play could not be ruled out, and appealed to the public for any further information.

When interviewed by reporters, Trevor Parker said: "[The body] was just lying there in plain sight. I didn't know whether the man was dead or alive, so I called the police and an ambulance. I was very frightened, I didn't want to be out there by myself. The body gave me a very eerie feeling. I have no idea how the man got in the yard, but I know one thing for absolute certain—there was no body on that coal pile when I loaded my truck earlier in the day."

Not only was the corrosive substance found on Adamski unidentified, it also appeared to have been carefully applied while the upper part of the body was naked. His face and clothes were entirely undamaged. Although his watch and wallet were missing, there was a £5 note in his pocket.

The sinister connection with UFOs came as a result of a number of sightings in the area around the time of Adamski's disappearance, one of which had been made by Alan Godfrey, who had been the first police officer to arrive at the scene following Parker's call to the authorities. Godfrey later said that Adamski's face held an expression of "fright or terror." He also noticed a deep, three-inch incision in the back of the neck, which contained a liquid later identified as boiled water. His hair had also been cut into a close crop (it had been of normal length when he left his house), and he was clean-shaven, which was not consistent with living rough for five days. His jacket was fastened incorrectly, perhaps implying that someone else had put it on him.

The body had apparently been placed with some care on top of the coal tip; in the opinion of one police officer who examined it, it would have taken a helicopter to achieve this, since there was absolutely no disturbance to the loose coal.

At the inquest into the death, coroner James Turnbull had this to say:

> As a trained lawyer, I have to rely on facts. Unfortunately, we have not been able to uncover any facts which may have contributed to this death. I tend to believe that there may be some simple explanation.
>
> However, I do admit that the failure of forensic scientists to identify the corrosive substance which caused Mr. Adamski's burns could lend some weight to the UFO theory. As a coroner I cannot speculate. But I must admit that if I was walking over Ilkley Moor tomorrow and a UFO came down, I would not be surprised. I might be terrified, but not surprised.
>
> I cannot believe that all the thousands of reports of this sort of phenomenon, covering almost every country in the world, and going back through the ages, result from human error. It is quite the most mysterious death I have investigated in 12 years.

A strange postscript to this tale occurred in March 1983, when Mark Birdsall of *UFO Magazine* received a telephone call from an individual claiming to be a relative of Zygmunt Adamski's. This individual, who has never been traced, informed Birdsall that after leaving his house, Adamski was met by a group of fellow Poles, whom he knew well, and who took him to a derelict hut a few miles away and imprisoned him there. He was kept there, apparently as a punishment for some unspecified transgression, until his death. He sustained the injuries to his hands and knees by clambering up a wall to a window in an attempt to escape.

According to Birdsall's informant, Adamski received his strange burns by grabbing a loose shelf and dislodging a tin of acid, which hit him on the head. His captors found him and, not having intended to harm him, panicked. They cleaned him up, but he died, and they then dumped his body on the coal tip.

The editors of *UFO Magazine* wisely hold back from making any sensational statements regarding this intriguing case, preferring to let the information we have (such as it is) speak for itself. There are many unanswered questions, perhaps the most important of which is: if Adamski spilled some form of acid or other burning solution on himself, why were the pathologists unable to identify it? Also, how could Adamski's associates place his body on top of a wet, seven-foot-high coal tip without leaving any trace of their activities? And why did the mysterious whistle-blower contact Mark Birdsall with his information instead of the police, who would doubtless have followed up on it?

Perhaps the answer is that they would indeed have followed up on it, and found it to be spurious. Could it be that the true purpose of the call (to a UFO-related publication) was to pour cold water on any connection with UFOs? This would make the caller's true identity of even greater interest.

Sometimes They Don't Come Back

One of the most astonishing cases of possible UFO abduction occurred on the shores of Lake Anjikuni, Canada, in the winter of 1930. The case is astonishing because it involved the disappearance of an entire Eskimo village, with a population of 1,200.

It began with the sighting of a strange object moving through the sky. Trapper Armand Laurent and his two sons were outside their cabin when they saw it. Laurent described the light as continuously changing shape as it glided overhead, from a cylinder to a bullet shape.

A few days after this sighting, two officers from the Royal Canadian Mounted Police arrived at the cabin. They were on their way north from their base at Churchill to Lake Anjikuni, and asked Laurent if they might shelter there for the night. According to the Mounties, there was a "kind of problem" at the lake. When Laurent mentioned the strange light he had seen, they asked him which direction it was moving in. He replied that it had been heading towards Lake Anjikuni.

For Armand Laurent and his sons, that was the end of the matter; not so, however, for another trapper, named Joe Labelle, who had snowshoed towards the Eskimo village on the shores of the lake a few days earlier. Labelle had many friends in this village, and it was with a sense of pleasant anticipation that he had made his way across the frozen landscape to spend some time with them.

That anticipation gradually turned to creeping dread as he drew nearer. Stopping at the edge of the village, he shouted a greeting. There was no one to be seen in the normally bustling little community, which Labelle found hard to understand. Peering through the icy gloom towards the lakeshore, he could make out a few kayaks, battered and torn by the wave action, lying on the beach.

Labelle entered the village and moved among the huts, glancing in increasing apprehension at the empty doorways, with their caribou skin flaps billowing forlornly in the icy wind. For more than an hour, he searched the village in vain for signs of its inhabitants. He discovered pots of congealed caribou stew hanging over the ashes of long-dead fires. He found sealskin garments, obviously belonging to a child, one of which had an ivory needle hanging from it. A mother must have been mending it, Labelle surmised, when something happened to make her stop.

Even more disturbing than this was the presence of the Eskimos' rifles, standing abandoned by the doors of the huts. To a seasoned trapper like Joe Labelle, this was truly astonishing: an Eskimo's rifle is his single most important possession; not one of the villagers would have gone anywhere without it in the hostile northern vastness, unless he were tired of living. And yet gone they had, without their only means of protection.

Labelle could stay no longer in that deserted place. He fled across the tundra to the nearest telegraph office and sent a report to the RCMP base in Churchill. The Mounties dispatched to the lake persuaded Labelle to return with them to the village. Labelle agreed, not least because he wanted to find out what had happened to the Eskimos' sled dogs, which were nearly as important to their survival as their rifles.

They found the dogs about a hundred yards from the village, tethered to some stunted trees. All were frozen solid, having died of starvation.

Mystery was compounded by mystery, and yet the greatest and most ominous puzzle was about to reveal itself. On the far side of the village, the Eskimos had previously buried a member of their community under the traditional cairn of stones. When Labelle and the Mounties came to the grave, they found that it was empty. The stones had been placed to one side in two neat piles, the ground had been opened and the body removed. None of the investigators could understand why this had happened, or indeed *how* since the ground was frozen solid. Animals were surely not to blame, since the stones had been *stacked* by the open grave.

A major investigation was launched, and a nationwide search conducted with the aid of experienced trackers, but no trace of the villagers was ever found. The only conclusion arrived at was that at some point everyone had left their homes, apparently attracted by something that was happening outside. They had left their rifles, their dogs, their food and clothing, and had not returned. Their kayaks had been left behind also, meaning that they had not set out across the lake.

In his 1989 novel *Majestic*, American author Whitley Strieber weaves the Lake Anjikuni incident into the narrative, and suggests an intriguing solution to the mystery of the empty grave. Since the Eskimos had great respect for their dead, might not their ancestor have been taken away also, as a sign of respect for their beliefs? This, of course, begs the question: *who* took them away, and why?

Although Eskimos have been known to migrate suddenly from their settlements, they do not do so without the means to ensure their survival. The questions surrounding this strange episode have never been answered, and the RCMP file on the disappearance of the Lake Anjikuni community remains open to this day.

The Hungry Sky

It was to have been an evening of celebration and joy. During Christmas Eve 1909, five inches of snow had fallen, covering the ground in an undisturbed carpet of white as far as the eye could see. At the Thomas farm near the town of Rhayader, Wales, a number of friends gathered for an evening of carol singing. As the evening wore on and midnight approached, they roasted chestnuts on the glowing embers of the fire and prepared to celebrate the arrival of Christmas Day. Around the hearth of Owen Thomas were his family, several close friends, the minister and his wife, the local veterinarian and an auctioneer from one of the neighbouring villages.

At about 11 o'clock, Owen Thomas noticed that the water bucket was empty. In those days, rural homes relied on wells for their drinking water. Mindful of his guests, whose joyful singing would doubtless bring on a thirst, Thomas turned to his 11-year-old son, Oliver, and asked him to take the bucket out to the well and fill it.

Oliver was a good lad, and despite the cheery warmth of the house, he was happy to pull on his boots and overcoat, and venture out into the icy night air. He had been gone only a few seconds, when the carol singing was interrupted by his frantic cries for help.

Shocked by the unexpected sounds, everyone rushed out of the house and into the snow-covered yard, which Oliver had been crossing on his way to the well, only a few moments before. The minister had seized a paraffin lantern, which he now held up, casting a flickering light on the empty yard. Oliver had gone. His footsteps, which could clearly be seen in the five-inch-deep snow, extending in a straight line in the direction of the well, stopped suddenly 75 feet away, as if something had swooped down from the sky and scooped up the unfortunate lad.

In abject horror, Oliver's parents listened as he screamed: "They've got me! Help, help! They've got me!"

Everyone tried to place the direction from which these terrified cries were coming, and soon they realized that Oliver's voice was coming from *above* them. The minister raised the lantern as far as he could, attempting to cast some light into the pitch-black sky. It was no use. Oliver was nowhere to be seen, but his cries continued to drift down to them, tormenting his horrified parents as they gradually grew more and more faint. Eventually, they ceased altogether, leaving the Thomas family and their guests alone in the yard beneath the silent, frozen sky.

There were no other tracks in the snow, and no signs of a struggle of any kind. The water bucket Oliver had been carrying lay about 15 feet away from where his footprints ended.

The following day, police from Rhayader appealed to local residents for help in locating the boy, and a search party was formed, which examined the Thomas's well and then scoured the surrounding countryside. The Thomas family and their guests of the previous evening were closely questioned; but the only conclusion to which the police could come was that Oliver Thomas had been seized on his way to the well, and taken directly upwards.

Although this conclusion was clearly not very satisfactory to the police, the physical evidence pointed strongly to it; but who or what could have done such a thing? No known animal could have done it without leaving tracks; certainly no known bird could have carried off an 11-year-old boy. Neither could any known flying machine have done so in 1909.

The only clue—and it is tenuous—is what Oliver Thomas himself cried as he was being taken up into the air: "They've got me!" Not "it," not "something," but "they." . . . As American researcher Brad Steiger says in his description of the case, this implies that Oliver got a good look at whoever had taken him. Oliver was never seen again. If he knew who or what his kidnappers were, he took the knowledge with him, into the sky....

Jumping Jellybags

Occasionally in the annals of ufology, one finds cases in which people have had narrow escapes from the kind of fate that perhaps befell the unfortunate Oliver Thomas. One such report was made in 1958 by two young Swedish men Hans Gustafsson and Stig Rydberg, who claimed that they were attacked by incredibly bizarre creatures from a UFO. Although largely forgotten today, the event made headlines across Europe at the time, and was reported in more than 70 newspapers.

The strange tale began early on the morning of 20 December 1958, as Gustafsson and Rydberg were driving from Hoganas to Helsingborg. At about 3.00 A.M., a thick mist descended over the highway, forcing them to slow their speed to less than 30 m.p.h. As they came to a wide clearing in the dense forest surrounding the highway, they saw an unusual light amongst the trees.

Curious as to what was causing it, Gustafsson and Rydberg left their car and walked slowly and carefully into the mist that was shrouding both the highway and the forest. According to Hans Gustafsson, "We saw a strange disc. It was resting on legs about two feet long. It seemed to be made of a peculiar, shimmering light that changed colour."

As the men gazed in shock at the object before them, they were confronted by several "blobs." The men described them as "like protozoa, just a bit darker... sort of a bluish colour, hopping and jumping around the saucer like globs of animated jelly."

Without warning, the creatures rushed at the men, enveloped them with their protoplasmic bodies and began to pull them towards the UFO. "The drag the things exerted was terrific. And they gave off such a terrible smell—like ether and burnt sausage," the men told investigators.

According to Stig Rydberg, to try to resist the creatures was worse than useless. "It almost seemed as if the creatures could read my mind. They parried every move before I made it. Their strength was not so great as the technique with which they wielded it."

Perhaps this lack of strength was what allowed Rydberg ultimately to save himself and Gustafsson, for after struggling frantically with one of the protoplasmic creatures, he managed to wrench himself free and made a dash for the car. Two of the creatures began to chase him as he opened the driver's door and sounded the horn in an attempt to attract somebody's—anybody's—attention to their terrible plight.

Meanwhile Hans Gustafsson was losing his battle with the jelly-creatures. He had grabbed hold of a fence post and was hanging on with all his might as they stretched him out horizontally in their attempt to break his grip. As his hands started to weaken and he prepared to meet an unimaginable fate, the car horn blared out, shattering the early morning silence.

This had an immediate effect on the dreadful "blobs," which reacted as if in pain or fear, and quickly retreated to their craft. With a piercing, high-pitched whistle, it rose into the air and shot away at a fantastic speed.

Exhausted by their awful struggle, Gustafsson and Rydberg fell into the car and continued on their journey, vowing not to breathe a word of their experience to anyone, for fear of the ridicule it would provoke. They would probably have remained silent, had it not been for that terrible stench, which clung to them, badly affecting their innards.

Eventually, they began to fear for their health. According to Gustafsson, "We endured it for three days, then we decided that we should see a physician. We were afraid that those monsters might have permanently damaged us in some way, perhaps internally."

Although the doctor could find no physical injuries, the two men were haunted by the memory of what they had experienced, not to mention the hideous stench that still seemed to cling to them. Eventually they decided to report their encounter, and braced themselves for the adverse publicity.

Gustafsson and Rydberg were questioned for 12 hours by representatives of the Swedish Defence Staff. Also present were doctors and psychologists, who attempted to trick the men into contradicting each other. These attempts were unsuccessful: the testimonies were absolutely consistent with each other.

The men then offered to take the defence officials and the press to the place where their nightmarish struggle had occurred. A large group went out to the forest clearing, and there they saw the three indentations in the soil made by the UFO's tripod landing gear.

After conducting several hypnosis sessions with the men, psychologists concluded that they genuinely believed what they were describing: they were not attempting to perpetrate a hoax.

Outrageous as this case sounds, soon after the story broke, Danish officials came forward with a request to interview Gustafsson and Rydberg. Apparently, their own files contained a report made by a Danish woman, who had described an almost identical encounter.

On these two occasions, the jelly-creatures thankfully failed in their attempt to carry off human beings. We might be forgiven for wondering how many times they have succeeded.

5

Official Reactions to the UFO Phenomenon

Project Sign

As might be expected, the authorities in the United States showed considerable interest in UFO reports. This is certain with regard to the early days of modern ufology and, despite subsequent assurances by the US Air Force to the contrary, intense interest continues to this day. The US Government's first entry into the subject came in 1947, in the form of Project Sign, which was established as a result of a letter from Lieutenant-General Nathan F. Twining, Commander of the Air Materiel Command, to Brigadier-General George Schulgen, Commander of the newly independent Air Force, who had requested a preliminary study of flying disc reports.

The letter, dated 23 September 1947, was as follows:

1. As requested by AC/AS-2 there is presented below the considered opinion of this Command concerning the so-called "Flying Discs." This opinion is based on interrogation report data furnished by AC/AS-2 and preliminary studies by personnel of T-2 and Aircraft Laboratory, Engineering Division T-3. This opinion was arrived at in a conference between personnel from the Air Institute of Technology, Intelligence T-2, Office, Chief of Engineering Division, and the Air Craft, Power Plant and Propeller Laboratories of Engineering Division T-3.

2. It is the opinion that:

   a. The phenomenon reported is something real and not visionary or fictitious.

   b. There are objects probably approximating the shape of a disc, of such appreciable size as to appear to be as large as man-made aircraft.

   c. There is a possibility that some of the incidents may be caused by natural phenomena, such as meteors.

   d. The reported operating characteristics such as extreme rates of climb, maneuverability (particularly in roll), and action which must be considered evasive when sighted or contacted by friendly aircraft and radar, lend belief to the possibility that some of the objects are controlled either manually, automatically or remotely.

   e. The apparent common description of the objects is as follows:

      (1) Metallic or light reflecting surface.

      (2) Absence of trail, except in a few instances when the object was apparently operating under high performance conditions.

      (3) Circular or elliptical in shape, flat on bottom and domed on top.

      (4) Several reports of well kept formation flights varying from three to nine objects.

      (5) Normally no associated sound, except in three instances a substantial rumbling roar was noted.

      (6) Level flight speeds normally above 300 knots are estimated.

   f. It is possible within the present US knowledge—provided extensive detailed development is undertaken—to construct a piloted aircraft which has the general description of the object in subparagraph (e) above which would be capable of an approximate range of 7000 miles at subsonic speeds.

   g. Any developments in this country along the lines indicated would be extremely expensive, time consuming and at the considerable expense of current projects and therefore, if directed, should be set up independently of existing projects.

h. Due consideration must be given to the following:

(1) The possibility that these objects are of domestic origin—the product of some high security project not known to AC/AS-2 or this Command.

(2) The lack of physical evidence in the shape of crash recovered exhibits which would undeniably prove the existence of these objects

(3) The possibility that some foreign nation has a form of propulsion possibly nuclear, which is outside of our domestic knowledge.

3. It is recommended that:

a. Headquarters, Army Air Forces issue a directive signing a priority, security classification and Code Name for a detailed study of this matter to include the preparation of complete sets of all available and pertinent data which will then be made available to the Army, Navy, Atomic Energy Commission, JRDB [Joint Research and Development Board], the Air Force Scientific Advisory Group, NACA [National Advisory Committee on Aeronautics], and the RAND and NEPA [Nuclear Energy for Propulsion Applications Program] projects for comments and recommendations, with a preliminary report to be forwarded within 15 days of receipt of the data and a detailed report thereafter every 30 days as the investigation develops. A complete interchange of data should be effected.

4. Awaiting a specific directive AMC will continue the investigation within its current resources in order to more closely define the nature of the phenomenon. Detailed Essential Elements of Information will be formulated immediately for transmittal thru channels.

It should be noted that sceptics have pointed to this letter as proof that no extraterrestrial spaceship crashed at Roswell, New

Mexico, in 1947. How could there have been, they ask, when Twining refers to the "lack of physical evidence in the shape of crash recovered exhibits"? The answer to this apparent inconsistency could not be simpler. Twining's letter to Brigadier-General Schulgen was classified Secret, and thus could only discuss information with that classification or lower. The alleged Roswell crash retrieval was classified above Top Secret and so could not have been referred to in a Secret communication.

At about this time, the Air Force had been engaged in an investigation of German aeronautical research during the Second World War. When they compared their information with the reported capabilities of the flying discs, they realized that no material on Earth could withstand the enormous stresses involved in disc manoeuvres. According to the US Air Force Aeromedical Laboratory, even if such vehicles could be constructed, the manoeuvres reported would be instantly fatal to any human pilot.

On 30 December 1947, approval was given for the establishment of a permanent flying disc investigation group, to deal with "sightings and phenomena in the atmosphere which can be construed to be of concern to the national security." The code name was "Project Sign," and it was given the lowest security rating: "Restricted."

Almost as soon as Project Sign was established, it started to cause serious problems for the Pentagon. So enormous was the number of reports coming in to the telephone switchboard that the Pentagon's ability to deal with other security matters was being dangerously undermined. Officials began to worry that the Soviet Union might take advantage of the public's increasing concern about the possible motives of the UFOs and the resulting clogging up of communication channels within the defence establishment. It was for this reason, combined with the secret status of the Air Force's conclusions as to the possible extraterrestrial nature of some UFOs, that a policy of official debunking was established, while in the background an intense struggle was set in motion to discover their true nature.

Soon after the Chiles-Whitted sighting (described earlier), the US Air Force Air Technical Intelligence Center (ATIC), based at Wright-Patterson AFB along with Project Sign, produced a formal "Estimate of the Situation," which was the closest the Air Force ever came to admitting the probability of the presence of extraterrestrial spacecraft on Earth. The document was classified Top Secret, and described in detail the history of UFO sightings up to 1948. These included the small, spherical UFOs, called foo fighters, that were reported by air crews of both Allied and German forces during the Second World War, and the Scandinavian ghost rocket sightings. The quality of the reports presented in the Estimate was extremely high, since they all came from reliable witnesses, including pilots and professional scientists. Seen from today's perspective of official dismissal of UFOs by the authorities, the document was astounding in its conclusion that we were indeed being visited by interplanetary craft.

Project Sign's Estimate of the Situation worked its way up the chain of command, eventually arriving on the desk of General Hoyt S. Vandenberg, the Air Force Chief of Staff. He decided that the evidence was not sufficiently impressive to warrant the extreme conclusions, and ordered the document to be destroyed.

This had an adverse effect on the morale of those working at Project Sign, who began to split into opposing camps, with those who still accepted the extraterrestrial explanation on one side, and others who had gradually become more sceptical on the other. This is understandable, in view of the continuing lack of (accessible) unequivocal proof, coupled with the success with which most UFO sightings could be explained in ordinary terms. This latter, sceptical view gained increasing predominance for the remainder of Project Sign's short life.

Project Grudge

On 11 February 1949, Project Sign became Project Grudge—a name that reflected its stance on UFOs. According to Captain Edward J. Ruppelt, who would later head the Air Force UFO investigation, this heralded the "dark ages," in which attempts were made to solve every case, no matter how unsatisfactory the official explanation. For example, J. Allen Hynek states that Grudge's public statements regarding specific cases "bore little resemblance to the facts.... If a case contained *some* of the elements *possibly* attributable to aircraft, a balloon, etc., it automatically became that object in the press release." (Emphasis added.)

In a move perhaps born of genuine apprehension, the military was no longer prepared to accept astonishing possibilities; it wanted easily understandable facts. New, less experienced personnel were brought in to run the project, and operated under the sceptical rubric: "it can't be, therefore it isn't." According to Ruppelt, "Everything was being evaluated on the premise that UFOs couldn't exist.... Good UFO reports continued to come in at the rate of about ten per month, but they weren't being verified or investigated. Most of them were being discarded."

In fact, Project Grudge took a path that was tantamount to dereliction of its assigned duties, in deciding to spend much of its time investigating the people who submitted UFO reports, rather than the reports themselves. The implication was clearly that the true nature of *any* sighting could be discovered exclusively through an examination of the state of mind of the person reporting that sighting, rather than an examination of the data gathered. The echoes of this attitude can still be felt today, when sceptics maintain that *all* UFO sightings *must*, without exception, be the results of the misidentification of various mundane phenomena.

While Project Sign was in the bureaucratic process of becoming Project Grudge, its staff completed and submitted their final report, which included two scientific overviews of the subject, by Professor George E. Valley of the Massachusetts Institute of Technology and the Air Force Scientific Advisory Board, and Dr. James E. Lipp of the Rand Corporation.

Part of Professor Valley's overview was as follows:

If there is an extraterrestrial civilization which can make such objects as are reported then it is most probable that its development is far in advance of ours. This argument can be supported on probability arguments alone without recourse to astronomical hypotheses.

Such a civilization might observe that on Earth we now have atomic bombs and are fast developing rockets. In view of the past history of mankind, they should be alarmed. We should, therefore, expect at this time above all to behold such visitations.

Since the acts of mankind most easily observed from a distance are A-bomb explosions we should expect some relation to obtain between the time of A-bomb explosions, the time at which space ships are seen and the time required for such ships to arrive and return to home base.

Dr. Lipp also commented on this apparent correlation between UFOs and nuclear tests:

The first flying objects were sighted in the Spring of 1947, after a total of 5 atomic bomb explosions, i.e., Alamogordo, Hiroshima, Nagasaki, Crossroads A and Crossroads B. Of these, the first two were in positions to be seen from Mars, the third was very doubtful (at the edge of the Earth's disc in daylight) and the last two were on the wrong side of Earth....

It is hard to believe that any technically accomplished race would come here, flaunt its ability in mysterious ways and then simply go away. To this writer, long-time practice of space travel implies advanced engineering and science, weapons and ways of thinking.... Furthermore, a race which had enough initiative to explore among the planets would hardly be too timid to follow through when the job was accomplished....

Although visits from outer space are believed to be possible, they are believed to be very improbable. In particular, the actions attributed to the "flying objects" reported during 1947 and 1948 seem inconsistent with the requirements of space travel.

Although Dr. Lipp's assertion that several atomic tests were visible from Mars does not mean very much (elsewhere, he points to the unlikelihood of a civilization there), his statement regarding the correlation between those tests and the birth of "modern" ufology has been reiterated by many commentators over the years.

In addition, the comments of both men point to the dichotomy of views that resulted in Project Sign's conversion to Project Grudge in 1949. The attitude of the scientific community, that alien civilizations were a possibility but were unlikely to be visiting the Earth, was echoed in Project Sign's final report, which erred on the side of scepticism while describing UFOs as if they were solid, manufactured objects, subject to the laws of physics and engineering.

Although Project Grudge was the Air Force's attempt to "brush off" the UFO problem, it was to give its name to one of the most hotly debated "revelations" of recent years, fuelling suspicions of a massive government cover-up of UFO-related information.

The Grudge 13 Affair

The affair first came to the attention of the ufology community by means of the Project Stigma memo, a strange document purporting to prove secret human knowledge of an alien presence on Earth. Project Stigma was founded in Texas in 1978 with the purpose of investigating cases of animal mutilation. In 1981 the organization received a curious document entitled "Memorandum." This is the entire text of the document:

An eyewitness has described an official Project Grudge Report Number 13, Top Secret, *Need To Know Only* classification, that was in fact published but then never distributed and was in fact subsequently destroyed. It consisted of 624 pages, typed, offset reproduced on white paper with a gray cover, and included whole pages of print by (name deleted) and Col. Friend. It covered US Government Official UFO Procedures, classifications, and all Top Secret UFO activity from 1942 through 1951. Among other information it included the following:

(1) (a) Significant UFO sightings.

    (b) UFO landings.

    (c) UFO/Alien Close Approaches, Abductions, Detentions.

    (d) Crashed UFOs and UFO Retrievals.

    (e) Sensitive Military/Industrial Areas where close encounters occurred.

    (f) Technical Details on Dismantled UFOs.

    (g) UFO Physics—Exotic, Nuclear, Weaponry.

        (1) Clean Breeder Reactor size of oval basketball.

        (2) Ultrasonic, Light, Ray and Beam Weapons.

(2) Photographic Section—All glossy pages, photos $3\frac{1}{2} \times 5$, 8×10.

    (a) Photographs of sensitive UFOs.

    (b) Color photographs of crashed UFOs.

        (1) Three in good condition.

        (2) One dismantled.

    (c) Color photographs of deceased aliens (Averaged $4\frac{1}{2}$ feet).

    (d) Color Photographs of 3 Living Aliens.

    (e) Color Photographs of Human Mutilations (head, rectum, sex organs, internal organs, blood removal). One military witness observed human abduction, body found a few days later. This case which had happened in 1958 had been added to the file.

(3) Covered Human and Humanoid Aliens.

    (a) Humanoid Species.

    (b) Humanoid Autopsies.

        (1) No indication of age.

        (2) Small species similar to humans, very similar, varied in height a few inches.

        (3) Liquid Chlorophyll Base Nourishment.

        (4) Food absorbed through mouth membrane, wastes excreted through skin.

(5) Language similar in appearance to Sanskrit, mathematical phrases.

(6) Live Alien communicated only desired answers to questions. Remained silent on undesired questions.

Classified summary of the report completed the text.

Note: The one copy seen had been annotated and updated by someone.

The author of the Memorandum was allegedly a Vietnam veteran who went under the pseudonym "Captain Toulinet." In a two-part article written for the British journal *Fortean Times* (numbers 75 and 76), researcher Peter Brookesmith relates how he decided to look into the affair, writing to Thomas Adams of Project Stigma for clarification of Toulinet's background.

According to Adams, Toulinet's real name was William S. English. While working as an intelligence analyst at RAF Chicksands in Bedfordshire, England, in 1977, he was instructed to examine and assign a "probability rating" to a 625-page-long document entitled *Grudge/Blue Book Report 13*. English claimed that he was subsequently separated from his wife and summarily deported back to the United States with no explanation. Once back in America, he was contacted by his former base commander from Chicksands, who informed him that he was about to go out to White Sands Missile Base in New Mexico to search for a large flying saucer that had been shot down and buried in the desert. English went and, while looking for the saucer, survived a missile attack which killed his former commander. He then went into hiding for the next eight years.

Brookesmith's well-argued exposure of the inconsistencies in English's claims regarding his time in Vietnam (including the discovery of a B-52 bomber that had been disabled by a UFO and set down intact in the jungle of Laos, together with its horrifically mutilated crew), not to mention the manner of his dismissal from his post at Chicksands, is too lengthy to set out in full here. I direct the reader to the relevant issues of *Fortean Times*.

Whether or not English was telling the truth, he is representative of a group of people who have come to be known as the "whistle-blowers": claiming to have secret knowledge of the alien threat to humanity, they have decided to put their own safety at risk to bring us the awful news.

Another whistle-blower is Bill Cooper, an ex-military intelligence operative who claims to have read the original *Grudge Report 13* (which, incidentally, was allegedly co-authored by J. Allen Hynek!). According to Cooper and others, the Greys come from a planet in the Zeta Reticuli star system (we may have Marjorie Fish to thank for this particular piece of information), which was devastated in a war with another race, and turned into a barren desert. This has resulted in an "evolutionary decline" and the atrophy of their digestive system. They have come to Earth in search of "new genetic material."

This information was allegedly supplied to the US Government by an alien named Krll, who was left on Earth after the UFO landing at Holloman Air Force Base, New Mexico (which will be discussed later). Whether or not *Grudge 13* really exists, and in spite of the obvious unlikelihood of alien beings being genetically compatible with humans, this scenario has gained wide acceptance in the field of ufology, being submitted as an explanation for both cattle mutilations and human abductions.

Project Blue Book

Officially, at least, Project Grudge came to the conclusion that UFOs did not present a security threat—indeed, that they presented no threat of any kind, since they could be explained as misinterpretations of ordinary phenomena. On 27 December 1949, the Air Force announced that the project had been terminated, and a final report was quickly issued, entitled "Unidentified Flying Objects—Project Grudge."

Dr. J. Allen Hynek submitted a report on the likely causes of the 237 best cases on file, which was included in an appendix to

the "Grudge Report." At that time, Hynek was an avowed sceptic, who confessed to enjoying the role of debunker. He found
that, while 32 per cent of the cases could be explained astronom-
ically, 12 per cent as balloons and 33 per cent as misidentified
aircraft, hoaxes or lacking sufficient information to make an
evaluation, this still left 23 per cent that "could not be identified
or classified in any of the previously mentioned categories."
Nearly one quarter of the cases were "Unknowns."

Unofficially, the Air Force was still deeply concerned about
the UFO problem, and assigned Captain Edward J. Ruppelt to re-
organize their study of the phenomenon in October 1951. By
March 1952, he had convinced the Pentagon to establish a new
project, which was given the code-name Blue Book. Far from
being a serious operation, however, Blue Book was a woefully
small-scale project, staffed by low-ranking officers who were
obliged to attend to other duties besides those pertaining to the
UFO problem. To make matters worse, the relatively low rank of
the officers in charge meant that they were in no position to
make demands for information. As Hynek states in his book *The
UFO Experience*, "The military is entirely hierarchical; a captain
cannot command a colonel or a major at another base to obtain
information for him. He can only request. As long as Blue Book
did not have at least a full colonel in command, it was impossible to execute its assigned task properly."

In addition, Blue Book's methods of storing data were totally
inadequate. They were filed according to date alone, with no attempt being made to process the data electronically, which
would have allowed patterns in the reports to be quickly dis-
cerned. Hynek and Jacques Vallée even offered to computerize
the data, but were turned down.

According to Hynek, "Blue Book was a 'cover-up' to the extent
that the assigned problem was glossed over for one reason or another. In my many years association with Blue Book, I do not recall even one serious discussion of methodology, of improving

the process of data gathering or of techniques of comprehensive interrogation of witnesses."

Air Force incompetence in dealing with UFOs did not square with the activities of the UFOs themselves, which demanded an all-out effort to solve the mystery. In his book *Report on Unidentified Flying Objects*, Captain Ruppelt describes the situation surrounding the famous "invasion of Washington" in 1952 (described earlier):

> When radars at the Washington National Airport and at Andrews AFB, both close to the Nation's capital, picked up UFOs, the sightings beat the Democratic National Convention out of headline space. They created such a furor that I had enquiries from the office of the President of the United States and from the press in London, Ottawa and Mexico City. A junior-sized riot was only narrowly averted in the lobby of the Roger Smith Hotel in Washington when I refused to tell the US newspaper reporters what I knew about the sightings.
>
> Besides being the most highly publicized UFO sightings in the Air Force annals, they were also the most monumentally fouled-up messes that repose in the files.

The great wave of sightings in 1952 was a cause of concern not only to the Air Force, but also to the CIA, which perceived a two-fold danger: first, that enemy agents might seek to clog the channels of military communications with false UFO reports; and second, that if the Pentagon got into the habit of dismissing reports of unusual objects in the skies, they might also dismiss a genuine enemy attack.

Thus, on 4 December 1952, the Intelligence Advisory Committee recommended that the CIA should "enlist the services of selected scientists to review and appraise the available evidence in the light of pertinent scientific theories." A panel was convened under the chairmanship of Dr. H. P. Robertson, a highly respected physicist with the California Institute of Technology. However, while the official reason for this panel was to evaluate the UFO phenomenon, the real reason was to "defuse" the large and growing public concern over UFOs.

The Robertson Panel opened on 14 January 1953, and examined the 75 best-documented cases from 1951 to 1952, which included the film footage of 12 bright objects taken at Tremonton, Utah, and the Great Falls, Montana footage, showing two objects following a level flight path.

The panel sat for four days. Its conclusions (in part) were as follows:

2. As a result of its considerations, the Panel concludes:
   a. That the evidence presented on Unidentified Flying Objects shows no indication that these phenomena constitute a direct physical threat to national security.

We firmly believe that there is no residuum of cases which indicates phenomena which are attributable to foreign artifacts capable of hostile acts, and that there is no evidence that the phenomena indicate a need for the revision of current scientific concepts.

3. The Panel further concludes:
   a. That the continued emphasis on the reporting of these phenomena does, in these perilous times, result in a threat to the orderly functioning of the protective organs of the body politic.

We cite as examples the clogging of channels of communication by irrelevant reports, the danger of being led by continued false alarms to ignore real indications of hostile action, and the cultivation of a morbid national psychology in which a skillful hostile propaganda could induce hysterical behavior and harmful distrust of duly constituted authority.

4. In order most effectively to strengthen the national facilities for the timely recognition and the appropriate handling of true indications of hostile action and to minimize the concomitant dangers alluded to above, the Panel recommends:

a. That the national security agencies take immediate steps to strip the Unidentified Flying Objects of the special status they have been given and the aura of mystery they have unfortunately acquired;

b. That the national security agencies institute policies on intelligence, training and public education designed to prepare the material defenses and the morale of the country to recognize most promptly and to react most effectively to true indications of hostile intent or action.

We suggest that these aims may be achieved by an integrated program designed to reassure the public of the total lack of evidence of inimical forces behind the phenomena, to train personnel to recognize and reject false indications quickly and effectively, and to strengthen regular channels for the evaluation of and prompt reaction to true indications of hostile measures.

The Robertson Panel Report is extremely important with regard to Project Blue Book, since it effectively dictated the group's policy for the remainder of its lifetime (it ended in 1969, finally succumbing to the entirely dismislve conclusions of the Condon Report). This resulted in two major disadvantages for Captain Ruppelt and his small staff: first, that they were now charged with the responsibility of proving, by whatever means necessary, that UFOs did not exist; and second, that the lack of defence significance caused what little resources they had to dry up.

In 1959, the Air Technical Intelligence Center (ATIC), based along with Blue Book at Wright-Patterson AFB in Dayton, Ohio, ordered a study of the project's future. The study concluded that the UFO investigation programme in general had "become an unproductive burden upon the Air Force...and has resulted in unfavorable publicity...." It suggested the need "to eliminate this costly, and to date unproductive, program."

Blue Book staggered on through the rest of the 1950s and 1960s, with several changes of leadership. When the Condon Report concluded in 1968 that the study of UFOs had no scientific justification, Air Force Secretary Robert C. Seamans announced that "the continuation of Project Blue Book cannot be justified either on the ground of national security or in the interest of science." The project was disbanded in 1969, ending 22 years of official government involvement with UFOs.

Blue Book Special Report 14

One of the mainstays of the sceptical argument against genuinely anomalous UFOs is that, given enough information, even those listed as "Unknowns" can be explained. In other words, they are "unknown" not because they represent a genuinely unexplained phenomenon, but simply because there are not enough data in the report to provide the mundane answer that is undoubtedly there. This would have been a fairly plausible argument, had it not been proved false by the research which resulted in Blue Book Special Report Number 14.

Towards the end of 1952, the Air Force commissioned the Battelle Memorial Institute in Columbus, Ohio, to conduct a secret, in-depth study of UFO reports from June 1947 to December 1952. The impetus for this seems to have been the "great flap" of 1952, which included the "Washington Invasion." The Battelle Memorial Institute was a private industrial research organization, with impeccable scientific credentials.

In his 1977 book *The Hynek UFO Report*, Dr. J. Allen Hynek provides an explanation of the methods used by Battelle in its study. The basic question to be addressed was: do those reports classed as "unidentified" differ fundamentally from those classed as "identified"? If similar descriptions are reported for each group, then it should be concluded that they belong to the same statistical "universe," in which case the sceptics are correct in their assertion that all sightings are ultimately amenable to mundane explanation. However, if the two classes differ significantly, then the opposite implication holds: UFOs represent a genuine mystery.

The statistical tool used by Battelle is known as the "chi-square" test which determines the probability that one set of things differs fundamentally from another. Hynek offers an example of this:

> If you were examining... two crates of apples (but didn't know they were apples), the chi-square test on sizes, weights, numbers of objects, etc., would tell you that the probability was very high that the same sort of things were in the two crates. But if one crate contained apples and the other tennis balls, the chi-square test would tell you that the probability that both crates contained the same thing was extremely small—not zero, but very small!

The Battelle Institute compared "unidentified" and "identified" reports in terms of six characteristics—colour, shape, number, duration of observation, speed and light brightness—and subjected them to the chi-square test. Hynek gives the results as follows:

> Probability that "Unidentifieds" Are the Same as Identifieds.
> COLOUR: Probability *less than 1%.*
> DURATION OF OBSERVATION: Probability *very much less than 1%.*
> NUMBER: Probability *very much less than 1%.*
> LIGHT BRIGHTNESS: Probability greater than 5%.
> SHAPE: Probability *less than 1%.*
> SPEED: Probability *much less than 1%.* [Original emphasis.]

Hynek explains that, although examination of any one characteristic, such as colour, might lead to an error as a result of subjective differences in the reports, it is very unlikely that all six of the characteristics described above could lead to the same errors. In fact, "the probability of all six UFO-characteristic chi-square tests giving the same results by chance (and thus making the conclusions drawn from the tests wrong) is much less than one chance in a billion."

Incredibly, the Battelle Institute disregarded these results in its final report, concluding: "The results of these tests are not conclusive since they neither confirm nor deny that the UN-KNOWNS are primarily unidentified KNOWNS, although they do indicate that relatively few of the UNKNOWNS are astronomical phenomena." This is rather puzzling, since statistical analysis is designed to establish *probability* not *certainty*. The above assertion states the blindingly obvious (statistics can neither confirm nor deny in absolute terms), while avoiding the implications of the very high probability that "knowns" and "unknowns" differ fundamentally from each other.

The Pentagon issued a press release on Blue Book Special Report Number 14, which stated, among other things, that it was "considered to be highly improbable that any of the reports of unidentified aerial objects examined in the survey represent observations of technological developments outside the range of present-day scientific knowledge." According to Hynek, the Pentagon sidestepped its responsibilities very neatly with the statement that "unidentifieds" do not represent "technological development." "Suppose they [UFOs] weren't 'nuts and bolts' hardware after all, but holographic images or projections from the human mind or from some intelligence far off? The Pentagon would then be safe in having made the statement they did. And since the Air Force's job *is* military, and deals with defense problems arising from possible enemy use of technological devices, they can always claim to have fulfilled their obligation to the public." (Original emphasis.)

Another surprising result of the Battelle Institute's study (and another rebuttal of the sceptical argument that "unknowns" tend to be reported by unreliable observers) was that 33.3 per cent of "unknowns" reported had been given an "Excellent" reliability rating. The complete table is given below.

Reliability Rating of Report	% Unknown	Total Number of Reports
Excellent	33.3	213
Good	24.8	757
Doubtful	13.0	794
Poor	16.6	435
		2,199

In other words, the study found that the reports that were of excellent reliability contained about twice as many "unknowns" as those of poor reliability. Although this was clear in the report itself, it was ignored in the report's conclusions and in subsequent press releases, upon which public attention would be concentrated.

While Hynek stresses the scientific integrity of the Battelle Institute, he nevertheless describes an unfortunate postscript to its UFO study. The report stated: "All records and working papers of this study have been carefully preserved in an orderly fashion suitable for ready reference." Yet, when Hynek visited the Institute in the 1970s, he was told that the records had been destroyed. It was, of course, most unfortunate that valuable original data, which could so easily have been stored on microfilm, had been disposed of. It was just one more example of the "It Can't Be, Therefore it Isn't" syndrome, from which orthodox science has suffered since the dawn of modern ufology.

The Brookings Institute Report

For those looking for evidence to support the contention that the reality of genuine UFOs is being withheld from the public, the Brookings Institute Report goes a long way towards providing it.

Perhaps the most unfortunate aspect of the Report is the implication that, even if we are *not* being visited by spacecraft from
another planet, it is unlikely that we would ever be informed by
the authorities, should a hypothetical alien race ever decide to
make their presence known exclusively to our leaders. In other
words, if they don't "land on the White House lawn," then the
chances are we won't get to know about them.

In 1959, NASA commissioned the highly respected Brookings
Research Institute in Washington DC to conduct a study which
was eventually entitled: "Proposed Studies on the Implications
of Peaceful Space Activities for Human Affairs." At that time,
NASA was a brand new agency, having been created by Congress in the 1958 Space Act so it was entirely logical that such
concerns should be addressed, and contingency plans drawn
up. Experts in a variety of disciplines, from all over the United
States, participated in the study, which took a year to complete.

The sinister implications for ufology and its related fields
came on page 215 of the final Report, which, according to science writer Richard Hoagland, was entitled: "Implications of a
Discovery of Extraterrestrial Life." In part, it concluded that
"cosmologists and astronomers think it very likely that there is
intelligent life in many other solar systems," and that "artifacts
left at some point in time by these life forms might possibly be
discovered through our space activities on the Moon, Mars, or
Venus."

The section on extraterrestrial implications dealt with "the
need to investigate the possible social consequences of an extraterrestrial discovery and to consider whether such a discovery
should be kept from the public in order to avoid political change
and a possible 'devastating' effect on scientists themselves—due
to the discovery that many of their own cherished theories could
be at risk[!]." The Report concluded that we should not be told. It
concluded that the risk to our civilization would be too great,
should alien artefacts ever be discovered in the course of our exploration of space. The main reason given was the unfortunate

history of our own species, in which many cultures had been devastated by contact with their technological superiors.

While the Brookings Institute Report ostensibly refers exclusively to abandoned artefacts discovered on our planetary neighbours, its recommendations seem to have been extended to cover all evidence of intelligent extraterrestrial life in the vicinity of the Earth, including the evidence gathered over the years by authorities all over the world during their studies of the UFO phenomenon.

The Freedom of Information Act

One of the most powerful tools in the arsenal of the UFO researcher is the Freedom of Information Act, which was created in a 1966 Act of Congress and designed to give the public greater access to government records. However, as Lawrence Fawcett and Barry J. Greenwood make clear in their 1984 book *Clear Intent*, the FOIA is not a skeleton key to open every single door behind which important information might lie. In fact, nine types of information are exempt from release to the public. The subjects covered are:

(1) (A) specifically authorized under criteria established by an Executive order to be kept secret in the interests of national defences or foreign policy, and (B) are in fact properly classified pursuant to such Executive order;

(2) related solely to the internal personnel rules and practices of an agency;

(3) specifically exempted from disclosure by statute . . . provided that such statute (A) requires that the matters be withheld from the public in such a manner as to leave no discretion on the issue, or (B) establishes particular criteria for withholding or refers to particular types of matters to be withheld;

(4) trade secrets and commercial or financial information obtained from a person and privileged or confidential;

(5) interagency or intra-agency memoranda or letters which

would not be available by law to a party other than an agency in litigation with the agency;

(6) personnel and medical files and similar files the disclosure of which would constitute a clearly unwarranted invasion of personal privacy;

(7) investigatory records compiled for law enforcement purposes, but only to the extent that the production of such records would (A) interfere with enforcement proceedings, (B) deprive a person of a right to a fair trial or an impartial adjudication, (C) constitute an unwarranted invasion of personal privacy, (D) disclose the identity of a confidential source and, in the case of a record compiled by a criminal law enforcement authority in the course of a criminal investigation or by an agency conducting a lawful national security intelligence investigation, confidential information furnished only by the confidential source, (E) disclosure investigative techniques and procedures, or (F) endanger the life or physical safety of law enforcement personnel;

(8) contained in or related to examination, operating, or condition reports prepared by, on behalf of, or for the use of an agency responsible for the regulation or supervision of financial institutions; or

(9) geological and geophysical information and data, including maps, concerning wells.

Fawcett and Greenwood list a number of amendments, which were attached to the Act in 1974, and which are relevant to the search for information on the government's alleged knowledge of UFOs:

1. Agencies were to release documents to someone requesting them with a *reasonable description* of said data. *Exact* information would not have to be given to gather information on a particular topic.

2. Time limits were placed on agencies in responding to requests.

They were allowed ten working days to respond to the first request, twenty working days for responding to an appeal of a denial of documents, and a single ten-day extension in responding to allow for administrative difficulties. Also, a thirty-day limit was placed on an agency in responding to a court case.

3. Set fees were provided for search and reproduction costs. This is rated at a 10c. per page photocopy charge, plus fees for hourly clerical and professional time applied in preparing a response to an FOIA request.

4. Courts could examine and render decisions on whether or not to release documents from agencies brought to court by those filing requests.

5. A full report on FOIA requests and their handling by each agency would be provided to Congress annually.

As an illustration of how the FOIA works in practice, Fawcett and Greenwood then provide a "test case," based on an article in the *National Enquirer* of 13 December 1977, entitled "UFOs Spotted at Nuclear Bases and Missile Sites." Although the authors readily concede that this publication is not the most reliable for serious UFO reports, the article nevertheless provided "places, dates, and some details which could be verified." So they filed an FOIA request on 26 December 1977 "for case files from Loring AFB, Maine, October 27, 28, and 31, 1975; Wurtsmith AFB, Michigan, October 30, 1975; [and] Malmstrom AFB, Montana, November 7 and 8, 1975."

On 6 February 1978, Fawcett and Greenwood received a reply from the Office of the Assistant Secretary of Defense, notifying them that the Office of the Joint Chiefs of Staff had identified 24 relevant documents. One of the documents was a National Military Command Center (NMCC) Memorandum dated 13 November 1975, which concerned "Requests for Temperature Inversion Analysis." In part, the memo stated:

The West Hem Desk Officer will act as the control officer for temperature inversion analysis requests initiated by the NMCC. These requests will be made in conjunction with sightings of unusual phenomenon along the northern US border.

Fawcett and Greenwood conclude that this is firm evidence that the US Air Force is continuing to investigate reports of UFOs in the vicinity of military bases (the Air Force has denied all involvement with UFOs since the closure of Project Blue Book in 1969). "Whenever a sighting occurred, the NMCC would phone the AFGWC [Air Force Global Weather Central] and ask whether an atmospheric temperature inversion existed in the area." (The reader will recall that temperature inversions can sometimes cause apparent UFOs, visible both by radar and eyesight.)

Interestingly, the authors also relate how another researcher, Robert Todd, filed FOIA requests for all records of temperature inversion analyses (TIAs) performed by the AFGWC for the NMCC, in the hope that this would yield a list of UFO incidents considered important enough to investigate by the military. The only information he received concerned the dates on which such analyses were done. However, subsequent requests filed in 1981 revealed that TIAs were no longer required by the NMCC. When the Department of Defense was asked why this was so, they denied all knowledge of the change in procedure. Fawcett and Greenwood wonder whether the TIAs "were discovered to be of little use in explaining the UFO reports being investigated and, therefore, were dropped...."

It can thus be seen that, while any ultimate documented proof of the reality of genuine UFOs will almost certainly be retained by the authorities under the exemptions listed above, much valuable evidence can nevertheless be gathered through carefully placed FOIA requests.

Afr 200-2 and Janap 146

The regulations issued by the authorities (particularly in the

United States) with regard to UFO sightings have been the subject of intense interest from ufologists over the years. This was especially true in the early 1950s, with the issue of Air Force Regulation 200-2, and Joint Army Navy Air Force Publication 146.

AFR 200-2 was issued towards the end of 1953, in response to the conclusions of the Robertson Report. In effect, the Regulation prohibited the release of any information regarding a sighting until a satisfactory explanation had been arrived at by the Air Force. Although ufologists concluded from this that the Air Force was engaging in a cover-up of "dangerous" information on genuine UFO activity, a more down-to-earth answer is evident, in the context of the Robertson Report. The reader will recall that the Report stated the danger of large numbers of UFO reports clogging government communication channels, together with the threat of genuine enemy activity being mistakenly dismissed in the wake of such reports. The Air Force also considered the "morbid national psychology" engendered by UFOs to be a real danger, with the threat ever present that "skillful hostile propaganda could induce hysterical behaviour and harmful distrust of duly constituted authority." In view of these facts, the true intention of AFR 200-2 was clearly to defuse the steadily increasing public concern, and its concomitant increase in officially-made reports.

Of somewhat greater interest is JANAP 146, which was issued in December 1953. Drawn up by the Joint Communications-Electronics Committee and put into effect by the Joint Chiefs of Staff, its full title was "Canadian-United States Communications Instructions for Reporting Vital Intelligence Sightings," and it set down the correct procedures for reporting information considered by the observer to require "very urgent defensive and/or investigative action." There were a number of categories of intelligence sightings, including hostile or unidentified aircraft, missiles, UFOs, submarines, ships and suspicious groups of personnel on the ground.

The instructions contained within JANAP 146 did not apply only to the military, but also to civil airline pilots who, should they encounter a UFO, were liable to a prison term of one to ten years and/or a fine of $10,000 if they discussed the sighting with the media or public. The JANAP restrictions were imposed on civil airline pilots in February 1954, after a meeting between intelligence officers and airline representatives.

In December 1958, according to Timothy Good, 450 airline pilots signed a petition in protest at the official policy of dismissing UFO sightings. One pilot described the policy as "a lesson in lying." Fifty pilots had reported sightings, "only to be told by the Air Force that they had been mistaken." And yet the pilots had *also* been warned "that they faced up to ten years in prison (under JANAP 146) if they revealed details of their sightings to the media"!

In February 1959 the Royal Canadian Air Force, which was just as concerned with the UFO problem as its American counterpart, issued its "Communications Instructions for Reporting Vital Intelligence Sightings" (CIRVIS), in co-operation with the US. In March 1966, (CIRVIS) JANAP 146 (E) was issued by the Joint Chiefs of Staff and the Canadian Defense Staff. Like its American cousin, it sets down the correct procedures for reporting information of "vital importance to the United States of America and Canada."

Timothy Good cites further evidence of official involvement with UFOs on the North American Continent, in the form of a memorandum dated 24 November 1967 from Royal Canadian Air Force (RCAF) Wing Commander D. F. Robertson, commenting on the intention to transfer the RCAF UFO files to the National Research Council. In part, the memo states: "If NRC accepts the responsibility of investigating UFOs and they work with the University of Toronto in co-operation with [the Department of National Defense], in my opinion we are on the right track." According to Good, "Robertson's file contained several reports which he had hoped would convince the NRC that *extraterrestrial activity was behind some of the sightings in Canada.*" (Original emphasis.) The reason for the RCAF's declining interest in UFOs was given thus: "The primary interest of UFOs lies in the field of science and, to a lesser degree, *to one that is associated with national security.*" (Good's emphasis.)

While ufologists point to the suppressive aspects of JANAP 146, sceptics such as Curtis Peebles remind us that the transmission of reports which might be considered of vital intelligence interest to national security was protected by the US Communications Act of 1934. In addition, reports with intelligence implications were protected by the Espionage Act in the United States, and the Official Secrets Act in Canada. *This* was why those reporting intelligence-related information were forbidden from discussing it publicly. According to Peebles, "These provisions were meant to 'emphasize the necessity for the handling of such information within official channels only.'" He continues: "Believers used these penalties [fines and/or imprisonment] to put a more sinister meaning on JANAP 146. The provisions for reports of airplanes, missiles, submarines, ships, and ground parties were ignored. UFOs were depicted as its only interest."

Although Peebles is here referring to the stance taken by Major Donald Keyhoe and other contemporary ufologists, this criticism is harder to level at UFO researchers today, many of whom do not ignore the other categories of sighting in JANAP 146, but merely point out (quite reasonably) that UFOs are listed as a category *entirely separate* from the other, more mundane sightings. The implication, of course, is that the US and Canadian Air Forces were well aware that some UFOs are not misinterpretations of man-made aircraft or natural phenomena.

Extraterrestrial Quarantine Law

In his 1986 book *Extraterrestrials Among Us,* researcher George C. Andrews draws attention to an arcane law, adopted in July 1969, which effectively prohibits US citizens from having any contact with alien spacecraft or their pilots. According to Title 14, Section 1211 of the Code of Federal Regulations, anyone found guilty of extraterrestrial contact can be jailed for one year and fined $5,000. People who have been "extraterrestrially exposed" can be quarantined under armed guard for an indefinite period. There is no limit to the number of people who could be detained thus, and there are persistent rumours among the more extreme UFO conspiracy theorists that the US Government has established a large number of detention camps for this contingency. According to Andrews, "The definition of 'extraterrestrial exposure' is left entirely up to the NASA administrator, who is thus endowed with total dictatorial power to be exercised at his slightest caprice, which is completely contrary to the Constitution."

The relevant sections of the text of the law are as follows:

1211.100 Title 14—Aeronautics and Space
Part 1211—Extra-terrestrial Exposure

1211.100 Scope.

This part establishes: (a) NASA policy, responsibility and authority to guard the Earth against any harmful contamination or adverse changes in its environment resulting from personnel, spacecraft and other property returning to the Earth after landing on or coming within the atmospheric envelope of a celestial body; and (b) security requirements, restrictions and safeguards that are necessary in the interest of national security.

1211.101 Applicability.

The provisions of this part apply to all NASA manned and unmanned space missions which land or come within the atmospheric envelope of a celestial body and return to the Earth.

1211.102 Definitions.

(a)"NASA" and the "Administrator" mean, respectively, the National Aeronautics and Space Administration and the Administrator of the National Aeronautics and Space Administration or his authorized representative.

(b) "Extra-terrestrially exposed" means the state or condition of any person, property, animal or other form of life or matter whatever, who or which has:

(1) Touched directly or come within the atmospheric envelope of any other celestial body; or

(2) Touched directly or been in close proximity to (or been exposed indirectly to) any person, property, animal or other form of life or matter who or which has been extraterrestrially exposed by virtue of paragraph (b)(1) of this section.

For example, if person or thing "A" touches the surface of the Moon, and on "A's" return to Earth, "B" touches "A" and, subsequently, "C" touches "B," all of these—"A" through "C" inclusive—would be extra-terrestrially exposed ("A" and "B" directly; "C" indirectly).

(c) "Quarantine" means the detention, examination and decontamination of any person, property, animal or other form of life or matter whatever that is extra-terrestrially exposed, and includes the apprehension or seizure of such person, property, animal or other form of life or matter whatever.

(d) "Quarantine period" means a period of consecutive calendar days as may be established in accordance with 1211.104(a) . . .

1211.104 Policy.

(a) Administrative actions. The Administrator or his designee . . . shall in his discretion:

(1) Determine the beginning and duration of a quarantine period with respect to any space mission; the quarantine period as it applies to various life forms will be announced.

(2) Designate in writing quarantine officers to exercise quarantine authority.

(3) Determine that a particular person, property, animal or other form of life or matter whatever is extra-terrestrially exposed and quarantine such person, property, animal or other form of life or matter whatever. The quarantine may be based only on a determination, with or without the ben-

efit of a hearing, that there is probable cause to believe that such person, property, animal or other form of life or matter whatever is extra-terrestrially exposed.

(4) Determine within the United States or within vessels or vehicles of the United States the place, boundaries, and rules of operation of necessary quarantine stations.

(5) Provide for guard services by contract or otherwise, as may be necessary, to maintain security and inviolability of quarantine stations and quarantined persons, property, animals or other form of life or matter whatever.

(6) Provide for the subsistence, health, and welfare of persons quarantined under the provisions of this part.

(7) Hold such hearings at such times, in such manner and for such purposes as may be desirable or necessary under this part, including hearings for the purpose of creating a record for use in making any determination under this part or for the purpose of reviewing any such determination ...

(b) (3) During any period of announced quarantine, no person shall enter or depart from the limits of the quarantine station without permission of the cognizant NASA officer. During such period, the posted perimeter of a quarantine station shall be secured by armed guard.

(4) Any person who enters the limits of any quarantine station during the quarantine period shall be deemed to have consented to the quarantine of his person if it is determined that he is or has become extra-terrestrially exposed.

(5) At the earliest practicable time, each person who is quarantined by NASA shall be given a reasonable opportunity to communicate by telephone with legal counsel or other persons of his choice ...

1211.107 Court or other process.

(a) NASA officers and employees are prohibited from discharging from the limits of a quarantine station any quarantined person, property, animal or other form of life or matter whatever during order or other request, order or demand an announced quarantine period in compliance with a subpoena, show cause or any court or other authority without the prior approval of the General Counsel and the Administrator.

(b) Where approval to discharge a quarantined person, property, animal or other form of life or matter whatever in compliance with such a request, order or demand of any court or other authority is not given, the person to whom it is directed shall, if possible, appear in court or before the other authority and respectfully state his inability to comply, relying for his action on this 1211.107.

1211.108 Violations.

Whoever willfully violates, attempts to violate, or conspires to violate any provision of this part or any regulation or order issued under this part or who enters or departs from the limits of a quarantine station in disregard of the quarantine rules or regulations or without permission of the NASA quarantine officer shall be fined not more than $5,000 or imprisoned not more than 1 year, or both.

In view of our continuing exploration of space, it seems reasonable enough that provision should be made for the day (which surely cannot be far off) when interplanetary probes will be designed to return to the Earth, after landing on the more distant planets in our Solar System. The recent discovery of what might well be microscopic fossils inside the Martian meteorite known as ALH84001, means that there *is* a potential danger from extraterrestrial life—even if that life cannot be seen with the naked eye.

George Andrews is disturbed by the fact that the provisions of the quarantine law do not refer *only* to NASA manned and unmanned spacecraft. Of course, while the absence of the word "only" could be construed as meaning that spacecraft from any nation on Earth could be potential carriers of dangerous extraterrestrial micro-organisms, and thus should be subject to quarantine procedures for the sake of humanity, it can also be construed to mean *any spacecraft*, whether from the Earth or another planet. According to Andrews, "NASA's general counsel, Neil Hosenball, has admitted that [the quarantine law] is applicable to space vehicles not originating from Earth."

It is extremely unlikely that the government would actually detain people who witness genuine UFOs and "aliens" under this law, since to do so would be blatantly to admit the reality of extraterrestrial spacecraft and beings, which surely is not on the immediate agenda! However, the "ET Law" has given rise to some very dark speculations in certain quarters, among which are that the US Government is well aware of the presence of aliens, and has formed a draconian contingency plan to deal with human reaction to any large-scale future landing. Also, there is a rather implausible theory that these detention camps will be used to imprison political undesirables, after a spurious official announcement that the Earth is under surveillance by hostile alien beings.

While the extraterrestrial quarantine law may well include provisions for dealing with exposure to potentially harmful material (living or otherwise) from other planets, to apply it to UFO contactees seems rather illogical: if alien beings have landed on Earth (as has been reported on numerous occasions), then it surely follows that any contamination will already have taken place. The implication is that if the aliens really are here, they must have taken their own precautions against harming our environment with extraterrestrial bacteria.

6

Operation Majestic-12

Background

The "Majestic-12 documents" have come to be regarded by many ufologists as the best evidence for government knowledge of the alien presence. Not surprisingly, for every researcher who accepts their authenticity, there is another who maintains that they are either a clever hoax, or else part of an elaborate campaign of disinformation designed to obscure the path to the truth.

The origin of the Majestic-12 controversy can be traced to Sergeant Richard C. Doty, one-time special agent with the Air Force Office of Special Investigations at Kirtland Air Force Base. In 1981, Doty leaked a document to researcher William Moore, who at that time was on the board of directors of the Aerial Phenomena Research Organization (APRO). The "Project Aquarius Document" was apparently a teletype message, dated 7 November 1980, from the Air Force Office of Special Investigations (AFOSI) headquarters in Washington, DC, to the OSI at Kirtland AFB. The message was classified Secret, and contained the results of the analysis of several UFO photographs taken by Dr. Paul Bennewitz. According to the analysis, the object in the photographs was "saucer shaped, approximate diameter 37 feet." There was also a "trilateral insignia" on the lower part of the UFO. (The trilateral insignia would come to be regarded by some researchers as the "flag" of the alien nation.) In part, the Aquarius Document stated:

...USAF no longer publicly active in UFO research, however USAF still has interest in all UFO sightings over USAF installation/test ranges. Several other government agencies, led by NASA, actively [investigate] legitimate sightings through covert cover.... NASA filters results of sightings to appropriate military departments with interest in that particular sighting. The official US government policy and results of Project Aquarius is still classified Top Secret with no dissemination outside official intelligence channels and with restricted access to "MJ TWELVE." ...

A subsequent AFOSI investigation of the Aquarius Document revealed that it was not authentic, being riddled with flaws in style and format. However, Moore explained this by saying that he had retyped the original document, and that this version had been inspected by AFOSI.

Throughout the early 1980s, Richard Doty met with several UFO researchers, informing them that he and the OSI were deeply involved with the UFO phenomenon. He himself had been assigned to investigate sightings and encounters, and he claimed to have access to a number of briefing papers dealing with the subject. According to Doty, the US Government had entered a "secret treaty" with the aliens, in which the government agreed to the abduction of humans (and the mutilation of cattle) in return for items of alien technology. (It is rumoured that the F-117A Nighthawk and the B-2 Stealth Bomber use alien-derived components, which does make one wonder why they are still powered by jet engines.)

In April 1983, Linda Moulton Howe (most famous for her excellent research on cattle mutilations) met with Doty in Albuquerque, at the Kirtland AFB AFOSI office. There she was shown several documents purporting to be briefing papers for the President of the United States. Doty told her that his superiors wanted her to see the documents, but that she could not take notes.

The information contained in the documents was astonishing, to say the least. Apparently, there had been a number of

UFO crashes in the late 1940s and early 1950s, mainly in the American south-west and northern Mexico. The cause of the crashes was radar, which interfered with the UFOs' flight control systems. A crash at Roswell in 1949 yielded six dead aliens and one still living, which survived at Los Alamos until June 1952. This creature, designated "EBE-1"(EBE stands for Extraterrestrial Biological Entity) told the Air Force investigators about the aliens' role in human evolution, which was quite extensive, including the manipulation of human DNA, beginning 25,000 years ago. Modifications were made 15,000, 5,000 and 2,500 years ago, and EBE-1 also said that the aliens had created a "being" 2,000 years ago, who would teach humans to love each other and renounce violence.

Also included in the documents Linda Howe examined was a list of UFO- and alien-related government research projects. For instance, there was Project Garnet, which succeeded in answering all questions regarding the origin and evolution of *Homo sapiens*. Project Sigma dealt with ongoing attempts to establish permanent lines of communication with the aliens; Project Snowbird dealt with the development and implementation of alien technology; and Project Aquarius was an overall effort to accumulate all available information on the aliens and their technology.

The sudden release of this information to Howe was allegedly a prelude to the release of several thousand feet of film, showing crashed spacecraft, alien bodies, the survivor of the Roswell crash (EBE-1) and a meeting between the military and a saucer crew that occurred at Holloman AFB (more of which later). Doty revealed that the aliens live on a hot desert world; their houses are carved from soil and rock, and they live like "Pueblo Indians." When asked if the aliens' home star system was Zeta Reticuli, Doty refused to answer, but claimed that there is an exchange programme, in which "research scientists [are] studying their planets like they study ours."

According to Doty, EBE-1 died from unknown causes, despite

efforts to save him. Howe asked if he had said anything about God; Doty replied that the alien said our souls "recycle," that reincarnation is real: "It's the machinery of the universe."

Unfortunately, the "several thousand" feet of film were never released, for "political reasons." As a result of this set-back, the UFO documentary that Howe had been planning had to be abandoned.

Although he admitted that he had met with Linda Howe, Richard Doty denied having shown her any secret documents, or having promised to release film footage. In a letter to researcher Barry Greenwood, he denied even knowing of any government investigation of UFOs. Howe maintained that this was not true, and signed a notarized declaration testifying that she was shown the documents. Timothy Good believes that Linda Howe was given disinformation (a certain amount of truth, mixed with a certain number of lies), perhaps for the very purpose of making sure that her UFO documentary "never got off the ground."

The next phase in the controversy occurred on 11 December 1984, when Jaime Shandera, a 45-year-old film producer based in Los Angeles, received a curious package in the mail. Inside the package was a canister containing a roll of exposed but un-developed Tri-X 35mm film. Shandera was due to have lunch with none other than William Moore (the two had met previously to discuss a UFO-related film project that never came to fruition, and had remained friends since), and he took the roll of film with him. When he showed the canister to Moore in the restaurant, describing how it had arrived, the two men immediately left and went to Moore's house.

There they managed to develop some sheets, which revealed seven pages of a typewritten document. At the top of each page was a stamp which read: "TOP SECRET/MAJIC/EYES ONLY." Apparently, the sheets contained a briefing document on "Operation Majestic-12," for the attention of President-elect Dwight D. Eisenhower. It was dated 18 November 1952; the briefing officer was Admiral Roscoe H. Hillenkoetter. The Majestic-12 had been established by President Truman, as a direct result of the Roswell UFO crash of 1947. According to the document:

> On 07 July, 1947, a secret operation was begun to assure recovery of the wreckage of this object for scientific study. During the course of this operation, aerial reconnaissance discovered that four small human-like beings had apparently ejected from the craft at some point before it exploded. These had fallen to earth about two miles east of the wreckage site. All four were dead and badly decomposed due to action by predators and exposure to the elements during the approximately one week time period which had elapsed before their discovery. A special scientific team took charge of removing these bodies for study. (See Attachment "C.") The wreckage of the craft was also removed to several different locations. (See Attachment "B.") Civilian and military witnesses in the area were debriefed and news reporters were given the effective cover story that the object had been a misguided weather balloon.

The document described Majestic-12 as a "TOP SECRET Research and Development/Intelligence operation responsible directly and only to the President of the United States." The group was "established by special, classified executive order of President Truman on 24 September 1947," nearly three months after the alleged Roswell UFO crash.

Membership of Majestic-12

According to the briefing document, the original members of the Majestic-12 group were as follows: Admiral Roscoe H. Hillenkoetter, Dr. Vannevar Bush, Defense Secretary James V. Forrestal, General Nathan F. Twining, General Hoyt S. Vandenberg, Dr. Detlev Bronk, Dr. Jerome Hunsaker, Rear Admiral Sidney W. Souers, Gordon Gray, Dr. Donald Menzel, General Robert M. Montague and Dr. Lloyd V. Berkner. Defense Secretary Forrestal committed suicide on 22 May 1949, after a nervous breakdown, and was replaced on 1 August 1950 by General Walter B. Smith. A few words on each member are in order:

Admiral Roscoe H. Hillenkoetter was the third Director of the Central Intelligence Group from 1947 to 1950, and the first Director of the Central Intelligence Agency (established, incidentally, in September 1947, the same month as Majestic-12). Hillenkoetter was convinced that UFOs represented a genuine mystery, and were most likely machines under intelligent control. He made no secret of his convictions, and accused the Air Force of censoring UFO sightings. He is quoted as saying: "It is imperative that we learn where UFOs come from and what their purpose is." Following his retirement from the Navy in June 1957, Hillenkoetter joined the board of directors of NICAP, which, as Timothy Good states, put him in an "excellent position to monitor the activities of this influential civilian group."

Dr. Vannevar Bush was a world-class scientist who advised President Truman throughout the Second World War. Dr. Bush organized the National Defense Resources Council in 1941 and the Office of Scientific Research and Development in 1943; the latter organization was instrumental in the creation of the Manhattan Project and the first atomic bomb. In his book *Above Top Secret*, Timothy Good draws our attention to a Top Secret memorandum released by the Canadian Government, in which scientist Wilbert Smith referred to Dr. Bush as heading a "small group" set up to investigate UFOs. Good then asks (not unreasonably) if this "small group" was actually Majestic-12.

Defense Secretary James V. Forrestal had been President Truman's Under Secretary of the Navy from 1944 to 1947. In September 1947, Truman authorized Forrestal and Vannevar Bush to set up Majestic-12 "with all due speed and caution." In 1947, Forrestal was appointed to the newly-created position of Secretary of Defense, from which he resigned in 1949, following a serious nervous breakdown. He committed suicide two months later.

General Nathan F. Twining was appointed Commanding General of Air Materiel Command at Wright Field (now Wright-Patterson AFB) in Dayton, Ohio, in 1945. In 1953 he was appointed Chief of Staff of the US Air Force, and in 1957 he became chairman of the Joint Chiefs of Staff. Timothy Good reminds us that Twining was of the opinion that UFOs were "something real and not visionary or fictitious," and reports that Twining suddenly cancelled a trip to the West Coast on 8 July 1947, less than one week after the alleged Roswell crash, "due to a very important and sudden matter." According to William Moore, reporters were told that Twining was, at this time, "probably in Washington, DC"; in fact, he was in New Mexico, where he remained until 10 July.

General Hoyt S. Vandenberg was appointed the second Director of the Central Intelligence Group (which became the Central Intelligence Agency in 1947). It was Vandenberg who had ordered the Air Technical Intelligence Center to destroy its classified "Estimate of the Situation," which had concluded that UFOs were interplanetary. According to sceptic Philip Klass, it makes no sense for Vandenberg to have dismissed the Washington Invasion as nothing more than temperature inversions if he knew that UFOs were alien spacecraft. On the other hand, in view of the absolute secrecy desired by the government regarding the true nature of UFOs, there was nothing else he *could* have done.

Dr. Detlev Bronk, another scientific advisor to President Truman, was chairman of the National Research Council, and was a member of the Medical Advisory Board of the Atomic Energy Commission. Dr. Bronk's qualifications in the fields of physiology and biophysics (with emphasis on the transmission of nerve impulses) led to his performing autopsies on the bodies discovered at the Roswell crash site. Dr. Bronk was also a member of the Scientific Advisory Committee to the Brookhaven National Laboratory, along with Dr. Edward Condon, Director of the National Bureau of Standards, and of the USAF-sponsored committee on the Scientific Study of Unidentified Flying Objects, which concluded that UFOs were unworthy of serious investigation.

Dr. Jerome Hunsaker held credentials that would have made

him invaluable in the analysis of the materials recovered at Roswell. A former head of the Departments of Aeronautical and Mechanical Engineering at the Massachusetts Institute of Technology, he was appointed chairman of the National Advisory Committee on Aerospace at the time of Majestic-12's creation.

Rear Admiral Sidney W. Souers was the first Director of the Central Intelligence Group from January to June 1946, and became Executive Secretary of the National Security Council in 1947. Although he retired in 1950, he was retained as a special consultant to the President on matters of security. Once again, Philip Klass is unhappy with Souers' staying in Majestic-12 after his retirement, and wonders why his replacement at the NSC was not recruited to the group instead. However, journalist C. D. B. Bryan makes a good point when he counters that the fewer people involved in the super-secret Majestic-12, the more secure the group would be.

Gordon Gray was another member who posed great problems for Philip Klass, according to C. D. B. Bryan. In 1947, Gray was an Assistant Secretary of the Army—hardly a position that would have commended him to the creators of Majestic-12. In fact, he was not appointed Secretary of the Army until two years later. Why, asks Klass, was he considered worthy of membership? Once again, Bryan may have the answer: "... in postwar Washington, Gray's reputation as a gentleman with intelligence, reliability, and without political ties or debts would have made him an attractive addition to any secret, Executive-Ordered intelligence-gathering committee." Bryan adds that Gray's legal and journalistic training would have made him a good investigator. In 1950, Gray was appointed as Special Assistant to President Truman on National Security Affairs. Investigator William Steinman states that in 1951 Gray directed the Psychological Strategy Board, which is mentioned by General Walter B. Smith (Forrestal's replacement in Majestic-12) in a 1952 CIA memorandum dealing with the psychological implications of UFOs.

Dr. Donald Menzel was one of the most outspoken of UFO sceptics, and wrote several books debunking the subject. This has led Philip Klass to suggest that the "hoaxer" of the Majestic-12 documents included Menzel in the committee as a perverse kind of "punishment" for his years of raining on the UFO parade. However, Dr. Menzel was also chairman of the Department of Astronomy at Harvard, and head of the Harvard Observatory for Solar Research. He was a world-class astronomer, and as such would have been an essential addition to the group. In addition, the redoubtable Stanton Friedman informs us in his 1996 book *TOP SECRET/MAJIC*, that Dr. Menzel had been the subject of loyalty hearings in 1951, and was in danger of losing his Air Force security clearance (Friedman wonders why he had such a clearance in the first place). As it turned out, one of Menzel's staunchest supporters had been none other than Vannevar Bush! After some intensive and painstaking research, Friedman discovered that Donald Menzel seemed to have led a double life doing consulting work for the National Security Agency (NSA), the CIA, the military and many corporations.

Menzel was also highly regarded for his "outstanding discretion" with regard to classified material. His supporters at the loyalty hearings maintained that he was totally trustworthy and extraordinarily discreet. (It should be mentioned that these loyalty hearings were merely a part of the general paranoia extant in the United States at that time, and were the result of insignificant events, such as Menzel's trip to the Soviet Union on an eclipse expedition in 1936.) Menzel was also an expert cryptographer, which surely would have been essential in the interpretation of any markings in the Roswell wreckage.

General Robert M. Montague was Director of the Anti-Aircraft and Guided Missiles Branch of the US Army Artillery School, and was Commanding General of the Atomic Energy Commission installation at Sandia Base in Albuquerque, New Mexico. As such, he would surely have been deeply involved with any attempt to monitor and track the movements of UFOs, or to assess their performance with a view to possible methods of combating them.

Dr. Lloyd V. Berkner was another respected scientist, who was

Executive Secretary of the Joint Research and Development Board in 1946, under Dr. Vannevar Bush. He also chaired a special committee to direct a study that led to the establishment of the Weapons Systems Evaluation Group, and served on the Robertson Panel.

Contents of the Documents

The introductory paragraph on page "002" of the briefing document is as follows:

> OPERATION MAJESTIC-12 is a TOP SECRET Research and Development/Intelligence operation responsible directly and only to the President of the United States. Operations of the project are carried out under control of the Majestic-12 (Majic-12) Group which was established by special classified executive order of President Truman on 24 September, 1947, upon recommendation by Dr. Vannevar Bush and Secretary James Forrestal. . . .

The document goes on to describe the Kenneth Arnold sighting of nine disc-shaped objects over Mount Rainier, noting that, although this was not the first such sighting, it was the first to gain widespread public attention in the media. Many such reports also came from military witnesses, and resulted in independent efforts by several elements of the military to obtain information on the origin and purpose of the objects, in the interests of national defence.

Nothing of substance was learned until the Roswell, New Mexico, incident, when a disc apparently crash-landed on the ranch run by "Mac" Brazel. This led to the formation of a secret operation, on 7 July 1947, to recover the wreckage of the disc for scientific study. The crew, which apparently had ejected from the craft, were found about two miles east of the crash site. All four of the beings were dead and decomposed due to predator action and exposure to the elements, and were also removed for study.

A secret analytical effort was organized by General Twining and Dr. Bush, on the direct orders of President Truman. This analysis concluded on 19 September 1947 that the craft was most likely a short-range reconnaissance vehicle, based on its small size and lack of identifiable provisioning. Dr. Bronk organized an analysis of the four dead crew members, which tentatively concluded on 30 November 1947 that, despite the humanoid appearance of the creatures, they were nevertheless the result of evolutionary processes that were quite different from those observed or postulated in *Homo sapiens*. Dr. Bronk's team suggested the term "Extraterrestrial Biological Entities" or "EBEs" be adopted as the standard reference term for the creatures until a more definitive designation could be agreed upon.

Accepting the extraterrestrial nature of the object and its occupants, speculation centred on their ultimate origin. Although it was considered possible that they might have come from Mars, Dr. Menzel thought it more likely that they came from another solar system altogether.

Although attempts were made to decipher the hieroglyphic-like markings discovered on parts of the wreckage, they were largely unsuccessful. The propulsion system of the craft also resisted attempts at analysis, as did the method by which power from the propulsion source was transmitted. There were no identifiable wings, propellers, jets or other identifiable methods of propulsion and guidance, or even internal wiring or electrical components. It was assumed that the propulsion unit was completely destroyed in the explosion which caused the crash.

In December 1947, Project Sign was established in an attempt to gain as much information as possible about the alien craft, their performance characteristics and their purpose. Tight security was preserved by the liaison between Project Sign and Majestic-12 being limited to two operatives within the Intelligence Division of Air Materiel Command, whose function was to pass certain information through channels. Project Sign became Project Grudge in December 1948, before being renamed Project Blue Book in 1952.

On 6 December 1950, a second object crashed in the El Indio–Guerrero area of the Texas-Mexico border after a lengthy flight through the atmosphere. A search team was dispatched, but found that the craft had been almost completely incinerated. The remains were transported to the Atomic Energy Commission facility at Sandia, New Mexico, for study.

The motives and intentions of the aliens remained completely unknown, which had serious implications for the national security. In addition, a significant upsurge in apparent surveillance activity of the craft in 1952 caused considerable concern that new developments might be imminent. It was for these reasons, as well as international and technological considerations and the need to avoid public panic, that the Majestic-12 Group maintained the need for strictest security to continue without interruption into the new administration. At the same time, a contingency plan—MJ-1949-04P/78 (Top Secret–Eyes Only)—was held in readiness, should the need to make a public announcement present itself.

The Majestic-12 Operations Manual

In his book *TOP SECRET/MAJIC*, Stanton Friedman relates how, in December 1994, he learned that Don Berliner of the Fund for UFO Research had received a package, mailed from Wisconsin. The package contained a roll of 35mm film which, when developed, revealed photographs of a document entitled *Majestic-12 Group Special Operations Manual: Extraterrestrial Entities and Technology, Recovery and Disposal*. The document was dated April 1954; like the earlier MJ-12 documents, it was marked "TOP SECRET/MAJIC Eyes Only." While the original Operations Manual contained six chapters, four appendixes, 30 pages of text and a photographic section (according to the contents page), not all of these had been photographed.

According to Friedman, Don Berliner informed the General Accounting Office (GAO)—Congress's investigative arm—of the existence of the document. The GAO was, at that time, in the process of searching for government records pertaining to the Roswell Incident, and in turn informed the US Air Force of Berliner's discovery. Neither the Air Force nor the GAO, however, made any reference whatsoever to the Operations Manual in the subsequent official responses to the extraterrestrial theory of the Roswell Incident.

The Operations Manual itself (or at least the extracts included in Friedman's book) adds another fascinating dimension to the Majestic-12 controversy, since it contains information on the alleged methods by which the group deals with the alien hardware (not to mention the aliens themselves) it recovers. For the extracts themselves, I direct the reader to Stanton Friedman's book; however, a brief summary is in order here.

After a brief background explanation of the origin and purpose of Majestic-12, the manual goes on to define "Extraterrestrial Technology" and to describe (based on "general shape") the types of craft that have been encountered and studied: elliptical or disc, fuselage or cigar, ovoid or circular, and airfoil or triangular. There follows a description of the two "distinct categories" of Extraterrestrial Biological Entities, based on the studies conducted on the crews of various crashed spacecraft. "Type I" entities are described as similar to human beings, to the extent that they might be "mistaken for human beings of the Asian race if seen from a distance." "Type II" entities correspond to the now ubiquitous Greys.

The recovered technology is then described as being composed of materials unlike any known to "Terrestrial science," which are extremely light and strong, of an appearance similar to "aluminum foil or aluminum-magnesium sheeting," but whose characteristics resemble more "some kind of unknown plastic-like material." This material displayed no measurable magnetic characteristics or residual radiation.

The next chapter covers "Recovery Operations," including cover-up methods, such as official denial, the discrediting of witnesses and the issuing of deceptive statements to explain UFO crashes in mundane terms (i.e. meteorites, downed military aircraft, etc.). Instructions are then given on how to secure the area around a crash site, and on the removal and transport of the wreckage. Should an intact and functional craft be encountered, extreme caution should be exercised, and it should be approached only by "specially trained MJ-12 RED TEAM personnel wearing protective clothing." Any live EBEs encountered should be taken into custody immediately, and every care should be taken to ensure their survival. The area should then be completely "cleansed," and every care should be taken that no traces of the incident remain.

A number of receiving facilities to which extraterrestrial material should be taken are listed, including "Area 51 S-4," "Blue Lab WP-61," "OPNAC BBS-01" and "Building 21 KB-88."

The next chapter includes highly detailed procedures for the packing, unpacking and handling of materials retrieved from a crash site, and is followed by a chapter dealing in greater detail with the EBEs themselves. There are two types of encounters with EBEs: those initiated by the aliens themselves (in which it is anticipated that the venues would be military bases), and those resulting from spacecraft accidents.

With regard to the interaction between human personnel and extraterrestrial entities, security is of paramount importance, and should be given a higher priority than the survival of any EBEs encountered, in spite of the desirability of that survival. Instructions are then given for the retrieval and preservation of deceased EBEs.

The final chapter in the extracts contains instructions for follow-up investigations of UFO sightings reported by members of the public.

Did Majestic-12 Ever Exist?

Not surprisingly with an organization allegedly dealing with an extraterrestrial presence on Earth, the only evidence for Majestic-12's existence is a kind of vapour trail of mysterious and tantalizing documents detailing its shadowy activities. For this reason, the reality (or otherwise) of Majestic-12 unavoidably rests on the question of the documents' authenticity. Equally un-surprisingly, these documents are themselves the subject of a heated and ongoing controversy, with proponents and sceptics alike expressing their opinions with intense enthusiasm.

From the sceptics' point of view, there are a number of seri-ous problems with the Majestic-12 documents, which would seem to point rather strongly to their being a hoax. One of the most detailed attacks comes from aviation historian Curtis Pee-bles. In his book *Watch the Skies!* Peebles relates how, in 1985, William Moore and Jaime Shandera made a discovery which they claimed provided proof of Majestic-12's existence. One of the "Attachments" in the documents mailed to Shandera was a memorandum dated 24 September 1947, from President Tru-man to Defense Secretary Forrestal, establishing the MJ-12 group. At the National Archives, Moore and Shandera discov-ered an unsigned carbon copy of a memorandum, dated 14 July 1954, from Robert Cutler, special assistant to the President, to General Nathan F. Twining. The text dealt with "NSC/MJ-12 Special Studies Project" and read: "The President has decided that the MJ-12 SSP briefing should take place *during* the already scheduled White House meeting of July 16, rather than follow-ing it as previously intended."

To Moore, this provided conclusive proof that a group called "MJ-12" existed in 1954. However, the so-called "Cutler Memo" was not quite so impressive to the National Archives. For one thing, the memo was classified Top Secret, yet it did not have the required Top Secret register number. Its label, "Top Secret Restricted Security Information," was an anachronism, since it would not be used at the National Security Council until nearly 20 years later, when Richard Nixon took office. Even the paper was problematical: according to Peebles, documents created by Cutler while at the NSC had an eagle watermark on onion-skin paper used for carbon copies, and yet there was no water-mark on the Cutler Memo.

Peebles refers to a "Reference Report on MJ-12," by Jo Ann Williamson of the National Archives, in his listing of further problems with the memo:

> There was no NSC meeting on July 16, 1954, and there were no NSC records dealing with MJ-12, Majestic, UFOs, flying saucers, or flying disks. There was no listing in President Eisenhower's Appointment Books for a special meeting on July 16, 1954. Even when he had off-the-record meetings, the Appointment Books listed the time of the meeting and the participants. Finally, Robert Cutler was not even in Washington, D.C., or the U.S. on July 14, 1954. He was visiting military bases in Europe and North Africa between July 3 and 15. A genuine memo, also dated July 14, 1954, was signed by James S. Lay.

According to the sceptics, the Majestic-12 briefing paper itself contains many inconsistencies, particularly in the method of writing dates with a "0" prefix, for instance "01 August." Curtis Peebles states that he has never seen a "0" prefix before a single-digit date in a government document. The briefing paper also uses a comma in its dates, for instance "06 December, 1950," whereas the proper format was "6 December 1950." Philip Klass and the American organization Citizens Against UFO Secrecy (CAUS) pointed out that William Moore had himself used the "0" prefix in his correspondence since 1983.

CAUS came up with more interesting evidence that all was not as it seemed with the briefing paper. The "TOP SE-CRET/MAJIC EYES ONLY" markings were identical to the rub-ber stamp used by Moore for his return address. The lettering on Moore's address stamp was removable, but real classification stamps do not have removable lettering. According to Peebles, "One obvious indication of this is the letter 'I.' In both the

'MAJIC' and the 'WILLIAM' and 'OLIVE' of Moore's return address, the 'I' is raised slightly."

In addition, the pages of the briefing paper are numbered "002," "003," etc. This is not consistent with the page numbering system used in genuine Top Secret documents from 1952, which carry the statement: "This document has __ pages," and thereafter: "Page __ of __ pages." The reason for this system is that Top Secret documents are checked periodically, to make sure that they still have all of their pages.

Peebles also points out a reference to "Roswell Army Air Base (now Walker Field)," which should be Roswell Army Air *Field* and Walker *AFB*. The term "Army Air Base" was not used after 1943, and "field" was not used after 1947, when the Air Force and Army became independent from each other.

Further anachronisms are evident in the use of the words "media" instead of "press" and "Extra-terrestrial" instead of "alien," the former words not entering popular usage until the 1960s. Perhaps one of the most revealing errors is the phrase "homo-sapiens," which should read Homo sapiens (a generic name in the Linnaean system of classification, for instance "Homo," should always begin with a capital letter). As science writer Edward Ashpole states, it is evident that no biologist checked the briefing paper before it was sent to Eisenhower, "yet biologists would have been intimately involved and two biologists were on the MJ-12 Committee, according to the MJ-12 document."

One of the most important of the MJ-12 documents is the "Truman Memorandum," dated 24 September 1947, which reads:

MEMORANDUM FOR THE SECRETARY OF DEFENSE

Dear Secretary Forrestal,

As per our recent conversation on this matter, you are hereby authorized to proceed with all due speed and caution upon your undertaking. Hereafter this matter shall be referred to only as Operation Majestic Twelve.

It continues to be my feeling that any future considerations rel-

ative to the ultimate disposition of this matter should rest solely
with the Office of the President following appropriate discussions
with yourself, Dr. Bush and the Director of Central Intelligence.

[Signed] Harry Truman

Towards the end of 1989, Philip Klass showed that the signature on the Truman Memo was "identical" to Truman's signature
on a letter to Vannevar Bush, dated 1 October 1947. Since it is impossible for two signatures to be identical (they will always carry
variations), Klass concluded that the signature on the 24 September 1947 memo had to be a photocopy of the signature on the
1 October 1947 letter. Klass was also informed by a document examiner that the memo had been typed on a Smith-Corona typewriter which was not available until 1963.

All of the above considerations have come to weigh heavily
against the authenticity of the Majestic-12 documents in the eyes
of many (if not most) serious UFO researchers. And yet one such
serious researcher has some interesting things to say on the subject of the MJ-12 documents.

Stanton Friedman has perhaps spent more time than any researcher going through the contents of various archives in his
search for verification of Majestic-12. According to Friedman, the
classification "TOP SECRET RESTRICTED SECURITY INFOR-
MATION" on the Cutler-Twining memo was "perfectly normal"
in 1954. In addition (and illustrating the confusion that abounds
in the UFO literature in general), Friedman states that the
"NSC/MJ-12 Special Studies Project" memo from Cutler to Twining was a "carbon copy in blue ink on onionskin paper." The paper
also had a watermark, in contradiction to the sceptics' claims.

Friedman also tackles the thorny question of date format in
the documents. After reminding us that Philip Klass pointed to
Moore's use of the "0" prefix in his correspondence as implying
that he forged the documents, Friedman then takes him to task
for neglecting to mention that Moore does not always use the
"0" prefix. Neither does Klass mention that this particular

method of writing dates is used in numerous other government documents of the period. "In addition," Friedman continues, "Hillenkoetter had served in Europe, and the French used this date format." (To which the sceptics might well reply: Hillenkoetter was in the United States—not France—when he allegedly wrote the briefing document.)

Friedman then goes on to state that there are many different date and letter formats to be found in archives, "and many different style formats emanating from the same office."

For example, in letters from MJ-12 member General Walter Bedell Smith to General George Marshall—personal notes, birthday notes, thanks for the greetings, and so on—there are four different date formats: 29 December 1952; 26 October, 1954 (note the comma); Oct. 7, 1954; and 12/29/54.

Friedman also collected copies of more than 20 different examples of Hillenkoetter's writings, and then submitted them for analysis to Dr. Roger W. Wescott, who holds a PhD in linguistics from Princeton, and who has lectured on the subject at Princeton, Harvard and Oxford. Friedman quotes Dr. Wescott's conclusions:

In my opinion, there is no compelling reason to regard any of these communications as fraudulent or to believe that any of them were written by anyone other than Hillenkoetter himself. This statement holds for the controversial presidential briefing memorandum of November 18, 1952, as well as for the letters, both official and personal.

However, Friedman points out that someone in the CIA could conceivably have imitated Hillenkoetter's style, which makes it impossible for Dr. Wescott to state categorically that Hillenkoetter definitely wrote the MJ-12–related material.

Then there is the question of Truman's signature, which sceptics claim is proof of forgery. Writing in the Winter 1987–1988 issue of *The Skeptical Inquirer,* Klass stated that the signature on the Truman-Forrestal memo is 1.032 times longer than that on the Truman-Vannevar Bush memo. The reason for this is that the photocopying process stretches the images (including type) in a document. According to Friedman, however, the two signatures are *not* identical. In addition:

> The Truman-Forrestal *Harry* is 1.012 [times] longer than the Truman-Bush *Harry,* the Truman-Forrestal *Truman* is 1.032–1.04 times longer than the Truman-Bush *Truman,* but the letterhead is exactly the same length for both. Clearly, to claim evidence of photocopying, the type on a sheet of paper would have to be stretched by the same ratio on all parts of the paper.

Another important factor to consider is that, occasionally, a person *will* sign his or her name virtually identically on two or more occasions over a given period. Thus, to point to the similarity between the signature on the Truman-Forrestal memo and that on the Truman-Bush memo as evidence of forgery is actually quite meaningless.

Likewise, the small accidental ink mark next to the "H" in "Harry," which is present in both signatures, has been cited by sceptics as further proof of photocopying. But Friedman states that he has "copies of at least three legitimate Truman signatures, all of which have the same kind of mark by the H." As to Klass's claim that a document examiner concluded the typeface on the Truman Forrestal memo was from a 1963 Smith-Corona typewriter, Friedman states that this examiner was a former CIA agent; and furthermore, other examiners disagree with his conclusion.

These fundamental differences of opinion as to the authenticity of the Majestic-12 documents (and thus of the organization itself) would seem to guarantee the continuation of the controversy well into the foreseeable future of ufology.

7

Military UFO Encounters

Extreme Measures

One of the commonest misconceptions among people who are unfamiliar with the history of ufology is that UFOs are only seen by "kooks," untrained observers, or starry-eyed dreamers yearning for a sign that all is well in the heavens, if not on Earth. However, as we have seen, this is far from being the case; and in this chapter we will take a look at some of the impressive encounters that have occurred between military forces and apparently genuine UFOs.

One such case is supplied by Captain Edward J. Ruppelt in his 1956 book *The Report on Unidentified Flying Objects*. Although Ruppelt does not provide the exact date or location of the encounter, it seems to have occurred in the summer of 1952, when an uncorrelated radar target approached a US Air Force base, prompting the scrambling of two F-86 Sabre jets. Presently, one of the pilots spotted a saucer-shaped object in the distance, and altered course to intercept. When he got to within 500 yards, the object accelerated away. The pilot began to fire at the object, which immediately climbed out of sight. The base intelligence officer who had passed the information to Ruppelt claimed that he had been ordered to burn all copies of the incident report, but had managed to keep one.

Occasionally, UFOs have been known to take more than merely evasive action when faced with hostile action by terrestrial pilots. In 1967, two Cuban jets were scrambled to intercept a strange object. Their radio communications were monitored by US Air Force agents, who heard one of the pilots tell his base that the other jet had opened fire on the object, and had then disintegrated without exploding. According to Stanton Friedman, the tapes of this conversation were sent to the National Security Agency, which listed the destruction of the Cuban aircraft as equipment malfunction.

The US Air Force suffered a casualty of its own 23 November 1953, when an F-89C Scorpion jet was scrambled from Kinross AFB to intercept a radar target over Soo Locks, Michigan. The jet was piloted by Lieutenant Felix Moncla Jr.; also aboard was an observer, Lieutenant R. R. Wilson. The Scorpion was vectored to the target by the controller at the Air Defense Command Ground Control Intercept station that had first detected the intruder. As the Scorpion approached, the UFO abruptly altered course. On his radar screen, the GCI controller saw the two blips of the jet and the UFO merge into a single blip, which vanished from the scope after a few moments. Assuming that the Scorpion had collided with the unidentified target, the controller alerted Search and Rescue teams, which searched the area that night, in the hope that the two pilots had managed to eject from their aircraft before the "collision." No trace of them or the Scorpion was ever found, however, and the Air Force has never been able to explain the fate of Lieutenants Moncla and Wilson.

On 18 October 1973, Captain Lawrence Coyne apparently managed to avoid a similar disaster during a helicopter flight from Columbus, Ohio, to Cleveland. The Air Force Bell Huey helicopter, carrying three additional crewmen (Crew Chief Robert Yanacsek, Co-pilot Arrigo Jezzi and Staff Sergeant John Healey), took off at 10.30 P.M. By about 11.10 P.M., the craft was flying at 2,500 feet over Mansfield, when Yanacsek saw a red light approaching rapidly from the east. Coyne immediately took evasive action, initiating a power descent to 1,700 feet, but the object remained on a collision course. Having no other alternative, Coyne braced himself for a probably lethal impact.

When it was no more than 500 feet away from the helicopter, the UFO stopped suddenly, and the Air Force crew were able quite clearly to discern its shape. It was dull metallic grey in colour, 60 feet long and was shaped like a fat cigar. The red light that had alerted them to the object's arrival appeared to be mounted on its nose, while the rear end contained a number of flickering green lights. At the centre of the cigar was a dome. The helicopter's cockpit was suddenly flooded with a green glow from one of the rear lights of the UFO.

Coyne called the control tower at Mansfield Airport to ask if there were any high-performance aircraft operating in the vicinity. There was no response from the tower, even though it had acknowledged the helicopter moments before. The radio had gone dead on both UHF and VHF frequencies. It was then that Coyne realized that although the controls were still set in the "full down" position, the helicopter was actually gaining altitude at a rate of 100 feet per minute, and had reached 3,500 feet by the time Coyne managed to regain control. The helicopter then completed its journey to Cleveland. Interestingly, this encounter was also witnessed by observers on the ground, who described the UFO as looking "like a blimp," hanging over the helicopter.

Civilians are occasionally put at mortal risk through military encounters with UFOs. One such tragic case occurred on 2 July 1954, when an F-94C jet was instructed to intercept a balloon-shaped UFO that had been sighted over Walesville, New York. The above description would seem to imply that the UFO probably *was* a balloon, but for the events that subsequently unfolded. According to the official report produced by Air Force investigators, as the pilot approached the UFO, the temperature in his cockpit increased abruptly, prompting him to check his instruments. The fire warning light was illuminated, so the engine was shut down, and the two crew members ejected safely.

The F-94 then crashed in Walesville, destroying two buildings and a car, and killing four people. The Air Force investigation concluded that the UFO was indeed a balloon, although this hardly squares with the tragic conclusion of the sighting, or the causes of that conclusion.

The Mystery of the Atlas Missile

According to Dr. Robert Jacobs, a former First Lieutenant in the US Air Force and subsequently Assistant Professor of Radio-Film-TV at the University of Wisconsin, an Atlas missile was destroyed by a UFO at Vandenberg AFB, California, on 15 September 1964. At the time, Dr. Jacobs was in charge of the filming of missile tests at Vandenberg; his team had set up a TV camera, affixed to a powerful telescope, on a mountain overlooking the base. According to Dr. Jacobs:

> We kept the telescope locked on to the moving missile by radar, and it was while we were tracking one of the Atlas F missiles this way that we registered the UFO on our film.
>
> We had a crew of 120 men, and I was in charge. As we watched the Atlas F in flight we were delighted with our camera, which was doing fine, in fact we were jumping around with excitement, with the result that, because we were doing this, we actually missed seeing the most important bit of all—our missile's close encounter, at an altitude of 60 miles, with a UFO!
>
> I only heard about it, in fact, a couple of days later, when I was ordered to go and see my superior, Major Florenz J. Mansmann, Chief Science Officer of the Unit. With him there in his office there were a couple of men in plain clothes. He introduced them to me only by their first names and said they had come from Washington, DC.
>
> Then Major Mansmann had the film of the test run through. And, just at that point where my men and I had been busy congratulating ourselves and each other, Major Mansmann pointed to the screen and said: "Watch this bit closely." Suddenly we saw a UFO swim into the picture. It was very distinct and clear, a round object. It flew right up to our missile and emitted a vivid

flash of light. Then it altered course, and hovered briefly over our missile . . . and then there came a second vivid flash of light. Then the UFO flew around the missile twice and set off two more flashes from different angles, and then it vanished. A few seconds later, our missile was malfunctioning and tumbling out of control into the Pacific Ocean, hundreds of miles short of its scheduled target.

They switched on the office lights again, and I found myself confronted by three very intense faces. Speaking very quietly, Major Mansmann then said: "Lieutenant, just what the hell *was* that?" I replied that I had no idea. Then we ran the film through several more times and I was permitted to examine it with a magnifying glass. Then Mansmann again asked me what I thought, and I answered that in my opinion it was a UFO. Major Mansmann smiled and said: "You are to say nothing about this footage. As far as you and I are concerned, it never happened! Right?"

Here then was the confirmation of what the UFO experts had been saying for years past—that the US Government was covering up on what it knew about UFOs.

The film was turned over to the two men in plain clothes from Washington, who I believe were CIA agents. The film hasn't been heard of since. Major Mansmann added: "I don't have to remind you, of course, of the seriousness of a security breach. . . ."

It's been 17 years since that incident, and I've told nobody about it until now. I have been afraid of what might happen to me. But the truth is too important for it to be concealed any longer. The UFOs are real. I know they're real. The Air Force knows they're real. And the US Government knows they're real. I reckon it's high time that the American public knows it too.

If we accept that the UFO witnessed in association with the Atlas missile was a genuinely anomalous object that was indeed responsible for the missile's failure, then two alternative explanations present themselves. One is that the "vivid flashes" emitted by the UFO were projected perhaps by some kind of weapons system, recalling the frequently-voiced claims that the aliens are intensely concerned with humanity's advances in military technology. "It" might even have assumed that the Atlas was being launched in a belligerent move against it. However, this does seem to have been an isolated incident (although there is some evidence to suggest that other such incidents have occurred elsewhere, for example the Ellsworth case, to be discussed later); in which case, one wonders why this particular missile was targeted.

The other possible alternative is that the UFO subjected the missile to some kind of sensor, in an attempt to gain information on the missile's various electrical and mechanical systems. The energy fields generated by this sensor may have proved too powerful for the delicate innards of the Atlas, resulting in serious damage to the missile's guidance system. Of course, this is extreme speculation, and it would doubtless be very helpful if the US Air Force released the results of the investigation it surely conducted into the missile crash. . . .

The Holloman Landing

One of the most impressive military encounters with a UFO and its occupants may not have happened at all. In his 1974 book *UFOs Past Present & Future*, Robert Emenegger includes a most curious chapter entitled "On Being Contacted," which takes as its premise the landing of an alien spacecraft at Holloman Air Force Base, New Mexico—an event that "might happen in the future—or perhaps could have happened already."

The "Holloman scenario" takes place some time in 1964, with the arrival on the base's radar scopes of three unidentified targets. The personnel assume that some kind of secret test is being conducted, perhaps of a prototype lunar module. Radio contact is attempted; the air traffic controller telling the intruders that they are in a restricted air corridor . . . but the craft continue their approach. When visual contact is made, however, the personnel quickly realize that the craft are unlike anything they have ever seen.

As the formation arrives, one of the craft breaks away from the others and hovers about ten feet above the ground for a few moments, before lowering its tripod undercarriage and setting down on the dry desert floor. By chance, two camera crews are working nearby; one in a helicopter on a routine mission, the other photographing a test launch. In all, about 600 feet of 16mm colour film is shot, capturing the disc-shaped UFOs with crystal clarity.

Accompanied by two officers and two Air Force scientists, the base commander approaches to within a discreet distance of the landed UFO, and waits. Presently, a door in the side of the craft slides open and the crew of three disembarks. Slightly shorter than an average human, and dressed in tight-fitting jumpsuits, the beings have blue-grey complexions, wide-set eyes and prominent noses. They also wear strange, rope-like headpieces.

The base commander steps forward to greet the beings, communication is established through "inaudible" means and the visitors are escorted to an "inner office in the King I area."

This, then, is the "Holloman scenario," and had it ended there, it might have become no more than a curious footnote in the history of ufology. However, it is a rumour that has refused to die away, and is still discussed by ufologists today (hence its inclusion in this book).

One possible reason for the rumour's survival is that Robert Emenegger himself submitted the "Holloman scenario" to a number of leading American psychologists, and asked them to comment on the likely outcome of such an event actually happening, and its details being released to the public. The results of this study, which was directed by Dr. Leon Festinger of the School for Social Research at the State University of New York, are presented by Emenegger in his book, but are too lengthy to include here. In short, the general consensus was that those who had believed in the reality of extraterrestrial visitors would, of course, feel vindicated, while those who had always been sceptics would suspect a hoax on the part of the government.

Another interesting aspect of the scenario is related by Jenny

Randles in her 1995 book *UFO Retrievals: The Recovery of Alien Spacecraft.* In a conversation with Dr. J. Allen Hynek, she learned not only of the scenario, but also that there had been an alleged plan to release the film of the UFO landing to the public, via an unnamed film producer. The producer was apparently shown the film by the US Air Force in the early 1970s, and was told that it would form the centrepiece of an "education programme," to be concluded at some point in the future, whereupon the truth of the alien presence would be revealed to the world. But the revelation never occurred: the producer was told that the film footage was a hoax, and that he should "forget all about it."

What is interesting about this story is that it is an obvious precursor of the strange 1983 encounter between Linda Moulton Howe (also a film producer) and Richard Doty, in which Doty promised her several thousand feet of film of the Holloman UFOs and alien beings. Like the unnamed film producer, Howe was ultimately disappointed (as were we all!). Doty subsequently told her that the footage would not be released for "political reasons."

The reason for these disappointments is allegedly that there are two factions within the US military: one wanting to release all UFO-related information to the public, and the other wanting to keep it secret. Apparently, in both cases, the latter faction won the day. The "Holloman scenario" is also representative of another long-lived rumour in ufology: that the time is close at hand when the doors of secrecy will finally be opened, revealing the incredible truth once and for all. Unfortunately, this rumour has been around since the early 1950s, and so seems unlikely to be realized, in spite of the fact that it is as prevalent today as it has ever been.

Phantom Encounter over Iran

As would be expected, encounters between the military and UFOs are usually very carefully reported and documented, and can provide impressive evidence for the researcher who is able to wheedle them out of the governments concerned. One such case, which Timothy Good understandably describes as "sensational," occurred in September 1976, when F-4 Phantom jets of the Imperial Iranian Air Force (IIAF) were scrambled to intercept a large UFO over Tehran. The encounter resulted in a report from the Defense Attaché at the US Embassy in Tehran, to the Defense Intelligence Agency (DIA) in the United States. Timothy Good informs us that the report was also distributed to the White House, the Secretary of State, the National Security Agency (NSA) and the CIA. In his 1996 book *Beyond Top Secret: The Worldwide UFO Security Threat*, Good includes the full text of the report, which I shall précis here.

The drama began at about 12.30 A.M. on 19 September 1976, when several people in the Shemiran area of Tehran telephoned the IIAF and reported unusual objects in the sky, one of which looked like a large bird, and the other like a lighted helicopter, although there were no helicopters in the area at that time. Although the initial explanation given to the citizens by the Assistant Deputy Commander of Operations was that the objects were just stars, he decided to look for himself, and saw a large, star-like object. He then decided to scramble a Phantom from Shahrokhi Air Force Base to investigate.

The jet took off at 1.30 A.M. and had no trouble finding the bright object, which was visible from 70 miles away, hanging in the sky to the north of Tehran. When the Phantom got to within 25 nautical miles of the object, the pilot lost all instrumentation and communication, so he broke off the interception and turned his aircraft back towards his base. When he did this (apparently no longer posing a potential threat to the UFO), he suddenly regained all his electrical systems.

At 1.40 A.M. a second Phantom was launched, and quickly acquired a radar lock on at 27 nautical miles, with a rate of closure of 150 nautical m.p.h. But when the Phantom got to within 25 nautical miles, the UFO manoeuvred to maintain that distance between it and the jet.

Although the visual size of the UFO was difficult to ascertain, owing to its brilliance, the radar return was comparable to that of a 707 airtanker. The flashing, strobe-like lights were arranged in a rectangular pattern, and alternated from blue to green to red to orange, at a speed sufficient for them all to be seen at once.

At this point, the UFO disgorged a smaller object, which headed directly for the Phantom at high speed. The pilot immediately attempted to fire an AIM-9 missile, but his weapons control panel and communications failed before he could do so. Having thus lost all defensive capabilities, the pilot threw his plane into a negative-g dive. The object trailed him before returning to its parent UFO for a "perfect rejoin."

Moments later, another small object emerged from the other side of the large UFO, and descended rapidly towards the ground. The Phantom crew, who by this time had regained their weapons instrumentation, expected it to crash, but it alighted gently, casting a bright light over an area of approximately two to three kilometres. After marking the object's position, the Phantom returned to base, but had difficulty landing owing to the brightness of the objects, which had undermined the pilot's night vision.

The Phantom continued to have considerable trouble with its communications system, a problem that was also reported by the crew of a civil airliner that was also in the vicinity (this crew, however, did not report any unusual sights). As the Phantom began its final approach, the crew saw another cylinder-shaped object with bright lights at each end and a "flasher" in the middle.

During daylight on 19 September, the Phantom crew was taken by helicopter to the site of the UFO landing, a dry lake bed. Although they could see nothing unusual, they did pick up a "very noticeable beeper signal," and found a small house at the point where they received the loudest return. They took the helicopter down and asked the occupants of the house if they had seen anything strange the night before. The people reported a very loud noise and a bright light like lightning.

Both the aircraft and the area of the UFO landing were

checked for radiation, although no results were given in the report, which concluded:

> (C) Actual information contained in this report was obtained from source in conversation with a sub-source, and IIAF pilot of one of the F-4s. More information will be forwarded when it becomes available.

Timothy Good informs us that the report, which was released to Charles Huffer in 1977 (after an initial refusal), also contained a DIA Defense Information Report Evaluation, a "rarity among documents released by the Agency." The Evaluation concludes:

> An outstanding report. This case is a classic which meets all the criteria necessary for a valid study of the UFO phenomenon:
> a) The object was seen by multiple witnesses from different locations (i.e. Shamiran, Mehrabad [airport], and the dry lake bed) and view points (both airborne and from the ground).
> b) The credibility of many of the witnesses was high (an Air Force general, qualified aircrews, and experienced tower operators).
> c) Visual sightings were confirmed by radar.
> d) Similar electromagnetic effects (EME) were reported by three separate aircraft.
> e) There were physiological effects on some crew members (i.e. loss of night vision due to brightness of the object).
> f) An inordinate amount of maneuverability was displayed by the UFOs.

Subsequent information revealed that just after they had attempted to fire the AIM-9 missile, the Phantom crew had attempted to eject, but were prevented by the malfunctioning of the eject buttons. In addition, 25 minutes after the encounter with the Phantoms, the UFO was seen by the pilot of an Egyptian Air Force jet over the Mediterranean Sea, and also by the crew and passengers of a KLM flight near Lisbon. According to

Good, Ron Regehr of the US Defense Support Programme (DSP) revealed that a "DSP (nuclear event monitoring) satellite picked up signals from an 'unidentifiable technology' over Iran on the night in question."

An Alien Intrusion at Ellsworth AFB?

An extremely unusual event (even by ufological standards!) allegedly occurred at about 9.30 P.M. on 16 November 1977, at Ellsworth Air Force Base in South Dakota. The case was researched by the redoubtable Linda Moulton Howe, and presented in her 1989 book *An Alien Harvest*.

According to Howe, the story began when a saucer-shaped object landed just outside the fence around a missile silo on the base. An "inner zone alert" was triggered inside the silo, whose concrete cap, weighing 150 tons, was closed. Two security personnel were dispatched to investigate, and drove out to "Site #L–9," where they saw a bright light shining upwards from behind a small hill about 50 yards beyond the fence line. One of the men, whose name was Jenkins, stayed with their vehicle while the other, Raeke, proceeded towards the hill to investigate the source of the light.

As Raeke approached the hill, he was confronted by "an individual dressed in a glowing green metallic uniform and wearing a helmet with visor." The individual walked towards the fence, ignoring Raeke's challenge. When Raeke raised his M-16 rifle and again gave the order to stop, the individual pointed an instrument at him and fired a bright flash of light, which instantly disintegrated the rifle and inflicted second and third degree burns to Raeke's hands.

After rapidly retreating, Raeke radioed Jenkins, who in turn radioed the situation to "Lima control." Jenkins then went to his colleague and managed to carry him back to their vehicle, before spotting two individuals walking *through* the fence around the silo. After challenging the intruders, Jenkins fired two rounds from his M-16; the bullets struck one intruder in the back, and the other in the helmet, felling them both.

Presently, however, both intruders stood up, apparently unharmed, and began firing their own weapons at Jenkins' position. They then fell back behind the hill. When Jenkins followed, he observed them entering a saucer-shaped object about 20 feet in diameter. The craft then began to glow with a greenish light, before ascending and disappearing over the eastern horizon.

After the craft had departed, Site Survey Teams were dispatched to the site and took radiation readings, recording levels between 1.7 to 2.9 roentgens. Maintenance teams also examined the missile and warhead, and discovered that several nuclear components had been removed.

As with the Atlas missile incident at Vandenberg AFB described earlier, if the Ellsworth incident really did occur, then it indicates the two possibilities also discussed with regard to Vandenberg: either the Ellsworth intruders recognized the missile as a potential threat, or they were curious as to its construction and operation, to the extent that they helped themselves to several vital components. Of course, there is a rather unsettling aspect to the Ellsworth incident, in that the intruders were quite prepared to use apparently lethal force against the human witnesses.

8

Alien Underground

Area 51/S-4

In recent years, stories of underground bases operated by both humans and aliens have not only come under the spotlight in the arcane field of ufology but also (thanks to Area 51) have received greater exposure to the general public. This was consolidated in 1996 with the release of the science fiction adventure *Independence Day*, although the top secret base in that film shared little more than its name with the real Area 51. Notwithstanding the possibility that there may indeed be alien-controlled bases throughout the world, it is not always fully appreciated that the very concept itself has a rich provenance in human mythology. Certain Native American peoples, for instance, believe that the human race was born inside the earth, and found its way to the surface through caves that are still considered to be sacred places. The notion of an "underworld," populated by non-human intelligences, forms a hugely important part of myth-systems from Classical Greece to Christianity, and on through the Theosophy of Madame Blavatsky, with its legends of the subterranean kingdom of Agharti, to the present fascination with underground alien bases. It is well beyond the scope of the present book to examine the development of the subterranean myth in any detail, so let us look at the "underworld" in the modern, technological context of the UFO phenomenon.

As mentioned above, by far the most famous of these bases is Area 51, which is located in Groom Lake, a dry lake bed about 120 miles north-west of Las Vegas, Nevada. Area 51 is something of a Mecca for aviation enthusiasts anxious to catch a glimpse of the sophisticated new aircraft that are undoubtedly being tested there. However, it is also the subject of intense fascination for those interested in UFOs, since countless strange aerial objects have been sighted in the vicinity, performing manoeuvres that seem to defy the laws of physics (not to mention the physiology of their pilots!).

The general consensus among ufologists is that Area 51 and its companion site, known as S-4, are home to both captured alien spacecraft and human-built craft based on reverse-engineered extraterrestrial technology. One of the main reasons for these suspicions is the intense secrecy surrounding the sites. For instance, Groom Lake officially does not exist; it is not listed on Federal Aviation Administration pilots' charts, and cannot be found on any US Geological Survey map. This does not stop at least ten Boeing 737 aircraft from busing workers and supplies into the area every day.

Groom Lake has always been shrouded in secrecy, ever since its construction in 1954, with the purpose of developing the U-2 spyplane. Its location in the remote Emigrant Valley was ideal for the test flights of the U-2; so much so that it was also the home of the U-2's replacement, the SR-71 Blackbird. In the late 1970s and early 1980s, Groom Lake was where the US Air Force built and tested the B-2 Stealth Bomber and F-117A Nighthawk fighter.

In 1984, the Pentagon applied to seize 89,000 acres of public land in Nevada, in order to banish the prying eyes of enthusiasts. When it was subsequently found that there were still three good vantage-points from which to view the facility, the Pentagon made a further application to seize an additional 4,000 acres which, like the earlier application, was quickly approved by Congress, in spite of vigorous public opposition.

According to one Congressional source, who was able to visit Groom Lake thanks to his high level of security clearance, a "mysterious technology" is under development there, one that is "not part of the official programme of the US Government."

Of course, the events described above are entirely understand-able in a top secret research and development facility. Many ufol-ogists point to the roving security teams and military helicopters that spy on sightseers as implying something deeply sinister. However, this activity would surely be expected at any military fa-cility. For that matter, anyone snooping around any half decent *hotel* should expect to be challenged by security sooner or later.

Nevertheless, there is still the problem of the numerous UFO sightings in the area, not to mention the testimony of the now world-famous Robert Lazar, who claims to have worked under contract at S-4 between 1987 and 1989. During that time, Lazar allegedly worked on at least one intact flying disc, and saw eight others, in various states of disrepair.

Lazar's story is at once astonishing and, in parts, utterly ab-surd, as Jacques Vallée points out in his book *Revelations: Alien Contact and Human Deception*. In an interview with Vallée, Lazar claimed that he was put to work on reverse- engineering the propulsion system of a flying disc; the only equipment he had to help him in this monumental endeavour was a digital voltmeter and an oscilloscope. Elsewhere, Lazar has alleged that a team of scientists was attempting to figure out how an antimatter reactor worked. Their solution: cut the thing open while it was up and running! The resulting explosion vaporized the scientists and obliterated several blast doors.

According to Lazar, the alien ships are powered by a transuranic element not found on Earth. In fact, he was even able to smuggle a sample of "Element 115" out of the facility and test it at his house (which, with its home-made particle accelerator, seems to have been rather better equipped than S-4). Interestingly, Lazar seems to know what he is talking about when describing the nature of Element 115. When Vallée mentioned that he didn't think super-heavy elements were stable, Lazar replied that there is a "zone of stability for higher numbers, above 110." This is in line with current theories on atomic physics, which indeed state that higher elements are expected to be relatively stable.

Unfortunately, Robert Lazar's credibility has been called into question in many other areas, notably his qualifications in the field of nuclear physics, and his claim to have been a consultant to the National Research Laboratory at Los Alamos. And yet he remains adamant that he worked on alien spacecraft at S-4, and his claims have been backed up by a host of other whistle-blowers, who have come forward with strange and disturbing information regarding the activities of the aliens in our midst. As we delve deeper into the subject of secret bases, we shall see that Area 51 and S-4 are among the least bizarre of these shadowy and mysterious facilities.

The Dulce Base

Perhaps the most outspoken writer on the subject of underground alien bases is a "former military intelligence operative" who calls himself Commander X. He has produced several books dealing with the alien presence on Earth which, regardless of their veracity, are a treat for anyone interested in Fortean subjects, not least because of their strange, stream-of-consciousness composition. The information he presents is worth considering because in many ways it is a distillation of both research and rumour, and as such represents the current state of the "subterranean legend."

Another well-known site of alleged alien activity is the base said to exist near the small New Mexico town of Dulce. It is here that the nefarious Grey aliens have ensconced themselves, since their secret treaty with the US Government, in which they were given permission to abduct humans and mutilate cattle in exchange for selected items of their own technology. In a bizarre twist to the "alien presence" scenario, the Greys are apparently native to the Earth, having descended from a reptilian species which cross-bred with early humans in the distant past. They are "Mercenary Agents" for these reptilians, known as the "DRACO," who are returning to the Earth inside a gigantic planetoid-starship. According to some of the more extreme ufologists, the unidentified object said to be accompanying comet Hale-Bopp on its journey towards the inner solar system is none other than the DRACO ship.

The primary function of the Dulce Base is said to be that of a genetic engineering laboratory, in which the hapless victims of alien abduction are experimented upon in a variety of hideous ways. For some reason which is not readily apparent, the Greys are fond of cross-breeding humans with various animals. People who claim to have worked there tell awful stories of beings that are half human and half octopus, half bat, or half reptile.

Other experiments centre on attempts to remove the soul from the body, and re-implant it elsewhere. These programmes are directed by the Defense Advanced Research Projects Agency (DARPA), and related projects are conducted by the "Jason Society," a group of elite scientists, working at the Sandia National Laboratories in Albuquerque, New Mexico.

One of the most appalling programmes under development at the Dulce Base involves "Disposable Biology": genetically engineered humanoid beings, created to provide a slave labour force "to do dangerous Atomic (Plutonium) Rocket and Saucer experiments." According to Commander X, the US Government has been doing its own share of impregnating human females, and removing the foetuses to produce "hybrid" beings. The results of these experiments receive brain implants which enable them to be controlled via radio frequency transmissions.

Human abductees are also implanted with "Brain Transceivers," which allow telepathic control and manipulation of thoughts and even memories. By these means, the people who are unfortunate enough to be implanted can be made to feel nausea, irritability, fatigue or even the sensation of death. Commander X tells us that this is basically the same thing as the deleterious ray described by Richard Shaver in his tales of the malignant Deros, who live far underground in vast cavern systems. (This is a further illustration of the immense influence that the so-called "Shaver Mystery" has had over UFO conspiracy theory.)

The base itself is said to be composed of a central hub, surrounded by many levels, which sounds suspiciously like the "Wildfire" facility in Michael Crichton's *The Andromeda Strain*. The complex can be reached through more than 100 hidden entrances, located at various points around the town of Dulce and the nearby Archuleta Mesa. The deeper levels of the base feed into huge natural cavern systems. According to one (naturally) unnamed source who had worked there, most of the aliens are on Levels Five, Six and Seven; "alien housing" is on Level Five. There are apparently more than 18,000 aliens living and working in the Dulce Base.

In 1979 (other sources give different dates), there was a serious confrontation at the base, between the aliens and the human personnel. Sixty-six humans were killed, apparently because they insisted on carrying loaded weapons through a certain force field, which caused the bullets to explode.

One of the most notable features of bases like Dulce and Area 51 is their size: the Dulce Base is supposed to be the size of Manhattan. And yet, here we run into another absurdity (as if we had not met enough already). When Jacques Vallée was first told of the New Mexico facility and its colossal size, he asked: "Who takes out the garbage?" This may sound like a rather facetious question, but it is a fair one. A base the size of Manhattan would produce an enormous amount of waste, which would have to be disposed of unobtrusively somehow. In addition, its heat signature would stick out like a sore thumb on any satellite imagery, including that of the old LANDSATS, which are available to universities all over the world. In short, it is unlikely that the Dulce Base exists; at the very least, it is certainly not the size of Manhattan.

The Superstition Mountains

The American south-west is home to numerous rumours and tales of subterranean realms, and their frequently unfriendly denizens. Although they are not always directly connected to the UFO phenomenon, belonging more to an occult tradition, they are frequently cited in books ostensibly dealing with UFOs and alien contact. This is indicative of one of the more curious current trends in ufology, which seems to be the drawing together of what hitherto had been a purely scientific mystery and a concept that is more at home in mythology and esoteric occultism.

Thus we have the Superstition Mountains in Arizona, which are shunned by those who know what lies beneath them. According to Commander X in his 1990 book *Underground Alien Bases*, several individuals have spoken of their experiences during ill-advised excursions in the Superstition Mountains. Two of them have gone insane, while the others "have either had nervous breakdowns or have vanished from their hometowns in order to go into seclusion." However, one brave man named Brian Scott came forward to tell his amazing story, involving hostile ufonauts, a domestic haunting, spontaneous combustion and demonic possession.

In 1971, Scott was vacationing in the Superstition Mountains when he was suddenly teleported on to a UFO, which was underground, and disrobed by several seven-foot-tall creatures. He described their skin as being "a cross between an elephant, rhinoceros and crocodile. [Their] ears would start at the top of their head and run all the way down the whole side of their face." Their breath reminded him of "dirty socks."

These rather unsavoury creatures used a box-like instrument to take X-ray pictures of their captive, who began to experience an unbearably intense headache, "like 10,000 migraine headaches all clumped into one." Paradoxically, this terrifying encounter resulted in Scott's brain "functioning much faster than usual"; he also seems to have been given a talent for drawing, and currently works as a draftsman.

After his encounter, Scott's home was invaded on several occasions by strange lights, and at one point he disappeared while inside the house, terrifying his wife, who called the police. He was found several hours later, wandering around his back yard in a daze.

Some time in the early 1970s a teenage boy who worked on a ranch in the area became separated from the rest of the round-up crew and wandered around the mountains for several days. During this time, he slipped into a "twilight between consciousness and unconsciousness." While in this altered state, he became aware of several small "men" who seemed anxious to help him, giving him directions on how to get back to the ranch. Eventually, he found himself in Gobe, Arizona, 50 miles from where he had become lost.

Mount Shasta

While most entities encountered underground are ambivalent at best and downright evil at worst, those said to live beneath Mount Shasta in northern California are definitely benevolent. In the vast caverns beneath this mountain, it is claimed, are a large number of UFOs, huge motherships and a crystal the size of a skyscraper.

Mount Shasta seems to constitute an extension of the myth of Agharti, the vast kingdom said to exist on the inner surface of a hollow Earth. It also represents the current revival of interest in the "Space Brothers," the benevolent, entirely human-looking aliens who are apparently working toward the salvation of earthlings and the saving of our planet. Consequently, the mountain has become a popular meeting place for those interested in New Age subjects, and has become home to several so-called "channelers," people who claim to be in contact through telepathic means with alien entities.

According to Commander X's sources, the city beneath Mount Shasta was built in the distant past by the Lemurians, that fabled race of superhumans whose Pacific continent suffered a similar fate to Atlantis. In fact, the Lemurians can still be seen in the area from time to time. Commander X offers us the apparently deadpan assertion that the Lemurians "can be recognized due to the fact that they are quite tall—in the eight and nine foot range." (Easy to recognize, indeed.)

Unlike most other subterranean realms, Mount Shasta benefits from a "highly charged aura" which keeps the forces of evil at bay. Like the denizens of Agharti, who use arcane methods to influence the course of events on the Earth's surface, the "Lemurians, Space Brothers and elementals" beneath Mount Shasta work in secrecy to ensure the future of the planet.

In 1977 the highly respected UFO researcher William F. Hamilton III met a beautiful young woman who claimed to be a resident of a golden city, called Telos, lying a mile beneath Mount Shasta. The girl, who called herself "Bonnie," described how the Lemurians and Atlanteans had fled underground from the catastrophes that destroyed their homelands, building huge cities within natural cavern systems and connecting them with a worldwide network of tunnels. Through this network, electromagnetic tube trains hurtle at speeds of up to 2,500 miles per hour.

Telos is a utopian society, once again along the lines of Agharti and its capital, Shambhala, in which food and resources are distributed freely among the population of one and a half million, in a "no-money economy." "Bonnie" informed Hamilton that certain cataclysms will bring about an alteration in the Earth's axis at the end of the century (a familiar millennial warning), after which "the survivors will build a new world free of worry, poverty, disease and exploitation."

In *Underground Alien Bases*, Commander X includes an interview conducted by Hamilton with "Bonnie," in which she describes the origin and nature of the subterranean realm. The Lemurians originally came from the planet Aurora, but their tenure on the Earth's surface (in the northern land known as Hyperborea) was interrupted by the Sun, which began to give off dangerous radiation. Some of these people fled to the interior of the planet, while many remained on the surface. The latter group "degenerated," presumably a process that led, ultimately, to humanity in its present form.

About 25,000 years ago, Atlantis seceded from its motherland, Mu, igniting a war which eventually destroyed the continent. Meanwhile, the Lemurians "developed into the Uighers, the Naga-Mayas, and the Quetzalcoatls," and many migrated to

North America and Scandinavia, while others went to Central and South America. According to "Bonnie," the Toltec civilizer-god, Quetzalcoatl, was actually a Venusian, while Viracocha, the "bearded stranger" who brought so much valuable knowledge to the Incas, was a Lemurian High Priest.

Atlantis met its fate as a result of unbridled scientific experimentation, especially with "monster crystals" which drew power from the Earth's atmosphere, and which generated energy which was beyond the scientists' ability to control. However, this power also drives the propulsion systems of the flying discs, which are based on "Ion-Mercury" engines. These ships can travel at many times the speed of light, reaching the far corners of the Universe through hyperspace. According to "Bonnie," there are many advanced intelligences near the "centre of the Universe," which she calls the "seat of God."

Brown Mountain

For hundreds of years, Brown Mountain in North Carolina has been the centre of much anomalous activity, mainly in the form of strange lights that flit through the air before plunging into the ground. As might be expected, the lights have given rise to numerous legends, one of which involves a battle fought between the Cherokee and Catawha tribes several centuries ago. It is said that the lights are actually the spirits of the braves from both tribes, which are wandering through the valley in search of their maiden brides.

Several residents in the area have taken an intense interest in the lights. Paul Rose, for instance, had his first encounter with them when he was a youngster way back in 1916. He believes that they are intelligently controlled, and probably radioactive. He bases this conclusion on an encounter that occurred one night in the late 1950s, when two of the lights approached a tower he had constructed for the purpose of observing them. The following day, he became extremely ill.

Ralph Lael, who ran for Congress in 1948 and now runs the Outer Space Rock Shop Museum near the town of Morganton, claims to have established communication with the lights. After several months of experimentation, Lael discovered that the lights would answer questions by moving up and down for "yes," and back and forth for "no." Eventually, the lights led Lael to a door leading to the interior of Brown Mountain.

Lael followed the lights to a room lined with a crystal-like substance, and heard a voice, which said, "Do not fear; there is no danger here." The voice then told him that the human race had been created on another planet, called Pewam. At some point in the past, our ancestors destroyed Pewam, reducing it to the rubble that now orbits the Sun between Mars and Jupiter. The light-beings claimed to live on Venus, "which is a planet of pure crystal" drawing sustenance from a gas called Pethine, which they absorbed from light.

In October 1962, Lael accepted the offer of a ride to Venus in a flying saucer, where he met the direct descendants of Pewam, including a beautiful woman named Noma, who was rather fetchingly attired in a matching bra and panties! While on Venus, he was shown images of the destruction of Pewam, followed by that of another Earth-like planet. This was apparently to illustrate the fact that there were certain "forces" watching the Earth, who would decide whether or not to eradicate our world. Lael was also entrusted with the preserved body of a tiny humanoid creature from a distant planet, which he kept in a glass case at the rear of his Rock Shop.

Lael's story, with its gentle Venusians, beautiful, scantily-clad alien women and warnings to the people of the Earth, is pure contactee material; and it is easy to see why ufologists in the 1950s and 1960s treated such claims with contempt. To be sure, serious researchers are still rather embarrassed by them today, and yet the entirely human-looking "alien" is making a strong comeback. Modern abductees frequently claim contact with such "Nordic" beings in the course of their involuntary adventures. Perhaps the image of the nefarious, all-powerful Greys is so unsettling that another force, for good, is required to balance the presence of a sinister and implacable enemy.

A Lost City beneath Death Valley?

Death Valley, California, is one of the most hostile regions on Earth, and yet far beneath the parched, heat-blasted landscape lies a vast network of tunnels and chambers containing treasures that would make any explorers unimaginably rich . . . if they could stay alive long enough to find the hidden entrances.

An intriguing tale about what lies there is told in an obscure book entitled *Death Valley Men*, in which two old prospectors of the 1920s, Bill Cocoran and Jack Stewart, describe an accidental excursion into this strange underground complex, made by three strangers who spent a few days with them, owing to trouble with their car.

One of the prospectors had been working in an abandoned mine shaft in the Panamint Mountains, when the bottom of the shaft collapsed, and he plunged into a tunnel. The prospector explored the tunnel later with his colleagues, and they found that it led into a huge underground city, with palaces, chambers and galleries. Some of the galleries ran alongside enormous window-like openings, from which the prospectors could look down on Death Valley itself. The prospectors came to the conclusion that the ancient people who built the city once moored their boats by the windows, which originally overlooked a prehistoric lake.

Throughout the city the explorers discovered gold and jewels, a treasure house beyond their wildest fantasies. In one enormous room, they found 100 men, dead and mummified, some of whom were sitting around a polished table, inlaid with precious gems. At one end of the room was a statue of the man sitting at the head of the table; it was solid gold, and stood nearly 90 feet tall.

The prospectors informed several academics of their find,

and an expedition into the Panamint Mountains was mounted. According to prospector Fred Thomason:

> ...we brought out more treasure and buried it close to the shaft entrance to the underground city before we went back to the Coast. I persuaded some university officials and some experts from the Southwest Museum to come out here with me. We got up on the Panamints and I could not find the shaft. A cloudburst had changed all the country around the shaft. We were out of luck.... The scientists became unreasonably angry with us. They've done everything they can to discredit us ever since.

Before the prospectors left the home of Cocoran and Stewart, they said that the windows overlooking Death Valley remained, a means of entrance into the underground city. All an explorer would have to do would be to climb roughly 5,000 feet up the side of the mountains along the west side of the valley. The prospectors said that this was precisely their intention: "We're going to take out enough gold to finance ourselves, and we'll open that city as a curiosity of the world."

Of course, this never happened, and the three prospectors were never seen nor heard of again. Perhaps this entire story is spurious; there never *were* any prospectors, and there is no lost city beneath Death Valley. On the other hand, if anyone reading this has the bright idea of searching for those peculiar "windows" in the mountainsides, they would perhaps do better to confine their explorations to their armchairs: Death Valley may only be dead on the surface....

UFO Bases in Canada

According to Commander X, "you'll find any number of UFO bases scattered throughout Canada," particularly underneath Toronto. In 1979, a man named "Ernest" accidentally discovered an entrance to an underground cavern system, while looking for a lost kitten on Parliament Street in the downtown area of the city. Having squeezed through the entrance into a dark cave, he encountered a three-foot-tall monkey-like creature with glowing orange-red eyes, which hissed at him: "Go away, go away." He promptly did so.

Some researchers believe that Toronto lies on top of an eons-old city, built by the "El race," and containing a huge array of instruments and machines, many of which are still in working order. The centre of the city lies beneath the junction of Gerrard Street and Church Street, the magnetic machinery apparently accounting for the above-average traffic accident rate there. A few years ago, the city was occupied by the villainous Deros, the highly malignant, dwarf-like creatures described by Richard Shaver in his rather dubious chronicles of Lemuria, first published in Ray Palmer's *Amazing Stories* magazine in the 1940s. Before they were forced out of the city by "positive Inner Earth Beings," the Deros were occasionally spotted on the streets of Toronto at night. Canadian researcher Ivan Boyes claims to have encountered one at 4.00 A.M., and describes it as having "no face except for eyes and two holes in his blank face for a nose...no mouth at all."

There is an old mine in Newfoundland Province that allegedly contains the entrance to another subterranean city complex. While the mine was in operation, many strange noises, like distant music, were heard. At other times, mumbling voices would drift through the galleries around the miners. One night, a miner was checking on some equipment, when he was jumped by several "small men," who pointed some form of instrument at him and rendered him unconscious. He was discovered the following morning and, although physically unharmed, he refused to set foot in the mine again, and soon left his job. Not long after this event, another miner who went underground alone disappeared. His lamp and helmet were discovered, but he was never seen again. Eventually, the remaining men became so unnerved by working in the mine that it was "condemned" and closed down.

Many years later, three amateur cavers, Arnold White, Rick Grayton and Don Lawrence, became interested in the abandoned mine and its sinister history. Their first expedition had to be aborted when two policemen threatened to arrest them if they entered the mine. However, they returned in the early hours of the following morning, approaching from a different direction, and found their way in.

Almost immediately, they heard a voice, apparently coming from far off in the mine, shout "Come!" This was followed by sounds of running, and although the three explorers searched the tunnel ahead with their flashlights, they could see no one. Making their way further into the mine, they gradually became aware of a blue light ahead, followed by the sound of a metal door closing. When they arrived at the place from which the light had seemed to radiate, they could find nothing. However, when they tapped the walls of the tunnel with their pick-hammers, they were rewarded with metallic clangs. After marking the place by chipping off several pieces of rock, they returned to the surface.

When they returned the following evening with more appropriate equipment, they discovered that the chipped rock of the tunnel wall had mysteriously been repaired. Undaunted, they used a battery-powered rock drill to reach the metal door that lay beyond. Using a different drill bit, they then penetrated the metal door. A blue light shone through the hole.

At that point, they heard a sound of moving machinery, and the section of wall on which they were working slid up out of sight, revealing a five-foot high corridor extending into the blue-lit distance. Finally overcoming their quite considerable apprehension, the three men entered the corridor, which seemed to be constructed of a seamless, plastic-like material. After some time, they came to a spiral staircase leading even further into the ground. They descended and found themselves in another corridor, this one pale green in colour.

Further exploration revealed a large chamber, filled with all manner of electronic equipment. At the far end lay a platform on which rested a disc-shaped object that the men took to be a UFO. Suddenly, the pale light in the chamber changed to a deep red, and one of the many monitor screens lining the walls flickered to life. Although they could not quite make out the shadowy image on the screen, they heard a high-pitched voice addressing them from the screen. As it was speaking, Don Lawrence managed to write down its message to them:

> You have been expected. You have been observed since first you entered our domain. You gaze upon the upper regions of our world. You are the first of your kind to be permitted this privilege. Let it be known this truth—we harbour you no ill will; we depend not upon your superficial world for our sustenance or pleasure. Those of your kind who make themselves the interpreters of our intentions are naught but the picayunish deceivers of your civilization. Let it again be said that we desire man no harm and wish only to pursue our independent existence on this, our mutual planet. We shall not influence nor bring to you discord in any medium. We are not doers of evil. Our world spans the inner gulf of your globe; we have existed since before your time. Had we wished harm upon you we would also have been its receivers. We beg you a friendly farewell and hope our message will be heeded and find wide acceptance among those of your kind who find it necessary to concern themselves with our domain.

As the screen faded, the three men suddenly felt light-headed, and then lost consciousness. When they came to, they found themselves outside the mine entrance, minus their caving equipment, but with their notebooks, wallets and so on intact. Several weeks after their strange adventure, the men discovered that the radium on their wristwatch dials had been affected, and no longer glowed in the dark.

9

Harassment of UFO Witnesses

The Mysterious Men In Black

The reader will doubtless appreciate, especially after reading the preceding chapter, that the world of ufology can be a place where fact and fiction blend into a complex and confusing unity, becoming a mystery that demands to be considered in an artistic as much as a scientific context. Indeed, UFOs are capable of casting a long shadow over those humans who are fortunate—or unfortunate—enough to come into contact with them; and the things that move within that shadow are not always amenable to explanation in terms that make sense to the late-twentieth-century mind.

Among the strangest of entities associated with UFO encounters are the Men in Black (MIBs), who have been reported on many occasions to visit witnesses soon after an encounter, claiming to be connected with either the government, military or UFO investigation groups in some way. Their identification, when shown, is always subsequently found to be false, as are the registration numbers on their immaculate, but out-of-date, black cars.

For one of the best examples of an MIB encounter, we can look to psychiatrist Berthold Schwarz, who discusses the strange case of Dr. Herbert Hopkins in his 1988 book *UFO Dynamics: Psychiatric and Psychic Aspects of the UFO Syndrome*. Dr. Hopkins had been engaged in investigating an alleged UFO encounter experienced by a man named David Stephens, through the use of regressive hypnosis.

On the evening of 11 September 1976, Dr. Hopkins's wife and son went out to see a movie, leaving him alone in their house in Orchard Beach, Maine. He received a telephone call from a man claiming to be a member of a UFO organization based in New Jersey, who asked if he might talk to Hopkins about the Stephens case. Hopkins agreed and invited him to the house.

Hardly had the physician replaced the receiver, when the caller presented himself at the front door. He was completely bald, and dressed in an immaculate black suit, black tie and white shirt. Apart from this, however, his pretence at normality was less of a success: he had no eyebrows or eyelashes, and when he later rubbed his mouth, it became evident that he was wearing red lipstick. The strange visitor walked stiffly and then sat perfectly still, like an automaton. He began to ask Hopkins various questions about the case, in the expressionless monotone used by most MIBs.

Presently, the man said that Hopkins had some coins in his pocket, and asked him to take one out. Hopkins held the coin in the palm of his hand. As he watched in amazement, its colour changed from bright silver to light blue, and it began to grow blurred to his vision. It then "became vaporous and gradually faded away." Hopkins told the man that he was impressed, and asked him to make the coin reappear. The man refused, saying, "Neither you nor anyone else on this plane will ever see that coin again."

He then asked Hopkins if he knew how Barney Hill had died. Hopkins replied that, as far as he could remember, Hill had died of a stroke. The man said: "No, Barney died because he had no heart, just as you no longer have your coin." Having made this bizarre and disturbing statement, the MIB told Hopkins to destroy all materials relating to the Stephens case.

Dr. Hopkins's encounter took yet another weird turn when his visitor said, with apparent difficulty, "My energy is running low...must go now...goodbye." He left, walking unsteadily around the corner of the house. As soon as the MIB was out of sight, Hopkins saw a blue-white light shining on the driveway. He searched for the MIB, but could find no trace of him.

When Hopkins's wife and son returned from the cinema, they found him in an extremely agitated state, sitting at the kitchen table with a gun, and with all the lights in the house switched on.

As it happens, Dr. Hopkins had been correct regarding Barney Hill's death: it had had nothing to do with his heart; and yet, as Richard L. Thompson tells us in his 1993 book *Alien Identities*, the MIB's threat had the desired effect, since Hopkins subsequently destroyed all his data on the Stephens case.

In his 1986 book *Visions, Apparitions, Alien Visitors*, Hilary Evans relates another curious story of the MIBs. In 1967 a man named Robert Richardson from Toledo, Ohio, was driving in his car when he collided with a landed UFO. When he later returned to the scene, he found a piece of metal lying on the road, which he collected and subsequently sent to a UFO investigation group.

On 16 July 1967, Richardson was visited by two MIBs, who questioned him about his encounter for about ten minutes. They had arrived in a black 1953 Cadillac which, despite being 14 years old, was in immaculate condition. Richardson wrote down the registration number of the car, and when he later checked it, he found that it had never been issued. In addition, Richardson said that it did not occur to him to check his visitors' identification. This is yet another interesting aspect of alleged encounters with MIBs, during which the percipients are rarely struck *at the time* by the unusual behaviour or lack of identification of their guests, who are frequently described as looking slightly Asian, or with olive complexions. Only later do they realize that all was not well, and that they had been talking to people who did not quite seem to be entirely human.

One week after Richardson's encounter with the MIBs, two different men called on him, again wearing black suits. After attempting to cajole Richardson into admitting that he had not had a UFO encounter, they asked him for the piece of metal he had picked up on the road. When he replied that he had sent it to a UFO organization, the MIBs said that he had better get it back, if he wanted his wife to stay as pretty as she was. This is a classic piece of heavy-handed B-movie dialogue, of which the MIBs seem to be inordinately fond.

There is something ghostly and folkloric about these bizarre personages: although they appear to be subtly non-human, they are almost certainly not "alien in the extraterrestrial sense. They seem to have more in common with the traditional spectre than the modern spaceman. Indeed, one of the theories put forward to explain the appearance of apparitions in "haunted houses" is that they are a kind of psychic recording of previous events and emotions, which are stored in the fabric of a building or other geographical location, and periodically "played back" through processes that are ill-understood. Anyone remotely acquainted with American history will be aware of the nightmare of paranoia that gripped the country in the 1950s, in which many suspected communists were ruined by means of highly publicized but frequently unfounded allegations. It may not be stretching the bounds of possibility too much to suggest that the trauma of these times could be described as the national equivalent of the past traumas said to result in more traditional hauntings. The subtle paranoia induced in percipients after a visit from the MIBs (such as Hopkins clutching his loaded gun) might well be a kind of psychic echo of the wider spread paranoia of the 1950s. This would explain not only the spectre-like quality of the MIBs, but also the fact that their B-movie gangster threats are never followed through.

Unmarked Helicopters

Although widely documented, visits by Men in Black are still rare. Altogether more common, and apparently on the increase, are the unmarked helicopters that are said to harass both UFO witnesses and ranchers whose animals have been killed by unknown predators. Typically, they are described as being similar, if not identical, to identifiable machines such as Bells, Hueys or Chinooks, although they carry no registration marks or other insignia (an offence under US Federal Aviation Authority regulations), and sometimes sport extremely unusual paint-jobs.

An early sighting, which is similar to the Cash-Landrum case described earlier, is recounted by John Keel in his 1970 book *UFOs: Operation Trojan Horse*. On 11 October 1966, a brilliantly-lit object was sighted over the Wanaque Reservoir in New Jersey. Among the numerous witnesses was police sergeant Ben Thompson, who told Dr. Berthold Schwarz: "This thing was so bright that it blinded me so bad I couldn't find my car. It was all white, like looking into a bulb and trying to see the socket, which you can't do." Sergeant Thompson was blinded by the light for "about 20 minutes."

About 15 minutes after the UFO had left the area, a formation of seven helicopters arrived and circled the area, accompanied by about 12 jet aircraft. The event was witnessed by dozens of people, who had parked their cars around the reservoir. The sighting was later investigated by science writer Lloyd Mallan, who made extensive enquiries in an attempt to track down the origin of the military aircraft. He checked with all Air Force bases in the area, as well as with the Pentagon. All denied knowledge of the event.

Keel also quotes a report in *Newsweek*, of 1 July 1968, written by the magazine's Vietnam correspondent, Robert Stokes, which describes military action against an unidentified helicopter:

It was 11 P.M. and US Army Captain William Bates sat in front of a radio set at his regimental headquarters at Dong Ha. Just then, a Marine forward observer came on the air reporting that he had spotted, through his electronic telescope, thirteen sets of yellowish-white lights moving westerly at an altitude of between 500 and 1,000 feet over the Ben Hai River which runs through the middle of the DMZ [Demilitarized Zone]. Bates immediately checked with authorities at Dong Ha to see whether there were any friendly aircraft in the area of the reported sightings. He was told there were not. Then he checked with the counterbattery radar unit at Alpha 2, the northernmost allied outpost in I Corps. Within minutes, the answer came back from Alpha 2's radar tracker: The "blips" were all around him, 360 degrees.

By 1 A.M., US Air Force and Marine jets were scrambling at Da Nang in pursuit of the unidentified objects. Forty-five minutes later a Marine pilot radioed that he had just shot down a helicopter. But when an Air Force reconnaissance plane, equipped with infrared detectors which pick up heat, flew over the area, it could find no evidence of burning wreckage. All it could confirm, the plane reported, was a "burned spot."

Bestselling author Whitley Strieber, who recounted his own "visitor experiences" in the books *Communion, Transformation* and *Breakthrough*, has described sightings of mysterious helicopters that seemed to be observing him and his family. Interestingly, in 1989, journalist Ed Conroy published a book entitled *Report on Communion*, which provides much background information on Strieber's life and career. Towards the end of the book, Conroy describes several very unsettling helicopter experiences of his own, which carry some strange implications regarding the origin of some of these mysterious aircraft.

He describes for instance, how he saw a helicopter fly behind the Tower Life Building in San Antonio, Texas ... and not appear on the other side. "I still have a hard time believing I saw that," he says. In August 1988, he saw "two Chinook-style helicopters, one with blue fuselage and white cab, the other painted brown with a red horizontal stripe, which flew out of the western horizon in perfect tandem, so close to one another that their blades must have been meshing as though they were eggbeaters."

Texas researcher Tom Adams, who publishes the *Crux* and *Stigmata* newsletters, has several cases on file, in which witnesses have reported helicopters that "shape-shift" into disc-shaped UFOs. Although the implication here is that non-human aerial devices have the apparent ability to camouflage themselves by assuming the shape of terrestrial aircraft, this begs the question: why do they only do so on certain occasions?

In November 1982, researcher Lawrence Fawcett managed to conduct an interview with a witness who claimed to have seen a black, unmarked helicopter land near his home on Long Island. The encounter occurred early one morning in 1974, when a Chinook helicopter arrived, disgorging a number of men dressed in black uniforms without markings. The men were armed with M-16 rifles, and began to set up a "perimeter" on the beach. The witness approached one of the men and asked him what he was doing, but received no reply.

At that point, a police car arrived, and the officer also asked the man what he and his colleagues were doing there. When he likewise received no response, he said that the men were carrying weapons and were wearing unidentified uniforms, and he would like to see some identification. Again, the man ignored him, so the police officer said: "If you don't answer me pretty soon, you're going to end up on the ground in handcuffs."

The man replied: "I don't think so; look around."

His colleagues had heard the exchange through the microphones attached to their shirts, and all had now trained their weapons on the police officer. Unsure how to proceed, he returned to his car and radioed his superior who told him to leave the area immediately. After the police officer had left, the helicopter crew suddenly returned to their craft and flew away.

The witness informed Fawcett that he later discovered a possible reason for the presence of the helicopter. The Air Force had apparently been removing missiles from warheads on Long Island, and was in the process of transferring them to a facility in New Jersey. One of the helicopters had developed mechanical problems, and was forced to make an emergency landing three miles down the beach. The men who had landed in front of the witness's house were security personnel assigned to protect the downed helicopter. This, however, does not explain the initial presence of only one helicopter.

Over the years, much speculation has centred on the idea that the mysterious, unmarked helicopters belong to an ultra-secret branch of the US Government, which has been charged with monitoring the activities of UFOs and cattle mutilators. Such a group would be able to respond quickly to genuine anomalous activity, and there is evidence to suggest that it has been involved in more than one UFO crash/retrieval. Although absolute secrecy would have to be maintained, there would doubtless be occasions where contact with the public would be unavoidable (as in the case described above), which would make it essential for both aircraft and uniforms to carry no identifiable markings whatsoever. In this way, the government could distance itself from the activities of these "rapid response teams," and thus could maintain its "plausible deniability" of involvement with the UFO phenomenon.

Abductions by Military Personnel

The harassment of UFO witnesses can take many forms, some of which merge seamlessly into one another: what seems like a discrete set of circumstances can contain certain elements common to other reported encounters. Thus, the activity of mysterious, unmarked helicopters is occasionally connected to one of the most disturbing aspects of witness harassment. Dr. Helmut Lammer, a scientist with the Austrian Space Research Institute, has coined the acronym MILAB for the *Military Ab*duction of UFO witnesses.

In an article entitled *Preliminary Findings of Project MILAB*, in the December 1996 issue of the Mutual UFO Network *MUFON UFO Journal*, Dr. Lammer raises and then dismisses the speculation that unmarked helicopters are comparable to the black Cadillacs of the Men in Black. Unlike the latter, the helicopters have frequently been photographed, and have been seen by people not directly involved with the UFO phenomenon. The clear implication is that, while the MIBs could conceivably be an essentially psychic phenomenon, the helicopters (and presumably their pilots) definitely exist in the concrete, rather than psychic, sense, and have their origin outside the human mind. In other words, they are *real*, and they show a *real* interest in those who have had encounters with genuine UFOs.

Lammer lists the elements in MILAB encounters, which usually begin with the arrival of the helicopters, and sometimes the presence of vans or other vehicles outside the homes of the victims, who are exposed to "disorienting electromagnetic fields" or drugs, and then transported in helicopters or vans to an underground facility of some kind. One of the principal differences between MILABs and alien abductions is that the military kidnappers do not seem to have access to the same level of technology as the aliens. For instance, instead of subduing their victims with the sheer power of their minds, as the aliens are reported to do, the military personnel will grab the victim and inject some substance into him or her with a syringe. Lammer also informs us that MILAB victims report being examined by humans in rectangular, hospital-like rooms, rather than the circular rooms commonly reported in alien abductions.

The examinations have much in common with those conducted by the aliens, including the often-described insertion of implants into the victims' bodies. According to Lammer, a small transponder bio-chip has been developed for use in humans by Dr. Daniel Man in the United States. The chip is similar to an earlier device developed by Destron-Fearing, for use as an identification tag for animals. Man's chip was developed to help locate missing children, and can be inserted with a syringe, the best place being just behind the ear. (Interestingly, this is the area-16 rifles, and began to set up a "perimeter" on the beach. cally, such devices could transmit physiological information about an abductee, in addition to his or her geographical location.

It will be clear to the reader that the journey to an underground facility is another element in common with certain alien abductions, notably the Judy Doraty and Myrna Hansen cases described earlier. American researcher Dr. Thomas Bullard has described the basic pattern of such journeys to the "Other-world." Lammer summarizses this pattern as follows:

1) *Preparation:* The alien beings put the abductee into a protective environment for the trip.
2) *Travel:* Actual transit to the Otherworld occurs.
3) *Underground:* The abductee passes underground.
4) *Landscape:* The abductee sees the surface of the Otherworld.
5) *Museum:* The tour of the Otherworld includes a stop at a museum or zoo.

Although there are definite differences between MILAB en-counters and alien abductions, such as the hard technology of the former, compared with the more subtle, mystical quality of the latter, the two scenarios contain interesting similarities. Myrna Hansen recalled seeing human beings working alongside aliens in the underground facility to which she was taken, and this is true of many MILAB victims. However, in the cases Lam-mer has studied, while some abductees have conscious flash-backs involving both aliens and human military personnel, during subsequent hypnosis the aliens seem to disappear from the victim's memory, leaving only the human beings. This could be due to a confusion in the abductee's mind between the initial alien abduction and the later encounters with the military.

Lammer puts forward the preliminary theory that "MILABS may be evidence that a secret military/intelligence task force has been in operation in North America since the early eighties, and is involved in the monitoring and kidnapping of alleged UFO ab-ductees." Their intention seems to be to withdraw any alien im-plants they find, and also to examine human females who have been impregnated and are carrying human/alien hybrid foetuses.

Whether this hypothesis is correct remains to be seen; but if military abductions really are taking place, they provide us with perhaps the most promising avenue of research in years—an av-enue that might, finally, lead us to the truth.

10

Bodies of Evidence

The Roswell Autopsy Footage

Early in 1995, word spread through the ufology community of an event that had long been dreamed about by researchers. The news was quickly picked up by the world's press, and within a few months was being reported both by respected broadsheet newspapers and supermarket tabloids. It seemed to have finally happened. There was, after all, conclusive proof that a UFO had crashed in Roswell, New Mexico in 1947. The evidence: genuine film of an autopsy conducted on the body of a UFO crew member.

Of course, as usual in the murky world of ufology, it wasn't quite as straightforward as that.

The man at the centre of this astonishing development was Ray Santilli, an independent film producer based in London, who claimed to have spoken with a former military cameraman, originally in connection with some 1950s footage of Elvis Presley. According to Santilli, after they had reviewed the film of Presley, the cameraman had mentioned that he had some other footage which might be of interest. It was what has come to be known as the "Roswell Alien Autopsy Film."

The cameraman, now in his eighties, explained his startling possession of this incredibly important record by claiming that he had always processed his own film, and the Roswell footage was no exception. He had thus made a copy for himself, which he had kept through the long decades since that fateful year,

1947. In fact, the only reason he had now decided to sell it was that he wanted to buy a wedding present for his granddaughter!

Needless to say, Stanton Friedman, as the first researcher to give serious credence to the "Roswell Incident," was intrigued when he heard of the autopsy film. To his credit, he was also extremely cautious, and was well aware of the damage that could be caused to ufology in general, and the work done on Roswell in particular, should the footage be discovered to be a hoax.

When Friedman finally managed to contact Santilli, the latter claimed that President Truman was clearly recognizable in the film, that the autopsy had been conducted in Dallas, Texas (not far from the 8th Air Force Headquarters in Fort Worth), and that it had been established that Truman had indeed been in Dallas at the time of the autopsy. When Friedman asked him if he had checked with the Truman Library, Santilli replied that he had. However, Friedman himself checked, and discovered that there were no records of Harry Truman being in Texas or New Mexico between June and October 1947. This made Friedman suspicious, for even if Truman had made a secret trip to Dallas, there was no record of it, which meant that Santilli had *not* verified his presence in Dallas, as he had claimed.

Eventually, Friedman was able to meet with Santilli in London. During their conversation, Santilli mentioned that the cameraman and his wife were living in Orlando, Florida, whereas he had told other people that they were living in Cleveland, and Cincinnati, perhaps to throw researchers off the trail.

On 5 May 1995, the film was screened at the Museum of London in front of a large contingent of journalists and UFO researchers. Although Santilli was present, he offered no introduction, no explanation of what was being presented, and he quickly left as soon as the film was over, thus depriving those present of the question-and-answer session to which they were entitled. In addition, although Santilli made numerous promises of access to the mysterious cameraman, these were never fulfilled. However, a name did eventually surface: Jack Barnett. Yet even this piece of verifiable information led to a dead end and even more suspicion. "Jack Barnett" did not appear in the lists of cameramen serving in any of the Armed Services in 1947.

Although Stanton Friedman was invited to the screening of the footage on 5 May, he did not receive his invitation until 24 hours before the event. Since he lives in Canada, it did not prove possible for him to make the transatlantic hop in time. On 3 May, he sent a fax to Santilli, challenging him to produce the information necessary to a full and proper evaluation of the footage:

Subject: Purported Roswell crashed saucer and autopsy film footage.

As the scientist who was the first investigator of the Roswell story and is still actively investigating it, I am very concerned that despite the almost 4 months that have gone by since the first public noise about the footage, you have provided NO evidence whatsoever to substantiate any of numerous claims.

You claimed in our first conversation back in mid-January, that the emulsion had been dated as of the right time frame; that you had been researching the case for over one year, and had all kinds of paperwork from the cameraman; that you had established that President Truman was in Dallas, Texas, when the autopsy took place including checking with the Truman Library; that you didn't know who I was despite my having coauthored what many consider the definitive book on Roswell (*Crash at Corona*) besides publishing many papers about Roswell and Majestic-12. When we met on April 4 in London, you claimed that cameraman JB [Jack Barnett] was given $100,000 US, but no receipt was obtained; that he was dominated by his wife, but that she didn't know anything about the deal. These both sound very unlikely. Surely IF the film were genuine, you would have had it examined in detail by someone like me who has been working on the story for more than 17 years and by film experts.

You would have provided as a minimum the following data:

1. The make and model of the film camera used.
2. The type of film used and the dates of the filming.
3. Evidence in the form of a written report from Kodak or whoever supposedly determined the vintage of the film.
4. JB's military discharge papers—DD 124.
5. A set or two of military orders from the right time frame indicating where JB was assigned, names of associates, etc.
6. A receipt for the $100,000.
7. Some kind of withdrawal slip showing from whence cometh the $100,000. Your small office gives no indication that you would find it easy to lay your hands on that amount of cash.
8. Evidence of a supposed showing to supposed religious leaders.
9. Any evidence that BBC [London] had ever intended to show the footage.
10. Evidence that there had been contact with the Truman Library and any indication that Truman was in Dallas any time in the period July 1–September 30, 1947. They tell me he wasn't in Texas.
11. Any evidence that your effort is other than an attempt to spread disinformation to discredit Roswell...similar to the US Air Force attack on Roswell in September, 1994...similar to the Doug and Dave Faked Crop Circle nonsense of several years back. [Douglas Bower and David Chorley claimed to have been behind a large number of hoax crop circles throughout southern England.]

In short, it seems to me you should put up, or shut up.—STF [Stanton T. Friedman]

The following day, 4 May, Santilli offered a rather short and terse reply to this challenge. "None of the above is of interest to me," he said.

Much controversy has centred on the actual dating of the film stock itself. For instance, Graham Birdsall describes, in the September/October 1995 issue of *UFO Magazine*, how the Kodak office in Copenhagen, Denmark, was asked to date the symbols on the spool edge. They concluded that the square and triangle markings gave 1947 as the year in which the stock was manufactured. However, according to Peter Milson, the Marketing Planning Manager with Kodak in England, the Copenhagen office was "very inexperienced, and didn't realize the symbols appeared on a twenty-year cycle."

Santilli had used Kodak's name in the commercial promotion of the footage, and this prompted Milson to issue the following statement:

ROSWELL FOOTAGE:

Comments from Kodak

The possibility of life-forms on planets other than Earth has always fired the imagination. This has been particularly true in the movie business and Kodak has been involved in supplying camera negative to such films, e.g. "E.T." and "Close Encounters of the Third Kind."

More recently, we have become involved in a more complex situation, namely, we have been asked to confirm the age of a piece of film known as "the Roswell Film," which allegedly shows Alien life-forms.

We have seen sections of either the film or its projection leader in 3 Kodak locations: UK, Hollywood and Denmark. The following outlines the conclusions of our examinations:

1. In our manufacturing process we put a code on the edge of the film which repeats every 20 years.

2. The symbols we have seen on the Roswell film samples suggest the film was manufactured in either: 1927, 1947 or 1967.

3. We are, therefore, unable to categorically confirm when the film was manufactured.

4. It should also be remembered that even if the age of the film manufacture is confirmed, this does not necessarily indicate that the film was shot and processed in the same year.

So, the bottom line is, that although we would like to know if

Aliens actually exist, Kodak cannot categorically confirm either the age of the film or when it was shot and processed.

Eventually, through TV producer Robert Kiviat, who had bought the rights to the footage, Stanton Friedman managed to view it, along with Dr. Bruce Maccabee, an experienced UFO investigator and film analyst. As it turned out, President Truman was not present after all; neither was there any footage of a disc on the ground, which had been described by other people. As Friedman states in *TOP SECRET/MAJIC*, the actual amount of footage was also different from what he had been led to believe. "Originally, Santilli had claimed there were fifteen 10 minute reels. Then the story was fourteen 7-minute reels. Then it became twenty-two 3-minute reels, but several had film that couldn't be used."

As Friedman and Maccabee carefully viewed the film at Maccabee's home in Washington, DC, it became clear to them that there were a number of discrepancies between what they were watching and the testimony of the many eyewitnesses to the Roswell Incident. For instance, the "alien" lying on the autopsy table bore little resemblance to the creatures described at Roswell. The body in the film had six fingers and six toes, whereas the Roswell witnesses had described beings with four long fingers, and no opposable thumb.

There was also a good deal of wrecked hardware in the film, including the famous "I-beams," with their strange symbols. But even these did not resemble very closely the material described by the eyewitnesses, including Dr. Jesse Marcel Jr., who had actually handled some of it when he was a small boy. These I-beams had been made of a strange, balsa-like substance, with purplish symbols; the I-beams in the film were obviously metallic, with the symbols stamped into them. The symbols themselves were reminiscent of Greek letters, but on close inspection seem to contain (rather damningly, it would seem) the word "VIDEO," albeit disguised by various additional geometric lines.

There was also a pair of apparent control panels, with large indentations in the form of six-fingered hands.

When challenged over these discrepancies, Santilli changed the date and location of the alleged crash several times. The cameraman was never located, and Friedman seriously doubts that he is even alive.

As far as the autopsy itself is concerned, there are serious problems here, too. There are three possible alternatives: the film shows a genuine extraterrestrial, or it shows a human corpse with some sort of abnormality, or it is a special effect—in short, an artificial model. The second alternative is not as outlandish as it sounds, since the "alien" in the film shows many signs of a genetic defect known as Turner's Syndrome. For instance, the body (which is apparently female) has no breasts, unusual earlobes, a wide chest and an excess of skin at the base of the neck—all suggestive of Turner's Syndrome, according to Friedman. In fact, these unusual features notwithstanding, the "person" on the autopsy table bore a much greater resemblance to a human being than a genuine extraterrestrial alien. "She" had a definite nose, rather than the air-holes described in aliens; pronounced ear flaps, which were not described by Roswell witnesses; and "her" eyes, although rather large, were much smaller than those of the creatures described at Roswell.

There are yet further problems with the manner in which the autopsy itself is conducted. For instance, as the medical personnel examine the cadaver's jet-black eyes, they quickly discover lens-like coverings over them—too quickly, in fact, as if they knew what to expect beforehand. These coverings are then taken out immediately, with no attempt made to discover how they might be attached, or whether their removal might damage the eyeballs. Avoiding any further unnecessary damage to the body would surely be the paramount consideration.

When the abdominal cavity is opened, a number of strange organs are revealed, along with a cartilaginous, wishbone-like structure in the chest. What follows is astonishing, given the premise that this is a being from another world. The examiner takes his scalpel and goes to work on the body with what looks like incredible ineptitude, as if he were filleting a joint of meat instead of carefully dissecting an utterly unique scientific specimen. The unidentified organs are excised with unseemly haste, pulled out of the abdominal cavity with no attempt to ascertain their supporting structures, and tossed into waiting specimen dishes.

It hardly takes a PhD in forensic medicine to see that an autopsy on an alien being simply would not have been conducted in such a laughably slapdash manner. A genuine autopsy would have taken days, weeks or even months to perform, with the subject preserved at each stage in the procedure, to the best of science's ability at the time. It would have been conducted with the utmost care, with the information gained from each step being collated and evaluated, before a decision on how to proceed could be made. The autopsy film shows no measurements being taken; the organs removed from the cadaver are not even weighed.

And what of Jack Barnett, the cameraman who allegedly took the film? French researcher Nicholas Maillard has discovered that a Jack Barnett did indeed film Elvis Presley in Cleveland in 1955, but he did not own the rights to that footage. They actually belonged to the disc jockey Bill Randle, who sold them to Santilli in 1992. According to Friedman, Jack Barnett had been employed as a cameraman by Fox Movietone News, and later by NBC. He had been a war correspondent in Europe during the Second World War, but he was never in the military. He died in Chicago in 1967.

Another name for the cameraman, Jack Barrett, popped up in the course of the Roswell autopsy affair, and Nicholas Maillard looked into this, also. Barrett worked as a grip for Columbia Pictures in Hollywood for 35 years, his military service having ended in 1945. He died in Los Angeles in 1995. Maillard submitted Barrett's signature to a graphologist, along with copies of the labels from the autopsy film canisters. The graphologist concluded that Barrett could have written the labels. Friedman asks if the "autopsy" could have been "stored in some Hollywood vault, perhaps from some science film?"

Speaking of Hollywood, the film has been shown to a large number of special effects experts, the vast majority of whom are of the opinion that the "alien" is a manufactured model. Interestingly, Friedman also reports a conversation he had with Richard Doty (whom we encountered earlier), who claimed to have seen the film in the early 1980s, "and even then it was known not to be of aliens."

The extraterrestrial alternative, then, slips out of the picture, leaving either the malformed human, or the special effects model. We will have to wait and see if any further information comes to light, which might enable us to make a definite decision on the true origin of this intriguing footage. In the meantime the extra attention that the UFO phenomenon has attracted as a result of the film is a rather mixed blessing in view of the virtual certainty that the Roswell autopsy footage is not, after all, the long-anticipated "smoking gun" that could reveal the truth to an expectant world.

Tomato Man

Although the Roswell autopsy footage has become world-famous, such alleged photographic evidence of dead aliens is not without precedent. Over the years a number of photographs have surfaced, purporting to depict dead or captured non-human entities; however, they are unfortunately more a lesson in the dangers of over-enthusiasm than categorical proof of an alien presence.

The situation is made yet more confusing when the results of apparently genuine incidents are photographed, as happened in Laredo, Texas, in 1948. It was not until 1978, however, that the photograph of the unfortunate individual referred to (rather gruesomely) as "Tomato Man" was released by Williard McIntyre, Charles Wilhelm and Dennis Pilchis, who belonged to an organization calling itself the Coalition of Concerned Ufologists of America. The photograph is extremely disturbing, since it apparently shows the victim of a genuine accident, who has been very badly burned and mangled, along with the twisted wreckage of whatever machine it was in when the catastrophic accident occurred.

The body seems to have its back to the camera, so the face cannot be seen. The skin on the top of the head has been burned away, revealing a hideous mass of scar tissue, covered with dark droplets of what is probably melted flesh. The victim's clothes have become fused with the body, and are thus unrecognizable. The body itself is surrounded by burned wreckage, including wires, small girders and struts.

McIntyre, Wilhelm and Pilchis also released a story with the photograph, which claimed that it had been taken by a young naval photographer who was based at White Sands Missile Range in New Mexico. Since his job was to photograph aircraft crashes, so that investigators could assess the wreckage for possible metal fatigue, he was ordered just over the border from Laredo into Mexico on 7–8 July 1948, to photograph a flying disc that had come down in the area.

The highly respected American researcher Leonard Stringfield (who tragically died in 1994) learned that a UFO had been tracked on radar, heading east towards Texas at 2,000 m.p.h. As it passed over Albuquerque, New Mexico, it was intercepted by two jets from Dias AFB, Texas. It is possible, although unsubstantiated, that the jets fired on the object, which then altered its course south and drastically reduced its speed to about 100 m.p.h., finally disappearing from radar at a point near the Texas/Mexico border.

According to the unnamed naval photographer, the wreckage was still smouldering when the retrieval team arrived and began their examination. Curiously, he mentioned that the craft's construction included numerous nuts and bolts, although the metal itself was said to be extremely tough, apparently composed of a honeycomb lattice. The photographer took about 500 pictures of the wrecked vehicle and its hapless occupant.

It was not until many years later that the photographer decided

to release some of the photographs, having made duplicate negatives. When they were submitted to Kodak for analysis, the company concluded that they had probably been processed 30 years
earlier, which would seem to support the photographer's story.

As to the identity of the body, opinion is divided, although
few researchers today claim that it is definitely an extraterrestrial being. Two alternatives remain: first, that it is actually the
body of a monkey that was used in an experimental V-2 rocket
flight, which crashed just over the Mexican border. This is not
as outlandish as it sounds, since monkeys were frequently used
in the very early days of space flight, to test prototype vehicles.
However, as Jenny Randles notes in her book *UFO Retrievals*,
the wreckage seems to resemble more closely the cockpit of an
aircraft than a V-2 rocket.

There is also a very important element in the photograph that
leads to the second alternative. Amid the wreckage, and close to
the victim's left hand, is a twisted pair of spectacles. Not only
does this definitely rule out an alien as the victim, it also virtually rules out a monkey. What we are left with is the extreme
likelihood that the Laredo photograph shows the unfortunate
pilot of an experimental Air Force aircraft that suffered from a
catastrophic malfunction and crashed. It thus seems equally
likely that the stories of flying discs and dead aliens were
merely the results of the ever-active ufology rumour mill, and,
as Randles suggests, may even have been encouraged by the Air
Force to protect its top secret tests.

The final nail in the coffin (if the reader will pardon the expression) of the extraterrestrial explanation for "Tomato Man"
came when McIntyre claimed he had wanted to test the credulity
of ufologists with the photograph.

A One-Legged Alien in Military Custody?

Another famous photograph shows what appears to be a captured alien walking between two military policemen. The crea-

ture was originally described as "strange...with only one leg moving about a rotating plate. His arms end in four stubby fingers." Its head is large and oval, and there is some kind of breathing apparatus in the form of a tube running from its mouth to a box, being carried by the MP behind it.

However, according to German ufologist Klaus Webner, the photograph is a hoax, an April Fools' Day trick arranged by William Sprunkel, then editor of the German newspaper *Wiesbadener Tagblatt* for its 1 April 1950 edition. The photographer was one Hans Scheffler, whose five-year-old son, Peter, stood between the two "MPs," to act as a kind of template, over which the image of the alien was later painted.

In the late 1970s, American UFO researchers were searching through some FBI files that had been released under the Freedom of Information Act, when they came across a reversed version of the photograph. Although extremely grainy after much photocopying, the little alien and its custodians were still easily discernible. According to the FBI papers, the photograph was received on 24 May 1950 from an intelligence officer at the New Orleans Port of Embarkation.

The photograph then found its way into the book *The Roswell Incident* by William Moore and Charles Berlitz, who included it without comment, thus adding to its apparent credibility. However, unlike the Templeton photograph described earlier, the one-legged alien photograph has most deservedly failed the test of time.

A Dead Martian?

The year 1950 also saw the perpetration of another famous hoax involving a dead alien, this time supposedly from the planet Mars. The tiny creature is shown being held up by its thin arms between two trenchcoat-clad "secret service agents." The story was that its spacecraft crashed near Mexico City and, for some reason, the dead pilot was sent to Germany for study. Early information on the photograph suggests it was taken in Cologne, perhaps as another April Fools' Day jape.

That there is something wrong with this photograph will become evident to anyone who gives it more than a cursory examination. For instance, the two men are holding the creature's tiny hands in their closed fists, instead of between their thumbs and fingers, which would have been more natural. The Danish UFO journal *UFO-Nyt* examined the photograph and concluded that the men were actually holding the handle of a pram, which had then been painted out of the image. The scrawny "alien" had then been inserted into the photograph.

Later rumours had it that the photograph was actually taken in America. However, there are several members of the public in the background looking at whatever the men are holding, and this hardly squares with the American authorities' famous reluctance to display publicly their captured extraterrestrials!

Another Autopsy

The vast majority of alleged alien photographs are, unfortunately, utterly laughable; and yet, very occasionally, a truly impressive image finds its way into the public domain, and forces researchers to wonder whether, this time, they have found the long-sought-after final proof. One such picture, showing a claw-like appendage and part of a torso, was allegedly taken during the autopsy of an alien creature in 1962. The photograph is of relatively poor quality, yet it clearly shows a long upper arm, an elbow joint, a disproportionately short forearm and a large, clawed hand.

Interestingly, before this photograph came to light, a former CIA operative claimed to have been present at a UFO crash/retrieval, during which he saw the hand of one of the crew members. His description and sketch of the hand is virtually identical to the photograph. In addition, Leonard Stringfield interviewed a retired doctor who claimed to have performed an autopsy on an alien body in the early 1950s. He also sketched the appendages of the alien, and they were identical to the CIA agent's sketch.

Montreal Hoax

There are times when certain ufologists play straight into the sceptics' hands, pointing to extremely dubious photographs as impressive evidence for alien reality. At times like this, the more responsible researchers in the field are left to limit the damage as much as they can, doubtless feeling great frustration at their colleagues' apparent lack of critical faculties.

Just such a lamentable case occurred in 1990, when a photograph came to light which prompted the more zealous members of the ufology community to claim that it was a "legitimate photo of an alien body recovered at the site of the Roswell UFO crash and stored in 'Hangar 18' at Wright-Patterson Air Force Base." The photograph clearly showed a small, hairless humanoid, dressed in a silver jumpsuit. The little man was strapped to a table, and was apparently dead. However, the suspicions of the more discerning UFO investigators were raised when it became apparent that the jumpsuit contained an ordinary zip fastener.

In addition, Wendy Holdsworth, a British researcher with Quest International, examined the figure closely, and noticed a similarity between the clothing of the "alien" and the fabric used by cavers. *UFO Magazine* then arranged for some tests to be done on the type of cloth Holdsworth mentioned, and it was found that it creased in exactly the same manner as the "alien's" jumpsuit.

According to *Fortean Times* editor Bob Rickard, the photograph had been known of in fringe UFO circles since 1970, when the Russian ufologist Marina Popovich revealed a black-and-white version at a UFO conference held in Munich, Germany. She claimed to have discovered it in the files of the late Professor Felix Zigel, an eminent Russian space scientist. She also claimed that it had been given to Zigel by none other than Dr. J. Allen Hynek at a secret Canadian conference in the 1970s.

In spite of this intrigue, the actual origin of the photograph was discovered to be rather more mundane. The little space man was a model that had been built as an exhibit at the "Man and his World" exposition in Montreal, Canada, which was closed down in the 1980s.

It is important to note that spurious "evidence" of this kind has always been shown to be wanting by discerning UFO researchers as well as sceptics. Serious ufologists are not afraid to pour cold water on dubious claims, showing up their lack of credibility for what it is. Indeed, it is clearly in the best interests of ufologists to ensure that this is done, when necessary. The serious and genuine mystery of the UFOs demands that hoaxes are exposed as quickly as possible, whenever they are perpetrated.

11

UFO Healings

The Strange Case of Dr. X

In some respects, the image that has grown in the public mind of evil Grey aliens abducting human beings and conducting hideous biological experiments on them, is somewhat misleading. It is increasingly becoming apparent that quite the opposite is frequently the case: many abduction researchers have cases on their files of people who have apparently been cured of various illnesses after a close encounter of the fourth kind.

Ironically enough, the most famous incident involved a man who, to this day, has diligently preserved his anonymity. He is known only as "Dr. X." His experiences are remarkable in a research context because his insistence on absolute anonymity allowed investigators (most notably the great French ufologist Aimé Michel) to conduct their examination of both the initial encounter and subsequent developments in isolation from the prying eyes of the press.

In the late 1960s, Dr. X, a highly respected biologist, was living with his wife and 14-month-old son in the countryside in the south of France. Late on the evening of 1–2 November 1968, the 38-year-old doctor was awakened by the cries of his son. The time was 4.00 A.M. Dr. X got out of bed and went to see what was disturbing the boy. He could only walk with great difficulty, owing to a leg injury he had sustained while chopping wood three days earlier. The wound had been a serious one: when his axe slipped, it had ruptured an artery in his lower leg, causing an internal haemorrage and resulting in a haematoma, a pocket of accumulated blood under the skin. On the afternoon of 1 November, a physician had examined the leg, and found that the wound had not healed; the swelling and pain had not subsided, and were still a serious problem for Dr. X.

Making his way to his son's bedroom, he noted that a thunderstorm was brewing, which might have disturbed the baby. When he entered the room, he saw his son standing in his crib and gesturing towards the window. Through the closed shutters, flashes of lightning could be seen. As he took his baby's water bottle and refilled it, it suddenly occurred to Dr. X that no sound of thunder followed the lightning flashes, although it was raining very hard and he could clearly see them through the closed shutters.

He gave his son the refilled water bottle, which seemed to satisfy the boy, and was about to return to bed, when he heard the sound of another shutter rattling in the wind somewhere else in the house. The troublesome shutter was in an upstairs room, and, after struggling upstairs, Dr. X opened the window to secure it. It was then that he realized the flashes of light were not caused by lightning. In astonishment, he looked out across the landscape to the south of the house (which was built on the side of a hill), at two silvery, disc-shaped objects hovering in the distance.

Each object shed a deep red light from its base, and each had a vertical antenna on top and a horizontal antenna extending from its side. As they slowly moved together across the rain-soaked countryside, further into the doctor's field of vision, each cast a cylindrical beam of bright white light on the valley below. At roughly one-second intervals, this light increased in intensity as an apparent electrical discharge flashed from the vertical antenna of one object, through its "hull" and across to the second object.

The two objects then began to approach the house (Dr. X was able to ascertain this by watching the path taken by the light-cylinders across the ground), and presently, their horizontal antennae touched, the flashing ceased and they merged into a single object. As the doctor continued to watch, utterly awe-struck, rooted to the spot by the open window, this single object continued its approach to the house, still casting its cylinder of intense light upon the valley floor. It then began a strange series of manoeuvres, flipping up on end and turning on its horizontal axis, until it appeared as a bright circle hanging eerily in the drizzling night.

The light-cylinder that had illuminated the valley floor now shone with all its intensity upon the window at which Dr. X was standing, bathing his face in its unearthly glow. At that point there was a loud bang, and the object vanished, leaving only a white glow that was gradually dispersed by the wind. As that too vanished, a single stream of light shot upwards into the sky and exploded high above the valley.

Although still in shock, Dr. X's scientific training came to the fore, and he immediately sat down and began to make sketches of what he had seen, accompanied by a detailed set of notes on the exact sequence of events. When he had completed this task, he returned to his bedroom, woke his wife and told her what had happened. She was nonplussed, to say the least, by this strange story, until she noticed something that, to her, must have been even more astonishing than her husband's notes and sketches. The swelling in his leg had completely disappeared! When she excitedly pointed this out, it occurred to Dr. X that the pain had likewise gone.

Although miraculous in itself, the disappearance of the painful haematoma was not the only apparent result of Dr. X's strange encounter. Ten years before, in the Algerian war, he had been badly injured in a mine explosion; his skull had been fractured, and the left hemisphere of his brain had been severely damaged. He had slipped into a coma, and subsequently suffered several months of partial paralysis, which considerably weakened the muscles in the right side of his body. However, in the days that followed his encounter with the UFOs, these debilitating after-effects of his battle injury also disappeared.

After a lengthy conversation on his experience, Dr. X and his wife returned to bed and, although she had difficulty sleeping, he immediately entered a deep slumber. He began to talk in his sleep, which was unheard of for him, and his wife took notes of what he was saying. Much of what he was saying referred to his encounter, and at one point, he mumbled: "Contact will be re-established by falling down the stairs on 2 November."

Dr. X slept in until two o'clock on the following afternoon. Although he felt extremely well when he awoke, he had no memory whatsoever of the events of the previous night. When his wife showed him the notes and sketches he had made, he was both surprised and alarmed.

The prophecy he had uttered while asleep was fulfilled when, later that afternoon, he tripped and fell down the stairs in the living room. He landed heavily, bumped his head, and suddenly regained his memory of his encounter.

On 8 November, six days after Dr. X's initial UFO experience, he was visited by Aimé Michel, whom he knew socially, and who found him tired and depressed. He had also lost weight, and was experiencing abdominal cramps. Later that day, he experienced an irritating itch on his abdomen, which was accompanied by a red rash in the shape of a triangle. A dermatologist examined the rash, which intrigued him so much that he expressed a wish to present the case to the French Academy of Medicine. However, fearful that the cause might become known to the public, thus putting his reputation at risk, Dr. X persuaded the dermatologist not to do so.

On the night of 13 November, Dr. X had a vivid dream of a flying disc and a triangle. Aimé Michel had wondered whether the triangular rash around the doctor's navel might have been some kind of psychosomatic phenomenon. However, this theory had to be discarded when a triangular rash subsequently appeared on the baby's stomach.

Although Dr. X's leg wound healed completely, and he was never again troubled by his war injury, the mysterious triangular rash recurred again and again in the years that followed, and was even recorded on film in 1986. A profound change in his outlook on life also occurred, a shift towards a spiritual world-view that was shared by his wife. This alteration was totally out of character for them, and mystified both their friends and family who, like the rest of the world, were still unaware of what had happened on that rainy evening of 1 November 1968.

Both Dr. X and his wife felt an ever-increasing appreciation of life in its totality; the eternal cycle of living and dying, the machinery of the Universe itself, became the centre of their consciousness. Not only did they empathize with the mysteries of reality; those mysteries apparently took up residence in their home. Poltergeist activity began to occur, and Dr. X experienced an episode of uncontrollable levitation, accompanied by an inner journey to distant places. At times, it seemed that non-human entities were present in the house, and clocks and electrical devices were affected by an unknown agency.

A Selective Blessing

Virtually every aspect of the UFO phenomenon—from the flight characteristics of the objects, to the conversations engaged in by human percipients and non-human entities—is characterized by absurdity. It must be understood that, by "absurdity," I do not mean to echo the sceptics who say that UFO encounters are not worthy of serious study, claiming that UFO witnesses tend to be stupid and frivolous dreamers who are prone to impose their own fantasies on sightings of mundane phenomena. Rather, I use the word in the same sense as researchers such as Jacques Vallée, who point out that, while genuine UFO-related events may resist our attempts to place them within a recognizable logical frame of reference, they nevertheless occur, and are experienced by perfectly intelligent and well-balanced people, who are just as bemused and disturbed by them as the people who later read of their encounters in books and magazine articles.

The apparent ability of these entities to cure some humans of a variety of ailments, from the superficial to the life-threatening, is another aspect of this essential absurdity. The obvious question to ask is: why are only *some* percipients healed? Why not all of them?

Preston Dennett is an investigator for MUFON, who has gathered more than 100 cases of UFO healings from the relevant literature, and published them in a book entitled *UFO Healings: True Accounts of People Healed by Extraterrestrials*. In an article in the October 1996 issue of the *MUFON UFO Journal*, he illustrates the central question of this subject by quoting the three best-known abduction researchers: Budd Hopkins, David Jacobs and John Mack. According to Hopkins, this is a sad and frustrating puzzle, since he has a number of abductees who have "serious medical problems who wish they were being healed, but are not." Although the "aliens" seem to be interested in the "most lovely aspects of being human," there is little evidence to suggest that they ultimately have our welfare at heart. As Hopkins reminds us, "we wouldn't perhaps have AIDS and the hole in the ozone layer and everything else if they were here to help us."

David Jacobs offers one possible answer, albeit one that does little to lift our spirits. He reports that the aliens will, on occasion, effect a cure of certain illnesses for the sole purpose of keeping the human specimens in good condition. In the words of one abductee: "It's equipment maintenance."

John Mack comments on the wide range of ailments that the aliens see fit to treat: "Many abductees have experienced or witnessed healing conditions ranging from minor wounds to pneumonia, childhood leukemia, and even in one case reported to me first-hand, the overcoming of muscular atrophy in a leg related to poliomyelitis."

According to Dan Wright, manager of the MUFON Abduction Transcription Project, preliminary statistical analysis reveals that 11 per cent of UFO-related physiological effects involve such healings. An idea of the wide range of procedures con-

ducted on abductees is given Dennett's partial list of conditions
that allegedly have been cured:

Aneurysm	Diphtheria	Myopia
Angioma	Fever	Paralysis
Arthritis	Flesh wounds	Pneumonia
Asthma	Heart condition	Polio
Back pain	Infertility	Rheumatism
Burns	Kidney disease	Tuberculosis
Cancer	Liver disease	Tumours
Candidiasis	Multiple sclerosis	Warts
Cold	Muscular dystrophy	

In order to illustrate the manner in which such ailments are
apparently cured, I will describe some of the cases presented
by Preston Dennett, after his own survey of the UFO and abduction literature.

Flesh wound: On 3 September 1965, two police officers were on
their way home after a high school football game. One of the
men, Patrol Deputy Robert W. Goode, had been bitten on the
finger by a baby alligator, and was experiencing considerable
discomfort from the swollen wound.

The other officer, Chief Deputy Billy McCoy, saw a formation
of lights ascending from the right side of the road, and pulled the
car over. The two men watched as the lights approached the car
and then projected a bright beam at them. Goode's arm was at
that moment hanging outside the car window, and his injured
hand was bathed in the light, which felt hot. The two officers decided to leave the area as quickly as they could.

A little later, Goode noticed that there was no longer any
pain in his finger. He later reported: "I suddenly realized it was
not bothering me and I pulled off the bandage. Hell, you
couldn't tell I had ever been bit."

McCoy confirmed this: "The swelling had disappeared and
the finger looked a lot better."

Colour blindness: Alien entities frequently exhibit an interest in human eyes, possibly because of a profound difference in the structure of their own. (Some percipients, notably Whitley Strieber, have commented on a strange structure that can sometimes be seen turning within the aliens' obsidian eyes.)

American researcher John Carpenter investigated the case of a 21-year-old man named Eddie, whose right eye was removed by aliens during a physical examination. After the beings had replaced the eye, he had the impression that they had "fixed" something, in the course of the operation. Carpenter later obtained a statement from Eddie's doctor, confirming that the young man had suffered from "profound colour blindness." After his encounter, his vision "had improved up to green colour blindness."

Hepatitis: In November 1967, Danish UFO researcher Hans Lauritzen was contacted by a Swedish girl, who informed him that he was on a "list" of humans due to be contacted by the "Space People." This prompted him to go on a series of sky watches with four of his friends, in the hope that the girl might be right, and they might encounter a UFO.

A year earlier, Lauritzen had contracted liver hepatitis, and had been forced to retire. This illness was, of course, not helped by sitting in damp fields waiting for the arrival of UFOs, and on the day of his encounter, his liver had become enlarged and he was tired and weak. On 7 December, he and his four friends spotted two dim yellow globes about 100 yards away. Lauritzen fell into a hypnotic trance and began to communicate with the entities inside the globes, who told him he had a great power to help humanity.

This lasted for about an hour, after which Lauritzen returned to normal consciousness and ran back to his friends, who were calling out to him. It was then that he realized he no longer felt tired. He later said: "I ran and ran so fast that my four friends could not follow me. I had to wait for them. I realized that I had been cured of my hepatitis."

To confirm this, Lauritzen went to his doctor, who examined

him and found that he had indeed somehow been cured of his illness. According to Lauritzen, "I passed a medical examination, not mentioning my contact, of course, and to the surprise of the doctors, ten centimetres of my liver had disappeared so that it was now normal size. The blood test showed that it functioned now as any other healthy liver [whereas] before I had a sick liver. At one time it was as much as 16 centimetres too large. . . . I am most thankful to the UFO for curing my otherwise chronic disease . . . I swear to God that I have told the truth as far as I can see it."

Diphtheria: Alice Haggerty was six years old when she contracted diphtheria in 1972. She had not been vaccinated against the disease, because of her parents' religious convictions; nor would they allow her to be treated, in spite of their doctor's protestations. Eventually, he informed them that their daughter had only a few hours left to live.

On the night she was expected finally to succumb to her illness, she was taken on board a UFO, where she encountered angelic beings in white robes, who passed a rod-like instrument over her body, and placed her inside a "blue cylinder." The aliens then informed her that she had been "cleansed," and returned her to her family.

Cancer: Preston Dennett informs us of the following little-known case. Licia Davidson of Los Angeles, was diagnosed with terminal cancer in 1989, and was given three months to live. She was also a repeat-abductee, having had UFO experiences for many years. During the next abduction she experienced, the aliens told her that they knew of her condition, and asked her to relax as they placed her on an operating table. An "excruciating" operation followed, and she was then returned to her home.

Like Hans Lauritzen, she went back to her doctor, who examined her and discovered that the cancer had been completely eradicated. According to her medical records, to which she later gained access, this apparently miraculous cure has been "verified by a major medical university." Interestingly, Licia Davidson is also a victim of alleged US Government harassment, perhaps because of the cure she received at the hands of the aliens.

Angioma (tumour caused by malformed blood vessels): "Ted," of Santa Clara, California, was diagnosed with angioma at the age of 18 months. The tumour put pressure on his brain, and by the time he was three years old, he suffered from double vision and partial paralysis. His life expectancy was put at virtually zero by doctors. However, his condition began unaccountably to improve, and he was admitted to hospital for exploratory surgery. The surgeons were astonished to discover that the angioma had actually reduced in size, an unheard-of occurrence.

In adulthood, Ted decided to undergo hypnotic regression, and recalled a UFO encounter in which beings put him on a table and focused intense, laser-like lights on his head. The beings also opened his skull and examined his brain. He remembers that "they touch all over and they find enlargement. And with the laser light, they're able to shrink it."

The beam of light apparently incinerated the tumour: a vacuum-like instrument was placed over his brain, and a fine substance similar to ash was removed. Another light beam was used to fuse his skullcap: "This time, instead of cutting it, it mends. It mends the skull back together. The atoms go back together and there's no scar tissue. And when it's finished, there's no indication that the skull has been opened."

Such alien technological feats seem so incredible as to be surely the products of human imagination or delusion, in spite of the unexplained healings that accompany them. However, perhaps they are not as incredible as we might think, in view of our own recent advances in the field of so-called "nanotechnology." We are, even now reaching the stage where we can manipulate atoms to form new structures. Already we have electric motors that are dwarfed by a pinhead; the atoms in a piece of metal have been rearranged to form the letters IBM; nerve cells have been grafted to computer chips, heralding the eventual union of human and machine. . . . With these technological wonders in mind, surely it is at least feasible that a culture perhaps millennia ahead of our own would have mastered these techniques, and would easily be capable of destroying a young boy's tumour and healing his skull atom by atom.

Electrocution: A real estate broker named Katharina Wilson had a healing encounter in 1989, which she described in a book entitled *The Alien Jigsaw*, published in 1993. On 7 August 1989, she was injured by a nearby lightning strike. She decided to postpone seeking medical attention until the next morning, since her injury didn't seem to be particularly severe.

That night, Katharina experienced an abduction, in which she was placed on a table. There was an agonizing pain in her chest. She was surrounded by Grey aliens, who cut a hole into her chest and inserted a black instrument. The aliens communicated with her telepathically, telling her: "We are repairing your heart. You will be OK now."

Katharina awoke the following morning in good health, apart from residual chest pains. She was able to remember the abduction consciously, and so searched for the expected scar on her chest. "I found nothing. No blood on my sheets and no scar. My chest was sore throughout the day, but it was not as sore as I would have expected it to feel after such a radical operation. I believe this machine they had over my head was realigning the electrochemical impulses in my heart because they had been altered by the lightning... somehow I believed the aliens were repairing the damage the high voltage of the lightning had done to my heart."

According to Katharina Wilson, the aliens have operated on her numerous times. "It was shocking to remember the different times the aliens had performed surgery on me.... What could the aliens be doing to me that would require my having surgery so often? It was not the first time I felt I may be a part of a huge experiment."

The common cold: In his 1977 book *Situation Red*, the late Leonard Stringfield recounts the case of Chuck Doyle of Florence, Kentucky, who was suffering from a bad cold when he went outside to check on his horse on the evening of 10 May 1975. He was astonished to see a metallic object, approximately 20 feet long and shaped like a "manta ray" hanging in the sky above his neighbour's garden. The object was projecting a thin beam of green light at the ground. Doyle described it as similar to a laser, in that its width was constant all the way down.

Suddenly, "the beam came at me. When it hit me, it was like being hit by a bucket of ice-water. I felt suddenly frozen. I couldn't move." This was quite literally so: Doyle was frozen in a running position as he tried to escape from the object. While he was paralysed, he received a series of strange mental images, including colours, mathematical symbols and scenes of another planet.

The beam then released him and he fell to the ground. As with the objects encountered by Dr. X, the UFO then disappeared with a flash and a loud report. As he returned to his house in shock, Doyle realized that he was no longer suffering from the cold. A few days later, he visited his doctor, who gave him a completely clean bill of health.

12

Conclusion: The UFO Phenomenon— Origin Unknown?

Faster-Than-Light Interstellar Travel

In the five decades since Kenneth Arnold's sighting near Mount Rainier, one of the cornerstones of the sceptics' argument against the extraterrestrial hypothesis (ETH) for genuine UFOs, has been the impossibility of faster-than-light (FTL) travel. The distances between the stars are so colossal, they say, that it would take thousands of years for any spacefaring civilization to traverse the gulfs between even the nearer stars. Thus, it would be far too wasteful, in terms of both time and resources, to make a habit of interstellar flight.

To speculate at any length on the developments in propulsion that might be achieved by an advanced alien civilization is beyond the scope of this book. Instead, let us look briefly at the developments in our own understanding of physics, which seem to refute the often-made claim that FTL travel is, and will always be, out of the question. In this way, we might at least begin, by association, to refute the sceptics' central claim that hypothetical aliens could not visit us because we cannot visit them.

It is, indeed, impossible for a spacecraft to travel faster than the speed of light by means of known propulsion systems. This is due to relativistic mass increase, which means that the faster a body travels, the greater its mass becomes. Although Albert Einstein's Theory of Special Relativity established him as the central figure in early twentieth-century physics, the relations which he derived to explain the behaviour of space, time and matter within a moving reference frame, were originally derived by a Dutch physicist named Hendrik Lorentz, through different means. For this reason, they are called the Lorentz transformations. In his 1988 book *Faster Than Light: Superluminal Loopholes in Physics*, the American physicist Dr. Nick Herbert summarizes the Lorentz transformations as follows:

> The Lorentz transformations predict four major changes that objects in a moving frame seem to undergo as viewed from a fixed frame: (1) Space shrinks in the direction of motion (Lorentz contraction); (2) time slows down (time dilation); (3) clocks desynchronize (relativity of simultaneity or "sync shift"); and (4) mass increases in the moving frame.

Herbert goes on to explain that at low speeds (compared to that of light), the Lorentz transformations are insignificant. However, as light speed is approached, the transformations increase by an amount proportional to the "Einstein factor." "The Einstein factor is equal to 1 for low velocities, is equal to 2 for 90 per cent of light speed, increases to 7 at 99 per cent of light speed, and becomes infinite at light speed itself."

Thus, the mass of a spacecraft accelerating towards the speed of light would increase, presenting increased resistance to further acceleration. Not only would the energy of the propulsion system be usurped by the increasing mass, but at the speed of light itself, the mass would become infinite; therefore, the amount of energy required to reach the speed of light would be infinite. In short, the spacecraft would have to carry an infinite amount of fuel, capable of delivering an infinite amount of thrust! To give some idea of the size of this problem, Herbert describes the behaviour of electrons inside a television set, which are accelerated to 30 per cent of light speed. For these electrons, which "paint" the picture you see on your screen, the Einstein factor is about 1.05, and they are 5 per cent heavier than electrons outside the television.

Electrons in a linear accelerator on the other hand, move a great deal faster; for instance, the mass of an electron passing through the Stanford linear accelerator would increase by an Einstein factor of 50,000. "A bullet travelling as fast as a [Stanford linear accelerator] electron would weigh as much as a dump truck."

It can therefore be seen that travel beyond the light barrier will never be achieved through "brute force." As Herbert states, "more artful strategies" are needed. However, by their very nature, these strategies are not amenable to easy utilization, and there are many false leads: instances where FTL travel actually occurs, but which are of little help in powering a hypothetical starship.

One such instance of FTL travel involves, believe it or not, radio waves. Herbert describes how, at the turn of the century, radio engineers discovered an astonishing property of these waves, which, although they travel at the speed of light, are capable of exceeding that limit. The reason for this is related to the behaviour of a beam of light passing between two transparent media of differing densities. If the beam is travelling from a high-speed to a low-speed medium (for instance, from air to glass), it bends downward at the interface. Conversely, if it is travelling from a medium where its speed is slow (glass) to one where it is high (air), it bends upward at the interface. However,

> . . . for incident angles greater than a certain "critical angle," the light beam for a slow-into-fast situation, instead of bending, doesn't even penetrate the second medium, but reflects from the interface as if from a perfect mirror. This phenomenon of "total reflection" is characteristic only of the slow-into-fast situation and never occurs in the fast-into-slow case.

The speed of light in water is 75 per cent of that in a vacuum, and in air is 99.9 per cent of vacuum speed, and this results in total reflection in certain instances, for example when the surface of an ocean appears as an undulating mirror to a diver below. When radio engineers discovered that ionized gas totally reflects radio waves, their inescapable conclusion was that, since this phenomenon only occurs from a slow to a fast medium (and since radio waves already travel at the speed of light), the waves had to be travelling faster than light in the ionized medium.

Bizarre as this conclusion sounds, it does not violate Einstein's universal speed limit. To explain this, Herbert uses the analogy of a stone dropped into a perfectly still pond. The result, of course, is an expanding, circular band; but within the band are smaller ripples moving from its trailing edge to its leading edge at about twice its speed. The velocity of these smaller ripples is called "phase velocity"; the velocity of the band itself is called "group velocity."

What those pioneering radio engineers had detected was the phase velocity within the radio waves, which were travelling faster than light, and thus were totally reflected by the ionized medium. Unfortunately, the group velocity of radio waves never violates Einstein's speed limit, even though the phase velocity does so with ease. Thus, although FTL travel is possible within radio waves under certain conditions (for example, when they are bounced off the Earth's ionosphere), the group velocity remains at light speed, and cannot be used to carry a signal faster than light. So much for FTL phase waves.

It would seem that we will have to look elsewhere for clues as to how we might, one day, bypass the apparently impassable light barrier, and journey to the stars. The mysterious—almost magical—realm of quantum theory might just hold such clues, since it describes, among other things, a curious phenomenon known as "quantum tunnelling," in which particles can move from one location to another without traversing the space between them. Another notion is the "quantum connection," which suggests, in Herbert's words, that "once two quantum systems have briefly interacted, they remain in some sense forever connected by an instantaneous link—a link whose effects are undiminished by interposed shielding or distance."

This continued instantaneous interaction seems to occur as a result of the mathematical probability waves which represent the quantum systems, and which do not exist in normal three-dimensional space, but rather in what is called "configuration space," which contains three dimensions for each particle. According to Herbert, "The quantum wave for a two-particle system, for instance, moves about in a six-dimensional space."

Herbert likens this faster-than-light quantum connection to the workings of voodoo, in that an action on one particle instantly affects the other particle, because they leave parts of themselves with each other during their initial interaction, and are still in contact with each other through those parts.

Many science fiction writers have used the notion of the "tachyon" in their FTL stardrives. Once again, we can turn to Nick Herbert for a summary of the properties of these hypothetical particles, and the differences between them and tardyons (slower-than-light particles) and zero-mass luxons (particles that travel at the speed of light, only three of which are currently known: protons, neutrinos and the hypothetical gravitons):

1. A tachyon possesses an imaginary rest mass; that is, the square of its mass is a negative number.

2. As it loses energy, a tachyon speeds up—a result already anticipated by Sommerfeld in 1904. Once a tachyon has lost all its energy, it must travel at an infinite velocity; that is, it occupies every point along its trajectory at the same time. Olexa-Myron Bilaniuk and E.C. George Sudarshan, authors of an early treatise on tachyons, call a particle that dwells in this strange state of omnipresence—zero energy/infinite velocity—a "transcendent" tachyon.

3. To slow a tachyon down requires the addition of energy. To slow a tachyon down to light speed requires an infinite quantity of energy. Thus for a tachyon, the speed of light is a lower limit to its velocity. Once a tachyon, always a tachyon—such particles can never go slower than light.

If a way could somehow be found to "translate" the matter of a starship into tachyons, it could then travel faster than light—indeed, it wouldn't have much choice! Of course, this may well be impossible, since, presumably, its rest mass would also have to be converted to an imaginary number, which would result in the starship becoming an "unphysical entity."

Finally, there is the old favourite of science fiction, the space warp. Recent speculation has centred on the idea that, since gravity "warps" spacetime (objects rest on the surface of the Earth because they are trapped at the bottom of its "gravity well"), it might be possible to construct a gravity amplifier. Installed in a spacecraft, a sufficiently powerful amplifier could be pointed ahead of the ship and switched on, resulting in the contraction of spacetime in the direction of travel. In this way, a distance of many light years might be squeezed into a distance of a few miles.

As it happens, this is the technique allegedly used by the alien spacecraft currently under inspection at the S-4 test site in Nevada—at least, according to Bob Lazar. If he is telling the truth, we might be a lot closer to building such ships for ourselves than physicists suspect.

Another possible method of travel through warped spacetime involves the use of "stargates," the postulated corridors through hyperspace, which can be entered via certain types of black holes. As the reader may well know, a black hole is a region of infinitely warped spacetime, the result of a sufficiently massive star that has reached the end of its life and has collapsed in on itself. When this happens, the collapse continues until the dead star's gravity is so great that its escape velocity exceeds that of light. In other words, even light itself plunges into the star, never to be seen again. So deep is the gravity well around a black hole that it could, conceivably, punch right through hyperspace and form a "wormhole" connecting the entrance with another region in the Universe, or perhaps another region in time.

Some physicists suggest that, if these wormholes exist, they probably have a very small diameter, perhaps as little as a few

Planck lengths. (The Planck length, named after the great German physicist Max Planck, is the smallest unit of distance that can be meaningfully described. It is a mindboggling 10^{-35} metres, or 1, over a 1 followed by 35 zeros.) This has led to further speculation that in the distant future we might discover a way to inject some form of "exotic matter" into such wormholes, widening and stabilizing them in order to permit transit by our spacecraft.

This kind of engineering is, of course, a long way off. Physicists have yet to solve the equations that would conclusively prove the very existence of wormholes and stargates, let alone solving the problem of how to travel through them. Even so, it can be seen that there are a number of tenuous possibilities for the future of interstellar flight. Indeed, there are doubtless myriad additional possibilities that have not yet even occurred to physicists.

And the possibility remains that the scientific discoveries surely awaiting us in our own future might be written in the history books of a distant planet. . . .

"They" Are (Probably) Not Aliens

By far the most widely accepted hypothesis for the origin of genuine UFOs holds that they are interstellar space vessels, piloted by scientific survey teams from another planet or planets. Ironically, this most prevalent of hypotheses is also acknowledged by the sceptics who, as mentioned in the previous section, use it to refute the notion that UFOs represent a genuine, unexplained phenomenon. The vast majority of ufologists accept the extraterrestrial hypothesis as the one which most successfully accounts for the mass of evidence, in the form of photographs, physical traces and eyewitness testimony, that has been accumulated over the years. But is this position justified? Does this evidence really point convincingly to an origin on another planet? In short: if they are there, are they coming here?

We may as well begin with the physical appearance of the "aliens." Although, as noted earlier in this book, not all aliens possess a humanoid form, it is described far more often than not in the UFO literature. This is even more true in the late 1990s, in which the ubiquitous Greys seem to have claimed exclusive visiting rights over our planet. Even when other types of beings are described, they are almost invariably associated with the Greys in some way. So, just how feasible is it that a being originating on another planet should look so similar to ourselves? (Don't let the huge craniums and gigantic black eyes fool you: such differences are negligible in terms of extraterrestrial evolution.)

In order to address this question, we must first take a look at the Earth itself. Our home planet has a sidereal period of revolution about the Sun of 365.26 days, its mean distance from the parent star being 92.96 million miles. Its axial rotation period is 23 hours 56.07 minutes, and its average radius is 3,959 miles. It has a mass of 13.17×10^{24} pounds. Its orbit occupies the so-called "habitable zone" about the Sun: any further away, and it would have become a frozen wasteland, like Mars; any closer, and the accumulation of greenhouse gases would have heated the surface, resulting in the hellish conditions observed on Venus.

The Earth is also blessed with the presence of a large natural satellite; very large, in fact, compared with the satellites of other planets in the Solar System. Its movement about the Earth causes tides, and its monthly orbital period may even influence the menstrual cycles of human females. The Earth's axis is inclined at approximately 23.5° to the vertical (this is called the "obliquity of the ecliptic" and gives rise to the seasons); however, there is a slight variation in this angle, a circular "wobble" that takes the axis from 22.1° to 24.5° over a cycle of 41,000 years. The fact that the obliquity of the ecliptic has a variation of just 2.4° is due to the presence of the Moon's steadying, gravitational influence. Without it, the obliquity of the ecliptic would have been much more severe; the seasons would have alternated between the unbearably hot and the intolerably frigid with great rapidity.

It can thus be seen that the present, life-bearing properties of our planet have been "fine tuned" to an incredible degree. If any of the above attributes had been missing, or at all different, life on Earth would certainly not have evolved the way it has, and perhaps would not even have evolved at all.

We are the products of three billion years of evolution, which in turn depended not only on the factors outlined above, but on countless others, including the radiation produced by the Sun, the intensity of the Earth's gravitational field and the means by which food is chemically produced (through photosynthesis on Earth). It is therefore virtually unthinkable that an intelligent being from another planet with conditions differing widely from those on Earth, would be as similar to ourselves as aliens are reported to be. By the same token, it is statistically very unlikely indeed that there are any other planets out there that are *identical* to the Earth (and thus capable of producing similar life forms to human beings); and even if there were, their inhabitants would *still* almost certainly look nothing like us, since our own evolution is the result of tens of millions of random genetic mutations, driven by the specific radiation output of our Sun; mutations that could not be duplicated *exactly*, no matter how similar conditions were elsewhere.

Let us now turn to the phenomenon of alien abduction. That something both disturbing and unexplained is occurring in many of these cases can, I think, no longer be seriously denied. Indeed, the phenomenon may well have an intelligent, non-human origin. But is it an extraterrestrial origin?

The typical abduction scenario involves the victim's removal to an enclosed space, in which a series of medical procedures are conducted, including the removal of biological material, such as skin, blood, sperm and ova. The general consensus among the majority of abduction researchers is that the aliens are doing this in order to create a new race of hybrid beings to bolster their own deteriorating genetic stock, to repopulate a doomed Earth, or to populate some other planet with a new variation of the human species.

However, the methods they are allegedly employing to achieve this goal are simply not consistent with the postulated activities of such a hugely advanced culture. There is simply no need to use such a traumatic method as the scooping out of a lump of flesh to secure a piece of human genetic material. As Jacques Vallée has stated more than once, human medical science as it stands today could secure such material without recourse to such radical measures. A single drop of blood, which could be taken without leaving any physical marks, would yield all the genetic material the "aliens" could need. In fact, they wouldn't even need to abduct a single human being: they could raid the blood or sperm bank of any decent research hospital and come away with all the material they would need.

Another often-reported element of the abduction experience involves the impregnation of human females, who are allegedly forced to carry human/alien hybrid foetuses for a period of several weeks, before they are abducted once again and the foetuses are removed. These women frequently report being taken to a room containing many transparent, fluid-filled vessels, inside which float the hybrid foetuses that have been taken from them.

Once again, not only is this incredibly cruel, it is also unnecessary, if we accept that these "aliens" are utilising a technology perhaps thousands of years in advance of our own. We have been using *in vitro* fertilization techniques for many years, and it seems logical to assume that the day will come when the biological womb becomes redundant. There seems to be no reason for such an allegedly advanced technology to require human females for this purpose.

They may well be abducting people all over the world; but it seems very unlikely that they are doing it for the reasons many ufologists assume.

We must now turn to the frequency of close encounters over the years since the late 1940s, for if we look carefully enough, we will perceive yet another enigma that weighs against the ETH as an explanation for UFOs. When Jacques Vallée examined the first catalogue of close encounter (immediate vicinity of the witness) reports to be compiled, in 1969, he noted that the total number of entries was more than 900. More recent estimates suggest that that number has grown to about 5,000.

This number, however, is almost certainly inaccurate by a factor of ten: as Vallée reminds us in *Revelations*, only about one in ten close encounters are ever reported, so the true figure is probably more like 50,000. Since the vast majority of these reports originate in the USA, Europe and Australia, and since it is extremely probable that UFOs are a worldwide phenomenon, we can conservatively multiply this number by two, to arrive at 100,000 close encounters.

Vallée discovered that "the geographic distribution of close encounters [indicates] a pattern of avoidance of population centres, with a higher relative incidence of landings in deserts and in areas without dwellings." Since the sparsely inhabited areas of the Earth vastly outnumber the densely inhabited areas, he suggests multiplying the number of encounters by ten, giving a figure of 1,000,000 landings. "In other words, if human witnesses were equally distributed over the surface of the land, and if they reported every close encounter they observed, the data universe should contain one million records."

However, even this vast number does not give a true picture of the frequency of UFO landings. Data from a number of researchers suggest that sightings reach a peak at about 9.00 P.M., then fall off through midnight, before reaching a lower, secondary peak at about 3.00 A.M. Since the vast majority of people go to bed at night, and are thus in no position to observe the phenomenon, it follows that the number of reports would rise dramatically if people were constantly vigilant. Vallée discovered that, were this the case, reports would rise continuously throughout the night, and would peak at about 3.00 A.M. The actual reported events would thus increase by approximately a factor of 14. In other words, we have "a total estimate of 14 million landings in forty years if we strictly adhere to the ETH."

Even if a culture were so technologically advanced as to enjoy unlimited resources, there could surely be no possible benefit to be gained by landing on a planet *14 million times*. A civilization capable of exploring interstellar space would certainly be past masters in the science of planetary survey. With our technology as it stands today, we can gather a colossal amount of information about a planet by placing satellites in orbit around it, and we can only speculate as to the remote sensing technology that would be used by advanced aliens. Although it can fairly be conceded that several landings might be necessary, for the physical collection of various samples of flora, fauna and minerals, any explorers who needed to do it 14 million times would surely not be worthy of the name.

In spite of these arguments against the ETH, there remains no logical justification for claiming that extraterrestrials have never visited the Earth in the past; likewise, it may well be that explorers from another planet have accounted for *some* close encounters over the years. The unusual features discovered on Mars and the Moon at least imply an ancient extraterrestrial presence, even if we will have to wait some years before this is either proved or disproved. Encounters such as those reported at Valensole and Rendlesham Forest (both of which were discussed earlier) would seem to point to technological activity, in view of the measurable traces left behind.

As we noted in the previous section, practicable interstellar travel is fantastically difficult—at least for twentieth-century human beings. The obstacles may be so great that they can never be overcome, by any civilization anywhere in the Universe. On the other hand, if there is an easy way (as yet undiscovered by us) to achieve faster-than-light travel, then nothing could be more natural than for alien explorers to survey our world. However, it seems very likely that if they are doing it now, they account for a vanishingly small percentage of those 14 million UFO events.

But what of the rest? What could account for all the encounters that resist identification in purely mundane terms? The answers may lie in realms that are at least as strange as a hypothetical alien planet.

UFOs and Near-Death Experiences

If we turn away from the extraterrestrial hypothesis to account for the majority of UFO and alien encounters, a vast and fertile theoretical landscape opens up before us, fed by mysterious rivers originating in the human unconscious and the wider Universe with which it is intimately and eternally linked. The fundamental characteristics of alien abductions have been compared with the phenomenon of near-death experiences (NDEs), and although many aspects of the NDE differ radically from abduction accounts, there does seem to be a paradoxical connection: they are, in a manner of speaking, opposite sides of the same metaphysical coin.

The NDE can be divided into two basic types: so-called deathbed visions, and out-of-body experiences resulting from serious injury or the immediate threat of death. In the huge number of cases studied, the percipients report that their experiences were incredibly real and totally objective. Interestingly, although sceptics have suggested that such visions are the result of random neural activity in the dying, oxygen-starved brain, there is evidence to suggest that NDEs are more likely to occur if the percipient's consciousness is unimpaired.

It is worth devoting some space to a description of what occurs during a typical NDE, and comparing it to the basic elements of the abduction experience. Dr. Kenneth Ring, Professor of Psychology at the University of Connecticut, has probably contributed more than any other researcher to our understanding of what happens during these experiences. In his 1992 book *The Omega Project: Near Death Experiences, UFO Encounters and Mind at Large*, he provides a useful comparison between the two basic scenarios.

Many of their aspects are diametrically opposed; for instance, the initial reaction to an NDE is one of peace, tranquillity and security, whereas the UFO abductee feels confusion and abject terror. The NDE percipient feels that he/she is experiencing something absolutely real, is surrounded by beings of light and deceased friends and relatives, and is encouraged to evaluate his/her life by a compassionate spiritual presence; the abductee senses a dreamlike quality to the experience, and yet is forced to submit to a grossly physical examination by dreadful-looking creatures, who are following some obscure and sinister agenda.

The NDE experiencer wants to remain in the "otherworld," although he/she is gently persuaded to return home (usually with the admonition that it is not yet the right time to stay), and complies with feelings of disappointment, even resentment, but also intense happiness. The abductee, on the other hand, is unceremoniously dumped back on Earth, with attendant feelings of relief, confusion and hatred of the kidnappers. The memory of an NDE is usually unimpaired, and is accompanied by strong feelings of a profound, spiritual component to the Universe, together with the desire to live a life that is useful and essentially good. Abductees usually (although not always) require the assistance of a hypnotherapist to access the memories of their experience, and frequently suffer from post-traumatic stress disorder.

Finally, an NDE usually occurs only once in a person's life, most commonly in adulthood, whereas abductions can occur many times, and usually begin in childhood.

These differences are indeed profound, and yet the sudden journey into another "reality" is common to both scenarios. Kenneth Ring suggests that such people possess "encounter-prone personalities," by which he means that their innate spiritual sensitivity indicates a visionary psyche that might represent the next step in human evolution. It should be emphasized that these people are not woolly-headed dreamers who are out of touch with reality, but rather a highly privileged group who have unconsciously recognized that, in the words of theoretical physicist Fred Alan Wolf, "mind is not confined to individual and separated persons, but is universal, singular, and beyond any conceptual limit we enforce, such as the notion of spacetime confinement." Wolf agrees with Kenneth Ring that NDEs and

UFO encounters might be an "evolutionary trend" leading to a human perception of unity between the "self" and the Universe.

Although the notion that, ultimately, "all is one" might be considered too "mystical" to have much relevance to what is essentially a scientific enigma, it is nevertheless gradually gaining currency in certain scientific circles. One of the most vocal proponents of this line of thinking is the British biochemist Rupert Sheldrake, whose theory of "morphic resonance" is considered by many to border on scientific heresy. The central assertion of this theory is that there exists in nature a collective memory, to which all life—indeed all organic matter—has unconscious access. This sounds rather like the Akashic Records of Theosophical theory, which holds that an eternal record of every event, thought and action that has occurred since the beginning of the Universe, is preserved in the *akasha*, a Sanskrit word meaning the fundamental fabric of space and time.

One of the illustrations Sheldrake provides of this storehouse of information in action, is his claim that people who do the London *Times* crossword at night do it more quickly than those attempting it in the morning. According to Sheldrake, this occurs because the answers to the crossword have entered the collective memory, and are being accessed by people through morphic resonance.

It is possible that those who experience NDEs and UFO abductions are, in effect, accessing this universal information record, especially in view of their sudden entry into the "otherworld," whether it be the putative afterlife, or an alien spacecraft. Indeed, Kenneth Ring notes that such reports are similar to dreams, in that there is considerable discontinuity in them. This is particularly true of UFO abductions, in which the percipient is taken from one location to another, to yet another, for instance from his/her bedroom to waiting area inside the UFO, to examination room, to foetus incubation room, with little recollection of what happens in between.

Of course, these encounters are not dreams as such: they

seem to have a much greater grounding in "reality," whatever the ultimate nature of that reality might be. In any event, it apparently is capable of interfacing with our conscious perceptions of the world at certain times, and is even capable of leaving physical traces on the bodies of percipients, such as scars and "scoop marks" from which tissue has apparently been taken, or the strange triangular rash experienced by Dr. *X*. If NDE experiencers and UFO abductees are accessing these records, which constitute another level of reality, this could account for the similarities between the various reports. However, the question remains: what *is* it that they are encountering? If the deceased relatives of NDE percipients really do exist in this transdimensional memory bank, then what are the Greys?

American philosopher Michael Grosso has suggested that they might be a manifestation of the collective guilt experienced by Western culture at an unconscious level, and which is related to the impact that modern science has had upon the face of our planet. The first image that naturally springs to mind is the terrifying arsenal of atomic weapons that humanity has accumulated. But an equally dreadful image is the abject suffering of the Third World. The almost nightly television images of starved and wasted innocents, succumbing to the ravages of disease and malnutrition, or perishing horribly in civil wars, have somehow resulted in a profound disturbance in the collective unconscious. This may have given rise to the reported dreamlike interactions with emaciated beings with wasted limbs and overlarge craniums, beings who, if the stories are to be believed, are dying. If this theory bears any relation to the truth, then perhaps it should come as no surprise that they treat their victims so cruelly, for the natural corollary of guilt is self-punishment. . . .

Northern Lights

Although so-called UFO "flaps," in which many different witnesses in a particular location report sightings of unexplained objects over a few weeks or months, have occurred frequently over the years, it is extremely unusual for the UFOs to return to the same area with such regularity that scientists can set up their equipment there, and be virtually guaranteed a sighting. However, just such a situation exists in the district of Hessdalen in central Norway.

The Hessdalen Lights were first reported by the local population in 1981, prompting the Universities of Oslo, Bergen and Trondheim, as well as the Norwegian Defence Research Establishment, to send several teams of investigators to tackle the mystery in 1984. They were intrigued not only by the reports themselves, but the frequency with which they occurred. Clearly, something very unusual was going on. The following testimony, from a miner named Bjarne Lillevold, is representative of the Hessdalen sightings.

As I was on my way home from work [on 24 September 1982], I and a colleague saw a light against the mountains near Hessdalen. We drove about five kilometres [three miles], and then the object began to descend towards the forest, near Alen. When we ourselves reached Alen, the object was hovering close to the trees. My companion, who hadn't seen the celebrated UFO of Hessdalen before, was very excited by the sight. We drove to the centre of Alen, and then saw a second object which came from the direction of Hessdalen and halted below the other. I then drove on my moped to Hessdalskjolen, where I saw an object near a cottage. At first I thought the cottage itself was on fire, but then I saw it was something else, which looked like an upside-down Christmas tree and bigger than the cottage beside it. It was about four metres [13 feet] above the hill, and had a red light on it which blinked: there also seemed to be a curious "blanket" over the whole thing. The object was moving up and down like a yo-yo for about 20 minutes; when it was close to the ground the light faded, but at the height of the manoeuvre it was so bright that I could not look at it for long. When the light was near the ground I could see through it as though it was made of glass.

At that time, the Hessdalen Lights were being investigated by the group UFO-Norge without any official help. They made several trips to Hessdalen, taking several different items of equipment, such as magnetic field detectors and spectrum analysers. Although these instruments yielded little valuable data, the teams were able to capture the UFOs on film. Behind the nebulous blobs of light, the researchers were able to discern a number of odd shapes, including rectangles and discs.

More recently, the teams have returned to Hessdalen with more sophisticated equipment, in an attempt to record the spectra of the lights, and thus determine the energy source behind them. However, these experiments have yet to yield any positive results. The research so far conducted suggests that the Hessdalen Lights may well be composed of ionized plasma, which would account for the strong radar reflections that have been recorded.

In his 1995 book *The UFO Phenomena: A Scientific Look at the Evidence for Extraterrestrial Contacts*, science writer Edward Ashpole summarizes a review paper by Professor Boris Smirnov of the Russian Academy of Sciences, who has studied light phenomena like those encountered at Hessdalen. According to Smirnov, they can be divided into three categories:

1. Small and strong white or blue flashes which could show up anywhere in the sky.
2. Yellow or yellow/white lights usually observed in the valley and below the horizon. (To be able to estimate size and distance it is necessary to observe a light against a solid background.) Sometimes they were just above rooftops and even down near the ground. They could be stationary for more than an hour before moving off slowly around the valley. Sometimes they accelerated to very fast speeds. They were also observed high in the sky.
3. Several lights together at fixed distances from each other. Mostly these were yellow or white lights with a red light in front. These lights moved slowly around the mountain tops.

One of the most interesting results obtained by the research teams was gained by projecting a laser beam at the lights. When this was done to one particular light which was regularly flashing, it began to flash with twice the frequency, until the laser beam was switched off, whereupon the flashes resumed their previous frequency. According to Ashpole, one possible reason for this surprising response is that, since dense plasmas can be highly reflective, "the physical vibration of the plasma is temporarily interrupted and changed by the arrival of a laser beam."

Ashpole has discussed these intriguing phenomena with several plasma physicists, who maintain that an explanation of them is within the bounds of our present knowledge of physics. All that is needed is more concentrated research. When asked why such research has not been done, their answers are both sad and unsurprising: since there is no discernible commercial value in discovering how the Hessdalen Lights work, no one will finance any research.

The Earthlights Hypothesis

It seems clear, then, that some UFOs are actually natural phenomena that definitely occur, but are ill-understood, placing them in a kind of twilight world between the known and the unknown. Another example of this is the so-called "Earthlights Hypothesis," which has been proposed to account not only for UFO sightings, but also for apparent contact with alien beings.

A Japanese researcher named Musya examined eyewitness reports from an earthquake that shook the Idu Peninsula on 26 November 1930. He discovered that 1,500 people had seen a variety of strange, luminous phenomena at the time of the quake, including lightning-like flares, shafts of light and round fireballs.

In 1977, Michael Persinger and Ghislaine Lafrenière published a book entitled *Space-time Transients*, in which they developed the theory that light phenomena can be generated by tectonic processes within the Earth's crust. Indeed, these processes need not be of the severity associated with earthquakes; even minor tremors can produce ionization effects in the atmosphere above the epicentre. This hypothesis is supported by the fact that many UFOs are sighted over regions known to contain geological fault lines, in which seismic activity occurs, for example Hessdalen, and the Pennine range in England. In addition, some UFOs have been observed to emerge from or plunge into the ground. Although this has resulted in some extreme speculation that such objects are in transit to or from their underground base, the theory put forward by Persinger and Lafrenière seems more promising.

Some researchers have even had some partial success in duplicating such phenomena under laboratory conditions. Dr. Bryan Brady subjected samples of quartz rock to extreme pressures, resulting in the discharge of small lights as the rock was crushed. However, it must be admitted that this experiment depends on unfeasibly high pressure, and also that the phenomena thus produced last for mere moments, unlike genuine light phenomena, which can be observed for many minutes. At any rate, what is certain is that further research along these lines is justified, not least because an understanding of the mechanics of seismic-related light phenomena could, conceivably, lead to a practical method of predicting earthquakes.

As mentioned above, it has also been suggested that the brains of human beings who find themselves in close proximity to such seismic discharges, might suffer from the "scrambling" effects of intense electromagnetic fields, resulting in a powerful hallucination. The salient features of this hallucination might well be determined by the percipient's cultural background. In other words, a person today seeing an unidentified light hanging low in the sky might well assume that it is some kind of technological device, and if its behaviour is inconsistent with any such device with which the percipient is familiar (such as an aeroplane, balloon, satellite, etc.), then he/she might well take it to be an alien spacecraft. As the electromagnetic field began to stimulate the brain's neocortex, the percipient would experience a hallucination profoundly influenced by the assumption that the light phenomenon was a craft from outer space, probably containing alien beings.

An interesting experiment was conducted on British television a few years ago, in which psychologist Dr. Susan Blackmore (who subscribes to the theory outlined above) was placed in isolation while wearing a helmet specially modified to produce an electromagnetic field around her head. When the helmet was activated, she experienced something akin to an abduction: suddenly extremely afraid, she "felt" something taking hold of her ankle, and reported that a powerful presence seemed to be in the room with her.

Although Blackmore's experience was nowhere near as profound and terrifying as that reported by genuine abductees, the fact that it had been induced by the electromagnetic stimulation of the temporal lobes of the brain would seem to indicate an avenue along which further serious abduction research might proceed.

The Time Travel Hypothesis

As mentioned earlier, the humanoid characteristics of ufonauts constitute a serious problem, one which perhaps more than any other militates against the extraterrestrial hypothesis. Of course, any fan of *Star Trek* will tell you of the notion that, aeons ago, the galaxy was seeded with life by a race of superbeings, thus accounting for the close similarity between intelligent creatures on various worlds. (I could mention that this has more to do with special effects budgets than ancient superbeings, but this would be a little churlish.) It could conceivably be that this happened in reality, and it has been tentatively put forward to explain the unfeasible humanoid alien. It is, however, extremely doubtful: even if the same building blocks of life had been distributed on worlds throughout the galaxy, the random mutations essential for its development towards intelligence would still come into play, forcing it along different evolutionary paths on different planets.

The time travel hypothesis puts paid to all these problems. It holds that UFOs are actually time machines (the Polish science fiction writer Stanislaw Lem calls them "chronotraction devices"), carrying our remote descendants on historical research assignments. This, of course, accounts quite elegantly for the physiological similarities between the ufonauts and ourselves. Even the frail and spindly Greys could be considered as our descendants of perhaps a thousand years hence, or ten thousand, or more. After all, they always seem to be harping on about the dismal future of humanity, how one day our species will become sterile through its irresponsible treatment of the Earth's biosphere, and that they are here to harvest genetic material so that the human race can be restarted elsewhere. This would, naturally, also account for the genetic compatibility (another serious problem with the ETH) between the Greys and their victims.

As mentioned briefly above, the ufonauts may be historians of the distant future who are travelling into the past to observe the Earth's history at first hand. This would account for several attributes of the UFO phenomenon, most notably its apparent ubiquity throughout history. It could also account for the observed ability of UFOs to materialize and dematerialize, which might occur as the onboard time machine is activated, and the craft heads off further into the past, or back into the future.

Time travel, like interstellar travel, is a commonplace in science fiction, and has always been considered a physical impossibility. But, like interstellar travel, it has received more serious attention from theoretical physicists in recent years. There are a number of possibilities that might, one day, lead to a practical time machine. For instance, spacetime is composed of four dimensions, three of space (left/right, forward/backward, up/down) and one of time. The three spatial axes extend at right angles to each other, and the time axis *also* extends at right angles to the spatial axes. This is extremely difficult to visualize, but can be described easily in mathematical terms. If the hypothetical gravity amplifiers described earlier could be made to distort a local region of spacetime sufficiently, the time axis could be warped to the extent that it becomes a spatial axis. Time travel would then become possible.

Intense gravitational fields also form the principle behind a theoretical device called Tipler's Infinite Rotating Cylinder. In 1974, the American physicist Frank Tipler suggested that a sufficiently massive cylinder, rotating at half the speed of light, could distort spacetime to the extent that "closed timelike loops" are created, through which past time would become accessible. British physicist John Gribbin has calculated that Tipler's cylinder would have to be 100 kilometres long, 10 kilometres in radius, have the mass of the Sun and the density of an atomic nucleus, in order to work.

There is, however, a problem with building such a device (quite apart from the obvious one): the rotating cylinder would be so dense that it would instantly undergo axial collapse (somewhat like a star collapsing), and would end up looking more like a giant pancake than a cylinder. It may be forever beyond our talents to construct Tipler's Infinite Rotating Cylinder, although Gribbin suggests that it may one day be possible to utilize natural objects (such as the so-called "millisecond pulsar" discovered in 1982) for the same purpose.

Another reason why time travel may be impossible is that nature may well refuse to allow us to create paradoxes. This is a well-known concept that, once again has an extensive provenance in the world of science fiction. Time paradoxes violate a putative law known as the Causal Ordering Postulate (COP), which insists that causes must precede effects. The most well-known of these paradoxes is that in which a psychotic time traveller goes back into the past to kill his own father before he (the time traveller) was conceived. Many physicists maintain that time travel will always be impossible because a scenario such as I have just described would violate the COP. Of course, one needn't choose such an extreme case to illustrate the time paradox. There is the old Ray Bradbury story, in which time travellers go sightseeing in prehistory, and return to find their democratic world transformed into a totalitarian hell. One of their number discovers the reason: a crushed butterfly on the sole of his shoe. Even a seemingly insignificant alteration in the past might have far-reaching consequences, which the COP would not allow.

However, all is not lost for the time travel enthusiast. It may just be that quantum theory has a way to avoid creating paradoxes. According to the so-called Many Worlds Interpretation, we do not live in a "Universe" as such, but in a "Multiverse" composed of an infinite number of "ghost" realities existing coterminously with this one. The Many Worlds Interpretation was arrived at through experiments with single photons (particles of light), but can be applied to events in the macroscopic world. In John Gribbin's words, we live amidst "a myriad array of ghost realities corresponding to all the myriad ways every quantum system in the entire universe could 'choose' to jump." So, in the macroscopic world, every time we make a choice (to cross a road at a particular point, for instance), the universe divides into an infinite number of slightly different "branches" in which we made a different choice.

If the Many Worlds Interpretation is an accurate description of reality, then the problem of time paradoxes would not arise. Any irresponsible time traveller intent on altering the past would create an alternate universe, quite separate from his own, which would thus be preserved. He could still kill his own father, but it wouldn't matter: it would just mean that in the new universe, he was not born. In his native universe, however, he *was* born. It can thus be seen that the initial groundwork, at least, for a workable theory of time travel has been laid. Whether it ultimately proves to be correct, only time will tell (if the reader will pardon the expression). If, on the other hand, it proves impossible to send physical objects (craft, explorers, etc.) back through time, this does not necessarily disprove the time travel hypothesis with regard to UFOs.

We know that there are certain fundamental particles that travel from the future into the past, and it may prove feasible to utilize them to carry information back through time. If our remote descendants ever find a way to do this, they may refine their technology to the point where they can send back themselves in the form of quasi-holographic images, capable of interacting with the target era, collecting information, and so on. If this turns out to be the case, the apparently ghostly behaviour of UFOs and their occupants (appearing and vanishing at will, etc.) would make more sense.

In his book *UFOs: Operation Trojan Horse*, John Keel speculates in a most interesting way along related lines. He theorizes that UFOs are themselves not composed of "matter" as such, but rather of an unknown form of energy that, once it has arrived, *simulates* matter in order to interact more fully with the environment. In this way, it is capable of leaving physical traces such as radiation, landing marks, and so on.

This is, of course, wild speculation, and may well turn out not to be the case! Indeed, the Time Travel Hypothesis suffers from a major drawback, which involves the intelligence (one might call it the common sense) of our remote descendants. If they really are returning to the various stages of the Earth's history in order to conduct research, they may well have rendered that information useless, by their very acts of temporal exploration!

The notion of "gods" from the sky is hugely significant in terms of our mythologies and our cultural development, which surely would have been very different had we not evinced an interest in the heavens and their denizens. Some ufologists have suggested that our mythological systems have been heavily influenced by visits from UFOs and their occupants. If so, this damages the Time Travel Hypothesis, since there would surely be little point in studying a history you yourself have created by your very act of studying. Although this statement could be countered by referring to the Many Worlds Interpretation, which would hold that the travellers are from an alternate universe, and thus have not polluted their *own* Earth's history, the question would still remain: why bother to study *ours*?

This is one of the many questions I would put to a ufonaut, were I ever lucky—or unlucky—enough to encounter one....

The Shamanic Hypothesis

One of the favourite assertions of those researchers who do not subscribe to the extraterrestrial or time travel hypotheses, is that the UFO phenomenon has always been with us, in one guise or another. What our ancestors saw as flaming shields in the sky, accompanied by angels or demons, we see as interstellar spacecraft, accompanied by scientific survey teams from other planets. In each case, according to the non-extraterrestrialists, the assumption is entirely erroneous. The natural progression from this position is toward a hypothesis that takes into account the historical ubiquity of such phenomena, with special regard to the human capacity for myth-making: the interaction with reality that is driven and informed by the imagination.

By "imagination," I do not mean to imply that UFO encounters are merely fictions. On the contrary, they constitute another order of reality, with which certain members of the human species have interacted throughout its history. Imagination, in this context, means, in the words of the British anomalist Patrick Harpur, the reversal of "our common notion of the imaginative as something unreal, something imaginary, [allowing] it an autonomous life that includes spontaneous apparitions."

In order to understand better how this interaction with reality might work with regard to UFO encounters, we can look at the visionary tradition of shamanism, which utilizes altered states of consciousness to contact the spirits residing in the natural world. Shamanism is essentially a benign and beautiful tradition, whose fundamental aim is the pursuit of sacred knowledge, combined with the power to heal and restore.

In his 1989 book *The Elements of Shamanism*, the anthropologist Nevill Drury describes how a person becomes a shaman.

> Shamans are called to their vocation in different ways. For some it is a matter of ancestral lineage or hereditary bonds establishing the person in that position or a situation where a would-be

shaman seeks initiation from one already established in this role. In other cases it seems almost as if the spirits have chosen the shaman, rather than the other way around. These are the "greater shamans"—those who have been called spontaneously through dreams or mystical visions to embody supernatural power. Those who have simply inherited their role are regarded as "lesser shamans" and hold a lower status in society, especially among the peoples of Siberia and Arctic North America.*

When a prospective shaman is chosen by the spirits, the process which then comes into play can be a very harrowing one. Indeed, many reach initiation through serious illness or injury, which brings them close to death. When death approaches most closely, contact is then established between human and spirit, the latter taking the form of entities from the underworld, the sky, or the souls of dead ancestors. At this time, he will be nursed by an experienced shaman, who will guide him along the perilous path to initiation.

Once this has been achieved, the shaman performs a vital service to his society, through his ongoing contact with the spirits of nature. One of the most important functions involves asking various spirits for permission to hunt animals. For a potent example of this, we can turn to the Eskimos, who occupy the area bounded by the Hudson Bay, the Bering Straits and Greenland. Like other shamanic peoples, the Eskimos believe that the world is controlled by invisible forces or spirits of nature, called "Innua." The Innua reside in all natural objects, including animals, the sea, the air and even rocks and stones.

When contact is made between an Innua and a human being, the Innua becomes a personal totem, or "Torngak." For instance, the spirit of a bear may become a man's Torngak, in which case,

---

* It is interesting to note that certain shamans gain their ability to contact the spirits of nature through hereditary means, just as certain UFO abductees are apparently contacted because their parents have had encounters.

if the man is killed by a bear, he will be restored to life, and will become a shaman, an "Angakok."

While the spirits of bears and stones are considered to be among the most powerful, those of the sea also hold a very important place in Eskimo mythology. The goddess of the sea, called Sedna, is extremely significant, since it is she who holds sway over all the animals of the deep, upon which the Eskimos depend for their survival. Sedna is the goddess most feared by the Eskimos, who are careful to placate her with sacrifices.

The *New Larousse Encyclopedia of Mythology* describes how the Angakok must endeavour to ensure the success of a sea hunt.

> Sometimes when the Eskimos fail to catch any seals the Angakoks dive down to the bottom of the sea to compel Sedna to set them loose. According to ancient Greenland legend, the Angakok who wants to reach her must first pass through the kingdom of the dead, and then an abyss where there turns ceaselessly a wheel of ice and a boiling cauldron full of seals. When the Angakok has managed to escape the huge dog guarding the entry, he has to cross a second abyss on a bridge as slender as a knife edge.

Some of the spirits are inimical to humanity. One legend tells of an Angakok who travelled too far out to sea, and suddenly found himself surrounded by the kayaks of some fire spirits, who were intent on capturing him. When it seemed he was lost, another kayak appeared, its prow opening and shutting like a mouth. The fire spirits immediately fled. The kayak belonged to the Angakok's protecting spirit.

How, then, can shamanism be compared to the strange journeys undergone by UFO abductees? One of the most profound connections is the incredibly harrowing operation conducted on the shamanic initiate, during which his body is dismembered by the attending spirits and his internal organs removed. The spirits then replace them with new organs, pieces of quartz and "iron bones." In his 1994 book *Daimonic Reality: A Field Guide to the Otherworld,* Patrick Harpur describes the case of a UFO abductee named Sandra Larson, who was travelling by car in North Dakota on 26 August 1975, when she saw a number of glowing UFOs approaching. She had a missing time period of about one hour, and sought the help of a hypnotherapist. Under hypnosis, she recalled being taken into a UFO. One of the "aliens" scraped the inside of her nose with a long instrument. Her skull was then opened, and her brain removed and replaced.

Other abductees recall being taken to underground caverns, in which painful physical experiments are performed. Part of the shamanic initiatory journey also involves a journey to the Underworld, where their bodies are destroyed and remade. Harpur suggests that the fragments of quartz inserted into the shaman's body (and whose function is to enable him to fly) are similar to the devices that are implanted into the bodies of abductees, again for specific purposes (most commonly, it is thought, to allow the aliens to monitor their victims' movements).

Part of the shaman's initiation involves a celestial journey, in which he converses with the spirits of the air, or the souls of dead shamans; abductees, too, are most commonly taken aloft, although conversation between them and the "aliens" is usually far more limited, if it occurs at all. If there *is* a link between the two experiences, then this is puzzling. It could, however, reflect the lamentable breakdown in communication that has occurred between our increasingly technological and materialistic culture, and the wider Universe in all its aspects, spiritual as well as material. Indeed, this may be the very reason why humanity (particularly in the West) is being forcefully contacted by representatives of the living consciousness of the Universe.

Speculations on the true nature of the UFOs and their occupants can and will continue for the foreseeable future. In the final analysis, all we can do is assume—and perhaps hope—that the truth, when we eventually learn it, will be more fascinating than any speculation we have yet made.

Bibliography and Suggested Further Reading

Andrews, George C.: *Extra-Terrestrials Among Us*. St. Paul, Minnesota: Llewellyn Publications, 1993.

Ashpole, Edward: *The UFO Phenomena: A Scientific Look at the Evidence for Extraterrestrial Contacts*. London: Headline Books, 1996.

Bernard, Raymond: *The Hollow Earth*. New York: Carol Publishing, 1991.

Boar, Roger and Blundell, Nigel: *The World's Greatest UFO Mysteries*. London: Hamlyn Publishing, 1991.

Bord, Janet and Colin: *Life Beyond Planet Earth? Man's Contact with Space People*. London: Grafton, 1992.

Bowen, Charles, ed.: *The Humanoids*. London: Futura Publications, 1977.

Brookesmith, Peter, ed.: *The Age of the UFO*. London: Orbis Publishing, 1984.

Bryan, C. D. B.: *Close Encounters of the Fourth Kind: Alien Abduction and UFOs–Witnesses and Scientists Report*. London: Orion Books, 1996.

Commander X: *Underground Alien Bases*. Wilmington, Delaware: Abelard Productions, 1990.

Drury, Nevill: *The Elements of Shamanism*. Shaftesbury, Dorset: Element Books, 1992.

Edwards, Frank: *Stranger Than Science*. London: Pan Books, 1963.

Emenegger, Robert: *UFOs Past, Present and Future*. New York: Ballantine Books, 1978.

Fawcett, Lawrence and Greenwood, Barry J.: *Clear Intent: The Government Cover-Up of the UFO Experience*. New Jersey: Prentice-Hall, 1984.

Fort, Charles: *Book of the Damned*. London: John Brown Publishing, 1995.

Friedman, Stanton: *TOP SECRET/MAJIC*. New York: Marlowe & Company, 1996.

Fuller, John G.: *The Interrupted Journey*. New York: MJF Books, 1996.

Good, Timothy: *Alien Liaison: The Ultimate Secret*. London: Arrow Books, 1992.

Good, Timothy: *Beyond Top Secret: The Worldwide UFO Security Threat*. London: Sidgwick & Jackson, 1996.

Gribbin, John: *In Search of Schrodinger's Cat*. London: Black Swan, 1993.

Harbinson, W.A.: *Projekt UFO: The Case for Man-made Flying Saucers*. London: Boxtree, 1996.

Harpur, Patrick: *Daimonic Reality: A Field Guide to the Otherworld*. London: Arkana, 1995.

Herbert, Nick: *Faster Than Light: Superluminal Loopholes in Physics*. New York: Plume Books, 1989.

Hoagland, Richard C.: *The Monuments of Mars: A City on the Edge of Forever*. Berkeley: North Atlantic Books, 1996.

Hopkins, Budd: *Missing Time: A Documented Study of UFO Abductions*. New York: Richard Marek Publishers, 1981.

Hopkins, Budd: *Intruders: The Incredible Visitations at Copley Woods*. New York: Ballantine Books, 1992.

Hynek, J. Allen: *The UFO Experience*. London: Corgi Books, 1975.

Jacobs, David M.: *Alien Encounters: First-hand Accounts of UFO Abductions*. London: Virgin Books, 1994.

Jung, C.G.: *Flying Saucers: A Modern Myth of Things Seen in the Sky*. London: Ark, 1987.

Keel, John A.: *UFOs: Operation Trojan Horse*. London: Abacus, 1973.

Mack, John E.: *Abduction: Human Encounters with Aliens*. London: Pocket Books, 1995

Maclellan, Alec: *The Lost World of Agharti: The Mystery of Vril Power*. London: Souvenir Press, 1996.

New Larousse Encyclopedia of Mythology. Twickenham, Middlesex: Hamlyn Publishing, 1985.

O'Brien, Christopher: *The Mysterious Valley*. New York: St. Martin's Press, 1996.

Peebles, Curtis: *Watch the Skies! A Chronicle of the Flying Saucer Myth*. New York: Berkley Books, 1995.

Randle, Kevin D.: *A History of UFO Crashes*. New York: Avon Books, 1995.

Randle, Kevin D. and Schmitt, Donald R.: *UFO Crash at Roswell*. New York: Avon Books, 1991.

Randles, Jenny: *Alien Contacts and Abductions*. New York: Sterling Publishing, 1994.

Randles, Jenny: *UFO Retrievals: The Recovery of Alien Spacecraft*. London: Blandford Press, 1995.

Sagan, Carl and Page, Thornton, eds: *UFOs: A Scientific Debate*. New York: Barnes & Noble Books, 1996.

Schnabel, Jim: *Dark White: Aliens, Abductions and the UFO Obsession*. London: Penguin Books, 1995.

Strieber, Whitley: *Communion: A True Story*. New York: William Morrow & Co., 1987

Thompson, Keith: *Angels and Aliens: UFOs and the Mythic Imagination*. New York: Fawcett Columbine, 1993.

Thompson, Richard L.: *Alien Identities: Ancient Insights into Modern UFO Phenomena*. San Diego: Govardhan Hill Publishing, 1993.

Vallée, Jacques: *Anatomy of a Phenomenon*. London: Tandem Books, 1974.

Vallée, Jacques: *Dimensions: A Casebook of Alien Contact*. London: Sphere Books, 1990.

Vallée, Jacques: *Revelations: Alien Contact and Human Deception*. New York: Ballantine Books, 1993.

Journals

Fortean Times, various issues.

UFO Magazine, various issues.

Mutual UFO Network *MUFON UFO Journal*, various issues.

About the Author

Alan Baker is the author of *Destination Earth: A History of Alleged Alien Prescence* (1998) and the upcoming *Encyclopedia of Alien Encounters* (1999), both published in Great Britain. He currently resides in Hove, East Sussex.